COUNSELING FOR WELLNESS AND PREVENTION

Counseling for Wellness and Prevention brings *Preventive Counseling*, one of prevention's founding texts, firmly into the twenty-first century. *Counseling for Wellness and Prevention* thoroughly updates and significantly expands on discussions of practical applications and emerging best practices. Counselors and counseling psychologists will find evidence-based, contemporary guidance to help them engage in needed efforts to help clients and the general population enhance their overall wellness and ward off future dysfunction. Author Robert Conyne demonstrates the ways in which the traditional model of one-to-one therapy can be expanded to embrace wellness and prevention as well as strategies for putting into practice a broad range of environmental and system change strategies, such as advocacy and community organization. The book is well suited for adoption in counselor-education courses and includes explicit connections to CACREP accreditation standards. It's also an excellent choice for programs in psychology, where the APA-approved prevention guidelines for psychologists are now available, and in social work, where prevention and community change have long been hallmarks.

Robert K. Conyne, PhD, is Professor Emeritus of the University of Cincinnati counseling program. He is a licensed psychologist, a licensed professional clinical counselor, and a fellow of several divisions of the American Psychological Association and of the American Counseling Association's Association for Specialists in Group Work.

COUNSELING FOR WELLNESS AND PREVENTION

Helping People Become Empowered in Systems and Settings

Third Edition

Robert K. Conyne

Routledge
Taylor & Francis Group
NEW YORK AND LONDON

Third edition published 2015
by Routledge
711 Third Avenue, New York, NY 10017

and by Routledge
27 Church Road, Hove, East Sussex BN3 2FA

Routledge is an imprint of the Taylor & Francis Group, an informa business

First edition published as *Primary Preventive Counseling* by Accelerated Development 1987

Second edition published as *Preventive Counseling* by Brunner-Routledge 2004

Library of Congress Cataloging-in-Publication Data

Conyne, Robert K., author.
[Preventive counseling]
Counseling for wellness and prevention : helping people become empowered in settings and systems / by Robert K. Conyne. — 3rd ed.
p. ; cm.
Preceded by Preventive counseling : helping people to become empowered in systems and settings / Robert K. Conyne. 2nd ed. 2004.
Includes bibliographical references and index.
I. Title.
[DNLM: 1. Counseling—methods. 2. Mental Health. 3. Mental Disorders—prevention & control. WM 55]
RA790
158'.3—dc23
2014045902

ISBN: 978-0-415-74313-6 (hbk)
ISBN: 978-0-415-74314-3 (pbk)
ISBN: 978-1-315-81384-4 (ebk)

Typeset in Bembo
by Apex CoVantage, LLC

The second edition of this book appeared 17 years following the first. Both editions were dedicated to my children, Suzanne and Zack. This third edition comes yet another decade later, reflecting the slowly maturing growth in the field. Now that my children are grown, I dedicate this book revision to all children everywhere and to all those others who may find themselves living in positions of vulnerability for which wellness and prevention initiatives are needed. And to the memory of my beloved and faithful dog companion, Lucy, who sat by my side as I wrote this (and other) books and who finally had to say goodbye—during the copyediting stage of this book—after 14.5 years: You helped keep me well over all these years. I miss you deeply, my Buddy, as does our whole family.

CONTENTS

List of figures and tables xiii
Preface xv
Acknowledgements xvii

SECTION I
Foundations of Wellness and Prevention **1**

1 Wellness and Prevention in Mental Health 3
Introduction 3
Lifestyle Diseases and Lifestyle-Induced Disorders Can Be Prevented 4
Being Well: Personal Actions 5
Being Well: Environmental Actions 6
Wellness and Prevention: General Goals and Intervention Strategies 6
Personal, Relational, and Collective Levels of Wellness Intervention 7
Wellness at All Levels 8
Prevention: Before the Fact 9
How Prevention and Wellness Interrelate 12
Behavioral Health Versus Mental Health 13
Return on Investment for Wellness and Prevention Programs 14
Issues for Reflection and Discussion 15
References 15

2 Everyday Wellness and Prevention: A Foundation of Positive Practices for People, Settings, and Systems 18
Introduction 18
Everyday Practice of Wellness and Prevention Is Possible and Important 19
What Is "Everyday Wellness and Prevention"? 19
The Emergence of Wellness and Prevention in Everyday Life 20
Person-Centered and System-Centered: Two Avenues for Daily Practice 21
Person-Centered Avenues 21
Settings- and System-Centered Avenues 22
Person-Centered Everyday Wellness and Prevention Practice Areas 22
Be Positive 22
Cultivate Resilience 23
Assess Your Positive Psychology Strengths to Assist in Leading the "Good Life" 23
Practice Wellness 25
Become Involved in the Wellness Domains 28
Develop and Use Life Skills 35
Carefully Consider Complementary and Alternative Medicine Health Care Approaches 36
Settings- and System-Centered Everyday Wellness and Prevention Practice Areas 38
Thirteen System-Centered Strategies for Everyday Wellness and Prevention 39
Role of the Counselor in Everyday Wellness and Prevention 41
Issues for Reflection and Discussion 42
References 42

3 Wellness and Prevention Strategies in Mental Health 48
Introduction 48
Public Health and the Medical Model in Relation to Wellness and Prevention 48
Public Health Model: Direct Support for Wellness and Prevention in Mental Health 49
Medical Model: Indirect Support for Wellness and Prevention in Mental Health 49
The Counseling Profession in Relation to the Two Models 52

History of Counseling and Counselor Education 52
Seven General Strategies of Wellness and Prevention 55
Wellness and Prevention Strategy 1: Education, Both Direct and Indirect 56
Wellness and Prevention Strategy 2: Social Competency Facilitation—Connecting With Resources 61
Wellness and Prevention Strategy 3: Natural Caregiving—Connecting With Helpful People 62
Wellness and Prevention Strategy 4: Community Organizing and Systems Intervention 65
Wellness and Prevention Strategy 5: Environmental Redesign—Altering Physical or Organizational Environment 70
Wellness and Prevention Strategy 6: Assist Developmental Transitions—Anticipating Predictable Needs and Challenges 72
Wellness and Prevention Strategy 7: Encourage Everyday Wellness and Prevention—Positive Practices for People, Settings, and Systems 73
Issues for Reflection and Discussion 74
References 74

4 Counseling for Wellness and Prevention 80
Introduction 80
General Behavioral Change Frameworks Supporting Wellness and Prevention 80
Individual- and Intrapersonal-Level Focus 81
Interpersonal-Level Focus 84
Community-Level Focus 85
Perspectives Supporting Wellness and Prevention 86
Ecological Perspective 86
Positive Psychology Perspective 90
Social Justice Perspective 91
Models Emphasizing Counseling and Aspects of Wellness and Prevention in Counseling 93
Change Models Emphasizing Counseling in General 94
Change Models Emphasizing Wellness in Counseling 95
Change Models Emphasizing Prevention in Counseling 97
Change Models Emphasizing Wellness and Prevention 98
Competencies in Wellness and Prevention Counseling 105
Seven Competencies: The "Big Ones" 105

Issues for Reflection and Discussion 108
References 109

SECTION II
Wellness and Prevention Applications **115**

Wellness and Prevention Approaches, Programs, and Initiatives 115
Program Selection Criteria Used in This Book 116
Online Resource Directories Containing Effective Wellness and Prevention Programs 117
Fit of Online Registries Within Planning of Wellness and Prevention Projects 118
References 119

5 Personal Wellness: Individual Counseling and Group Work 120
Introduction 120
Wellness and Prevention Through Individual Counseling 120
A General Process for Wellness and Prevention Approaches in Individual Counseling 122
Step 1: Form Beginnings of a Sustainable Helping Relationship 122
Step 2: Conduct a Wellness and Prevention Assessment 122
Step 3: Develop a Personalized Wellness and Prevention Counseling Plan, Including Pertinent Strategies 124
Step 4: Apply the Plan 133
Step 5: Evaluate Process and Outcomes 133
Wellness and Prevention Through Group Work 133
Group Work Foundations 133
Supporting Research 134
Wellness and Prevention Groups: Psychoeducation Format 136
A Detailed Plan for a Wellness and Prevention Group 138
Example of a Stand-Alone and of an Embedded Wellness and Prevention Group 140
Issues for Reflection and Discussion 142
References 142

6 Relational Wellness: Family and School Programs 146
The Family Setting 146
Functional Family Therapy 148
FAST Track Prevention Project 151

Triple P: Positive Parenting Program 154
Conclusion: Family Programs 156
The School Setting 157
Life Skills Training 160
Seattle Social Development Project 163
Olweus Bullying Prevention Program 169
Conclusion: School Programs 171
School Counselors Are Needed for Wellness and Prevention Counseling in the Schools 172
Issues for Reflection and Discussion 173
School 173
Family 173
References 174

7 Relational Wellness and Prevention: Community and Workplace Programs 179
The Community Setting 179
Big Brothers/Big Sisters of America 181
Communities Mobilizing for Change on Alcohol 185
Families and Schools Together: Protecting Hearts and Minds 189
Conclusion: Community Programs 191
The Workplace Setting 191
The Healthy Workplace Program 195
Coping With Work and Family Stress Project (Formerly Known as the Yale Work and Family Stress Project) 199
The JOBS Project for the Unemployed 202
Conclusion: Workplace Programs 205
Issues for Reflection and Discussion 207
References 208

8 Wellness and Prevention Initiatives With Collectives: Systems 212
Systems Strongly Influence Our Lives 212
One Example: Incarceration Tied to Policy 213
Some Public Policy and Legislative Gains 214
The World Health Organization's Comprehensive Mental Health Action Plan: An Initiative for the World 217
National Prevention Strategy: Moving From a System of Sick Care to One of Wellness and Prevention 219
Gun Violence Prediction, Prevention, and Policy: Addressing an Urgent Societal Problem 222

The Importance of Public Policy and Legislative Awareness for Counselors 225
A Successful Initiative: Preventing Cigarette Smoking 225
An Initiative Yet Unfulfilled: Suicide Prevention 228
Public Policy and Legislation Systems-Level Resources of Professional Associations 228
APA Web Site Resources: Public Education and Outreach 229
American Counseling Association Web Site Resource 229
Additional Systems-Level Involvement and Change Approaches 231
Final Thoughts on Counseling for Wellness and Prevention 233
Issues for Reflection and Discussion 234
References 234

Index 237

FIGURES AND TABLES

Figure 4.1	Behavior change wheel.	86
Figure 4.2	Person in context.	88
Figure 4.3	A broad perspective of health determinants.	89
Figure 4.4	Counseling for wellness and prevention model.	100
Figure 5.1	Individual counseling session.	121
Figure 5.2	Meeting of support group.	134
Figure 6.1	Enjoying family time outdoors.	147
Figure 6.2	Classroom.	158
Figure 7.1	Urban park.	180
Figure 7.2	Two carpenters working on wood.	192
Figure 8.1	National Prevention Strategy: America's plan for better health and wellness.	221
Table 8.1	Illustrative Public Policy and Prevention Initiatives: Programs and Outcomes	226

PREFACE

It was necessary in this third edition to produce a nearly complete rewrite of the second edition of *Preventive Counseling* to accommodate exploding knowledge over the last decade in the areas of heath care, wellness, ecology, social justice, and prevention as they relate to counseling and the helping professions. So this new version of the book also sports a new main title that accurately embraces all of this new material: *Counseling for Wellness and Prevention.*

This new edition incorporates an ecological orientation toward mental health care in which full attention is given to both human and environmental strengths and weaknesses. It is supported by extensive sets of chapter references that draw from theory and evidence bases, classics in the wellness and prevention field, applications from across the disciplines that contribute to wellness and prevention, and information that literally is ripped from today's headlines. Underscoring the importance of social justice in wellness and prevention counseling, the book's contents ask practitioners to consider both the immediate and broader contexts of their clients' lives. As such, this model of counseling avoids being restricted to a deficit-driven medical interpretation of psychological health by emphasizing a holistic, wellness perspective.

As the book's subtitle, *Helping People Become Empowered in Systems and Settings*, suggests, the intent is to show how counselors and other professional helpers can work with others to make substantial positive differences with clients and in the world. Its contents demonstrate not only how the traditional model of one-to-one therapy and small group work can be expanded to embrace wellness and prevention but also how a broad range of environmental and system change strategies, such as advocacy and community organization, can be included centrally within the helping repertoire. The new counseling for wellness and prevention model comprehensively incorporates the necessary elements and is intended to be of practical and heuristic value for practitioners, theorists, and academics.

The four chapters of section I address the foundations of wellness and prevention counseling. Concepts drawn from public health and the medical model and the evolution of wellness and prevention in health care are considered in chapter 1. How wellness and prevention can be expressed through daily life ("Everyday Wellness and Prevention") is the subject of chapter 2. Seven broad wellness and prevention strategies are explored in chapter 3, with the following chapter examining how counselors and other mental health professionals can apply these strategies in their work. The new counseling for wellness and prevention model is presented, along with other models, to provide direction.

Detailed information is presented in section II about specific evidence-based wellness and preventive programming in family, school, community, and work settings and in systems associated with public policy and legislation. (Note to Instructors: When assigning readings, you may find splitting chapter 6 (families, schools) and chapter 7 (communities, the workplace) to be helpful.) The introduction to section II contains valuable information about how the programs were selected and presents sets of resources that readers will find helpful in their own research.

I have tried throughout these pages to provide a needed road map for challenging the status quo and substantially altering the training and practice of counseling. See the book's ending, especially for suggestions about how to positively alter counseling training programs to more fully embrace wellness and prevention.

For practitioners, students, and professors interested in the expanded role of counseling for wellness and prevention in education, health care, and throughout the helping process, my hope is that this book will provide valuable guidance.

ACKNOWLEDGEMENTS

To Anna Moore, senior editor of Routledge Mental Health for the United States and North America, for supporting and guiding this third book revision; to George Zimmar, publisher of Routledge Mental Health for the United States and North America, for sponsoring the second edition; and to Joe Hollis (in memoriam), the founder of Accelerated Development, for taking a risk on the first version way back in 1987, when prevention and wellness were mere blips on a somewhat distant horizon.

To Seattle University and its College of Education, for all the support and kindness. The university was my home away from home as I revised this edition while serving as its Boeing-William M. Allen Endowed Chair and Distinguished Professor during 2013–2014.

To the Boeing Corporation, for providing the endowment that supported my invited position at Seattle University.

To Dr. William O'Connell at Seattle University, who shepherded my appointment and then my stay for the year at the university, and to my other terrific colleagues at Seattle.

To Perry Firth, my graduate assistant at Seattle University. Her resourcefulness, good cheer, and creative ideas contributed markedly to this revision.

To all at Illinois State University and the University of Cincinnati who supported my work in prevention over many decades.

To Richard H. Price and the community psychology program at the University of Michigan, from whom I learned much about prevention during my visiting scholar year in 1979–1980.

To my colleagues and friends in the Prevention Section of the Society of Counseling Psychology of the American Psychological Association, whose insight and dogged determination about prevention serve as a model for us all.

And last, but definitely not least, to my wife, Lynn, who supported this venture all along the way.

SECTION I

Foundations of Wellness and Prevention

We all want to live healthy lives in nourishing environments. A noticeable shift is occurring in counseling and general mental health practice to align with this impulse. This evolving direction is termed *wellness and prevention*, and it is the subject of this book.

The contents of chapters 1–4 in this first section lay down the foundations supporting a wellness and prevention approach to counseling and mental health practice. Chapter 1 traces the emergence of wellness and prevention and elaborates these terms' definitions.

The thesis of chapter 2 is that persons can proactively pursue wellness and prevention in their own lives through participating in counseling or other mental health services and by acting on their environments to produce needed health-oriented improvements. This is not an argument against counseling by any means but rather an affirmation of the responsible actions individuals can launch in their own lives and in society to attain a healthier existence, while also benefiting others. I term this personal initiative *everyday wellness and prevention.* It refers to the positive practices we can all use to improve our health status and our capacity to function satisfactorily and, indeed, happily in the settings and systems of our lives.

Chapter 3 explores major wellness and prevention strategies for promoting wellness and prevention. Seven significant strategies are identified and elaborated.

Chapter 4 asks a big question: How can counselors and other helpers use wellness and prevention strategies to promote healthiness in people, settings, and systems? To answer this question, a number of behavior change approaches are reviewed, followed by an examination of several counseling models that are especially sensitive to wellness and prevention, including the new counseling for wellness and prevention model, which includes interrelationships among prevention, wellness, ecology, and social justice. The chapter, and section I, conclude with attention to the wellness and prevention competencies that training programs need to address.

SECTION I

Foundations of Wellness and Prevention

1

WELLNESS AND PREVENTION IN MENTAL HEALTH

> Live in rooms full of light
> Avoid heavy food
> Be moderate in the drinking of wine
> Take massage, baths, exercise, and gymnastics
> Fight insomnia with gentle rocking or the sound of running water
> Change surroundings and take long journeys
> Strictly avoid frightening ideas
> Indulge in cheerful conversation and amusements
> Listen to music.
>
> Aulus Cornelius Celsus (25 BCE)

> Health starts in our homes, schools, workplaces, neighborhoods, and communities
>
> Healthy People.gov (2014)

Introduction

I begin this revised edition by relaying a message I hear from so many counseling and mental health professionals and professors. It goes something like this:

> It's more than time that counselors and other mental health professionals take the steps necessary to elevate wellness and prevention to occupy a prominent place in mental health delivery that effectively complements the important role of treatment.

This first chapter begins that discussion by introducing some important initial contextual information accompanying wellness and prevention in mental health. This information is expanded in subsequent chapters within section I. Then, section II of the book focuses on how counselors and other mental health professionals can apply wellness and prevention concepts in what I term *counseling for wellness and prevention*. Let's begin by considering issues surrounding the important place of lifestyle in wellness and prevention.

Lifestyle Diseases and Lifestyle-Induced Disorders Can Be Prevented

Noncommunicable conditions account for nearly two-thirds of deaths worldwide. Therefore, the emergence of chronic diseases as the main challenge to global health is unquestioned. In the United States, chronic diseases are the main causes of poor health, disability, and death and account for most health care expenditures (Bauer, Briss, Goodman, & Bowman, 2014).

As mentioned earlier, the very good news for counselors and their clients is that lifestyle diseases and chronic disorders, sometimes referred to as *lifestyle-induced disorders*, are preventable. In fact, up to 80% of illness is accountable by lifestyle choices (Ford et al., 2009). Lifestyle-induced disorders are those that are substantially impacted by how we live our lives and by the ongoing daily choices we make. A particular concern, and opportunity, for counselors and other mental health professionals in the United States adopting a wellness and prevention perspective is that *unmanaged stress* strongly adds to lifestyle-induced dysfunctions; this lifestyle variable is an area where counselors can make a substantial positive contribution.

Disorders attributable to lifestyle evolve through exposure, often intentional, to risk or certain health-compromising factors. It might be surprising to realize that heart disease, cancer, stroke, and diabetes are not the *causes* of illness and death, as may be commonly understood. Rather, they are the *effects* of people making unhealthy life choices day after day, year after year (McGinnis & Foege, as cited in Katz, 2013); of toxic environmental conditions; or of genetic causes. Examples of unhealthy choices and influences that may be subject to personal control include cigarette smoking, excessive use of alcohol or other drugs, lack of physical exercise, poor nutrition and dietary habits, low social support, ineffective thought processes, and responses to continual and/or accumulative stress. Encouraging and supporting individuals' positive lifestyle choices is a central tenet of wellness, where people learn how to take increased personal responsibility for their life trajectories.

Notice the long list of lifestyle-induced diseases in the following box. All of them can be positively affected through wellness and prevention interventions.

Lifestyle-Induced Disorders

Heart disease
Hypertension
Stroke
Type 2 diabetes
Some cancers (e.g., colon cancer)
Obesity
Diseases strongly associated with smoking, excessive alcohol consumption, and drug use
Emotional disorders not attributable to organic causes
(adapted from Matthews, 2011)

Being Well: Personal Actions

There is much that individuals themselves can do to get and stay well, however, and that counselors can promote with their clients and through programmatic offerings. Daily life choices, or everyday wellness and prevention practices (see chapter 2), are critically important. For example, people can choose not to smoke cigarettes or, if they do smoke, to participate in a smoking cessation program to become smoke free. They can choose to move more and to become more active, appropriate to their life situation and with doctor preapproval, leaving a sedentary lifestyle behind.

Katz (2013), in his book *Disease Proof*, amassed research to support a basic prescription for individual healthiness: *Do not smoke, eat well, be active, and maintain a healthy weight.* (Mental health professionals also recognize the critically important contribution of managing stress.) As Katz put it, "we are all making life-or-death decisions every day in terms of what we choose to put into our bodies and how we choose to use them" (p. 8). At the same time, these risk factors can be counteracted by conscious exposure to protective factors and behaviors such as Katz's: not (or never having started) smoking, eating nutritiously, and engaging in a regular pattern of physical exercise that is appropriate to life stage and age.

Walsh (2011) has crystallized how what he terms *therapeutic life changes* (TLCs) can promote wellness. TLCs are evidence-based lifestyle actions that individuals can take to improve their mental health and that counselors and other helpers can use in working with clients for that purpose. He maintains that TLCs can be as effective as psychotherapy or pharmacotherapy, offering unique and significant therapeutic advantages. Ivey (2012) has cogently illustrated how TLCs can promote new neural connections in the brain, suggesting that counseling and medicine connect. I discuss TLCs more extensively in chapter 2 as they relate to everyday wellness and prevention.

Positive alternative choices exist, therefore, to be made in the various wellness domains of life, and once made and maintained, they can contribute substantially to improving the quality of life. New research from the Centers for Disease Control and Prevention shows that life expectancy in the United States reached an all-time high of 78.8 years in 2012, but this marker varies by ZIP code, with those living in more affluent areas living longer, on average, than those living in poor areas.

Lifestyle choices also can contribute significantly to these results, according to observations solicited from Dr. Suzanne Steinbaum, a preventive cardiologist: "The most common causes of death are due to how you choose to live. If we can get how we eat and how we exercise under control, we can prevent many major causes of death. We can stop being a treatment-oriented country, and become a prevention-oriented country and extend life tremendously" (Healthfinder.gov, 2014).

Being Well: Environmental Actions

However, it's important to remember that becoming healthy is not solely a matter of individual choice. "Because people's lives are a complex kaleidoscope of experiences that influence what they believe and do, focusing merely on individual experiences leaves individuals trying to understand their lives out of context" (Prilleltensky, Dokecki, Frieden, & Wang, 2007, p. 32).

In fact, people live in context and are subject to multiple interactive forces constantly, some of which might support a healthy lifestyle, such as the availability of walking paths nearby, others of which might detract from a healthy lifestyle, such as high unemployment coupled with the lack of good jobs. Recall the second quotation at the chapter's beginning: "Health starts in our homes, schools, workplaces, neighborhoods, and communities" (Healthy People.gov, 2014). People can take steps to directly influence and improve many aspects of their environment.

As well, when counselors consider helping people and systems to become and stay healthy, an individual model of change, while important, makes only partial sense. An ecological model, concerned with people-in-systems, is more reflective of reality because humans experience their lives in relation to other people and to a variety of settings and systems. Counselors, then, need to help people learn how to use their knowledge, awareness, and skills to function effectively interpersonally *and* in the range of other environments in their lives. There are many implications emerging from this perspective, including, for example, that wellness and prevention goals apply both to people and to environments.

Wellness and Prevention: General Goals and Intervention Strategies

Wellness and prevention are interconnected goals for health care, for personal living, and for settings and systems. They also are accompanied by sets of intervention strategies that mental health professionals use to help clients and client systems reach desired goals. Both wellness and prevention are aimed at producing the "good life and the good society." Wellness refers to a health status of abundance, where persons or settings are not only free from dysfunction but also are maximizing healthy functioning across all important domains. Prevention refers to living life in such a way as to avoid significant problems and disorders and to intentionally improve the major settings of life: family, work, school, neighborhood, and community.

In terms of intervention strategies, counselors and other professional helpers can assist clients to engage in specific activities and behaviors that can elevate wellness in their lives and to modify their environments to become more empowering. Doing so has been endorsed in a number of ways, including through an official resolution, *The Counseling Profession as Advocates for Optimum Health and Wellness*, adopted by the Governing Council of the American Counseling Association (then known as the American Association for Counseling and Development) on July 13, 1989 (Myers & Sweeney, 2008).

Numerous ways are available for counselors to assist in promoting wellness. For instance, they can teach clients, train other professionals, and consult with agencies about the importance of lifestyle choices and how environments can support positive choices. Two major sets of empowerment strategies are available: (a) helping people to learn before the fact how to implement wellness strategies in their lives and (b) collaborating with others to facilitate system changes aimed at supporting wellness initiatives.

Personal, Relational, and Collective Levels of Wellness Intervention

As Prilleltensky and colleagues (2007) argued, wellness and quality of life are attainable when three primary sets of needs are met and mutually influence each other in an ecological system: (a) personal, (b) relational, and (c) collective. The personal and relational are very familiar to counselors. We counsel individuals, groups, and families all the time; those approaches have been, and remain, our bread and butter. From this viewpoint, the goal is to help individual clients to activate self-esteem and mastery through counseling and to promote support, caring, and positive relationships at the group and family levels. Less familiar to counselors is focusing on the collective level, where the approach is to influence positive change in settings and systems that may negatively affect people, using community organization and system intervention (COSI) strategies. It is important to emphasize that these three nodes, personal, relational, and collective, are not exclusive. In fact, they overlap and are interconnected, as is the case in any ecological system.

Give special attention to the *collective* node. This one is situated at the civic properties of life, on social justice, and on social systemic dynamics. Its province is spreading opportunities for all, creating equity and access to services and opportunities, and diminishing or eradicating assaults on the human spirit such as oppression, racism, sexism, and ageism.

Addressing the collective level is no doubt considerably less familiar right now for counselors and other helpers, and probably less comfortable to effect. Consultation, advocacy, and social justice strategies are attuned to facilitating needed social system change in such dimensions as culture, policies, procedures, and legislation.

Wellness and prevention efforts need to be informed by—and often to include directly—social justice. George Albee, a central figure in the development of mental health prevention, strongly asserted that prevention involved social justice, where the settings and systems of life—collective entities—are proactively altered to produce just and equitable environments that support the health and wellness of all citizens. Closing the have–have not gap represents one such area to be addressed from the social justice perspective. Indeed, wellness and prevention are goals for human *and* societal functioning—both—and they interrelate.

Let's take a closer look at both wellness and prevention.

Wellness at All Levels

Wellness is dynamic, comprehensive, and holistic, and its essence can be understood as the integration of the mind, body, and spirit. At the nub of the issue for understanding wellness is that health is far more than the mere absence of diagnosable illness or noxious environments, as important as those conditions are. After all, no one wants to be coping with diabetes, or depression, or urinary incontinency, or academic failure, or to be subjected to community environments that are oppressive, unjust, and sick—the list, unfortunately, seems endless. Yet healthiness, or wellness, involves the absence of personal illness or environmental dysfunction and also the presence of functioning at or near the potential for well-being across all domains.

Moreover, wellness is not languishing, not being free from a disorder or from inequity, not "just getting by," or not being "just enough." Rather, wellness refers to optimal functioning within and across personal, relational, and collective levels. Another way of stating it is that wellness represents the ultimate state of well-being and health that is capable of being achieved by individuals, groups and families, organizations, and communities (for additional definitions, see Myers & Sweeney, 2005, 2008; Prilleltensky et al., 2007). Keyes and Lopez (2002), in fact, discussed the concept of *flourishing*, a state of experiencing high levels of well-being in the emotional, social, and psychological domains.

So, there can be healthy individuals, healthy groups, healthy organizations, healthy communities, and so on. By being "healthy," it is much more likely that life will be satisfying, enjoyable, productive, and fair and equitable, and that a host of major life dysfunctions will be avoided or prevented.

Sometimes people comingle prevention and wellness. While the concepts are highly related, each stakes its own turf. As O'Connell, Boat, and Warner (2009) put it, prevention emphasizes the avoidance of risk factors at systemic levels (individual, group, family, organization, community), whereas health promotion/wellness promotes supportive family, school, and community environments and seeks to develop in people protective factors—resources that enhance well-being and provide competencies to avoid deleterious behaviors and emotions. Thus, a wellness and prevention counseling model (see chapter 4) needs to take into account proactively (before problem onset) the goal of reducing risk and increasing protective factors within and across personal, relational, and collective levels.

When considering wellness, most attention and research have been concentrated on the individual level: actions that a person can take to enhance her or his wellness or individual counseling addressing wellness issues. Note that the subsequent discussion follows that approach. Later, the discussion of prevention will emphasize the collective perspective, with a focus on social system change issues.

Prevention: Before the Fact

When I introduce the concept of prevention to those who are unfamiliar with it, I often draw from the classic fable referred to variously as the "river story," the "upstream/downstream" story, or some other similar descriptor. Its origins are attributed to various sources, most commonly to Julian Rappaport, the community psychologist, or to Saul Alinsky, the community organizer. Its specific contents also vary, but the essence of the message remains similar. In any case, its contents set the stage nicely for introducing prevention to an audience.

A Classic Prevention Fable

Imagine a warm, sunny afternoon. You are in a local park, lounging indolently on a blanket, with a bottle of wine and a good book on the grassy banks of a river below a swimming area. Suddenly you hear thrashing sounds and a cry for help from the river. Startled, you look over to see a person struggling unsuccessfully as the water sweeps him away. You courageously dive in, rescue him, and then return to the serious business of soaking up the sun. There is to be no respite for you, however, for you find yourself repeating this performance with several other drowning people throughout the afternoon. As you are ministering to the final victim, an observer asks a question that is startlingly powerful in its logic and simplicity: "Would it not ultimately be much easier and less dangerous to go to the swimming area and teach those people, collectively, how to swim than to rescue each individually?"

(Conyne, 2004)

Can we any longer afford the luxury of gearing our helping services around the model of "rescue each individually"? Of always swimming upstream, in a sense, against the prevailing current of treatment after the fact? Wouldn't it be more effective to take the advice of the observer in the previous anecdote and begin to teach people collectively the *wellness competencies* they will need in the future (in this case, floating and swimming) so that they can successfully cope with the demands of life later (again, in this case, so they can successfully handle a rough current)? Additionally, although the astute observer did not mention this, would it not have been useful for a railing to have been erected around the swimming area to keep the nonswimmers away from the danger of falling in and drowning? That is, as a general rule, can we begin *designing environmental improvements* to protect and enhance human functioning?

Teaching wellness competencies and accomplishing prevention through the design of environmental improvements, both conducted before the onset of problem formation, represent important ways to promote wellness and prevent dysfunction.

Social justice. I mentioned earlier how Albee (1986) called on mental health personnel engaged in prevention to help produce a "just society." His vision of such a society meant that oppression, such as exertion of privilege, sexism, racism, consumerism, ageism, patriarchy, and homophobia, must be eliminated. Counteracting oppression would allow settings and systems to develop more humanely, with positive effects on people. Social justice is a chief antidote to oppression, and it is a central tenet of prevention justice (Hage & Kenny, 2009; Kenny, Horne, Orpinas, & Reese, 2009; Ratts, 2009; Shriberg, Song, Miranda, & Radliff, 2013; Vera & Kenny, 2013; Vera & Speight, 2007). Its presence within wellness and prevention initiatives needs to be increased; it is important for social systems to be well, too. As Conyne, Horne, and Raczynski (2013) put it: "Prevention of disease is not contained in the doctor's office, but it starts in our communities and at home" (p. 51). It is the same for wellness, which is not limited to the efforts of individuals to remain healthy or to maintain a state of optimum health; rather, the wellness of a person is dependent on participating in a proficient health care system, through proactive individual efforts, and—importantly, but frequently not addressed—through environments in addition to health care that themselves are healthy.

Incidence reduction: A classic prevention approach. Albee (1982, 1985) adapted a public health approach known as *incidence reduction* to prevention in mental health. He emphasized that prevention is realized when the occurrence of *new* cases of a disease or disorder, or the rate of development of such new cases, is stopped, a kind of "No mas!" Some have proposed that such an understanding of prevention—prior to the onset of a mental, emotional, or behavioral disorder—is *true* prevention (O'Connell et al., 2009). "Before-the-fact" interventions and programs, then, are an outgrowth of incidence reduction as a goal. Incidence reduction typifies a view of what I would term "classic" prevention.

See the incidence reduction formula in the following box.

Classic Prevention Means "No Mas!"

$$\text{Incidence Reduction} = \frac{\text{Decrease: Organic Factors + Stress + Exploitation}}{\text{Increase: Self-Esteem + Coping Skills + Suppport Groups}}$$

Essentially, the formula suggests that prevention occurs when *new* cases of a disorder, such as obesity, are stopped (or slowed significantly) by decreasing risk factors contained in the numerator while increasing protective factors contained in the formula's denominator. Therefore, in broader terms, this approach can be understood as IR = Reduce Risk Factors/Increase Protective Factors. Interestingly, as we have learned more about wellness, the denominator of this formula needs to include the major wellness components.

The prevention fable presented earlier and the discussion about incidence reduction beg the question, "What is prevention?" The last edition of this book (Conyne, 2004) contained an extensive review of various prevention conceptions and definitions—and there are many, because the concept of prevention is an elusive one.

An inclusive definition of prevention was offered by Romano and Hage (2000):

1. stopping new cases of a mental, emotional, or behavioral (MEB) disorder, which is the classic view, called *primary* prevention
2. delaying the onset of a MEB, known as *secondary* prevention
3. reducing the impact of a MEB, its duration and severity, known as *tertiary* prevention
4. strengthening the coping capacities (wellness) of an identified individual, group, or population, otherwise known as strengthening protective factors to reduce risk factors
5. supporting institutional, governmental, and community policies to promote wellness (indirect strategies at the collective level to reduce risk); note, although not mentioned by Romano and Hage, that advocacy efforts to positively change policies and practices at this collective level also are within the purview of prevention

A sixth approach, not specified by Romano and Hage, is the universal approach, in which information and skills are made available to everyone in an entire population through such means as a targeted mass media campaign.

Guidelines for Prevention in Psychology. The Society of Counseling Psychology of the American Psychological Association (APA) sponsors a Prevention Section (Society of Counseling Psychology, 2011) aimed at furthering theory, research, training, practice, advocacy, and policy initiatives in prevention among counseling psychologists. The *Guidelines for Prevention in Psychology* (American Psychological

Association, 2014), which offer potential benefits to the public and the professional practice of psychology, emerged initially from that Prevention Section.

The guidelines give increased attention to prevention within APA and encourage psychologists to become involved with preventive activities within their areas of practice. Hage, Schwartz, and Murray (2012) discussed the prevention guidelines in terms of how they can guide efforts to improve the well-being of individuals, families, and communities; they also provided specific and helpful examples of how the guidelines connect with practice, research, training, and social action.

Obviously, these guidelines are geared to psychologists specifically. However, they are applicable to theorists, researchers, professors, practitioners, and students in other human service professions and disciplines, such as counseling and social work, who are concerned with wellness and prevention as a major approach to bettering people and systems (Romano, 2014).

The nine guidelines are summarized in the following:

Guideline 1: Psychologists are encouraged to select and implement preventive interventions that are theory and evidence based.

Guideline 2: Psychologists are encouraged to use culturally relevant prevention practices adapted to the specific context in which they are implemented.

Guideline 3: Psychologists are encouraged to develop and implement interventions that reduce risks and promote human strengths.

Guideline 4: Psychologists are encouraged to incorporate research and evaluation as integral to prevention program development and implementation, including consideration of environmental contexts that impact prevention.

Guideline 5: Psychologists are encouraged to consider ethical issues in prevention research and practice.

Guideline 6: Psychologists are encouraged to attend to contextual issues of social disparity that may inform prevention practice and research.

Guideline 7: Psychologists are encouraged to increase their awareness, knowledge, and skills essential to prevention through continuing education, training, supervision, and consultation.

Guideline 8: Psychologists are encouraged to engage in systemic and institutional interventions that strengthen the health of individuals, families, and communities and prevent psychological and physical distress and disability.

Guideline 9: Psychologists are encouraged to inform the deliberation of public policies that promote health and well-being when relevant prevention science findings are available.

How Prevention and Wellness Interrelate

No "right" way exists to capture the relationship between prevention and wellness. Which, for instance, is part of the other? Or do they coexist independently to be drawn together, as needed, by practitioners? A case can be made for either of these perspectives.

It is important to recognize that wellness and prevention are interrelated and mutually supportive. Prevention goals always have included two main strategies: (a) What typically has been known as *health promotion* and strengths-based approaches, on one hand, and (b) *system change*, aimed at deficit reduction, risk and harm reduction, and social justice, on the other. You saw this clearly in the Albee incidence reduction formula, where the numerator contains factors associated with risk reduction (such as negative stressors and oppression), whereas the denominator contains factors associated with health promotion (such as support groups and enhancing life competencies). In effect, these are social system and social justice change factors and wellness factors, respectively.

However, prevention has been more clearly linked over time with system change approaches, such as community empowerment strategies to help change policies and culture, than with health promotion. At the same time, wellness is much more clearly understood as a person-level variable, with interventions tied most closely to individual attitudes and behaviors (eating well, for instance) that can buttress wellness, with relatively little attention given to contextual and environmental variables. So linking wellness and prevention provides both a mutual balancing point and a more comprehensive approach for counseling.

Needed is an understanding, therefore, of wellness and prevention that clearly connects *both* of them, as they are twin approaches for counseling. The following definition suggests how prevention and wellness connect:

> *Wellness and Prevention initiatives seek to avert future significant health problems through promotion and system change strategies and to enhance optimum health and justice in people, settings, and systems.*

Wellness and Prevention

AIM: Avert future dysfunction through health promotion and system change and enhance optimum health and justice in people, settings, and systems.

STRATEGIES: Health promotion. . . system change

PEOPLE & ENVIRONMENT ECOLOGICAL LEVELS: Personal, relational (settings), and collective (systems)

TIME: Priority given prior to MEB onset or as early as possible, but at any point on the health continuum

Behavioral Health Versus Mental Health

A discussion is under way about whether the term *behavioral health* aligns more closely with wellness and prevention than does the traditional term *mental health*, which remains traditionally closely connected to disorder reduction and laden with stigma. Ivey (personal communication, March 8, 2014) represents those who are beginning to suggest that behavioral health might well become the preferred nomenclature to use when referring to wellness and prevention. According to SAMHSA (2011), *behavioral health* refers to a state of mental/emotional being and/or choices and actions that affect wellness, which can be advanced through a comprehensive intervention spectrum containing promotion, prevention, treatment, and maintenance.

Behavioral health as a concept and term seems to a growing number of expert observers to inclusively and more naturally embrace both promoting wellness and well-being and preventing dysfunction and mental illness, as well as substance abuse or other addictions. It also is argued from this perspective that the possibility of changing or developing new behaviors is more optimistic to people than the fear that illness may be a permanent aspect of one's life.

This developing discussion is well worth keeping our collective eyes on as we think about wellness and prevention and work toward finding the best ways to describe it and to enhance it through counseling and outreach programs. For the rest of this book, though, I will continue to reflect dominant convention by referring to wellness and prevention in mental health.

Return on Investment for Wellness and Prevention Programs

As we have seen, the U.S. health care system comes up short on attention to lifestyles, even though—as we have seen—as much as 75%–80% of chronic disease is said to be traceable to lifestyle and behavioral factors (Matthews, 2011). If noticeable improvements could be realized in promoting healthy lifestyles and behaviors, then it is likely that a significant proportion of disease prevention would result, as would a healthier population.

Improved wellness within the populace also saves money. Consider workplace wellness and prevention programs as an example, using a ratio drawn from the world of finance, return on investment (ROI). ROI is a bottom-line index that captures the financial amount saved by a program divided by the amount spent on it. In one critical meta-analysis of costs and savings for worksite wellness and prevention programs (Baicker, Cutler, & Song, 2010), the ROI for health care cost reductions was 3.27:1 (i.e., $3.27 saved for every dollar spent), and for reducing absenteeism of 2.73:1. Wellness and prevention benefit both people and society in real, tangible ways. To state this point in a different way, effective wellness and prevention programs can literally "pay off" for individuals and for society.

Positive signs are emerging in relation to costs and benefits of wellness and prevention. For example, health care spending seems to be beginning to level off, with amounts expended in 2012 even with those in 2011. This is big news, indeed. Health care dollars saved could be spent in other needed ways. For example, financial decisions could be made to expand access to health care services for more people. In another example, Americans reported eating more fruits and vegetables from 2009 to 2011, while consuming fewer calories. These behaviors contribute positively to a healthier lifestyle and lowered illness. In a third illustration, the prevalence of childhood obesity, a particularly vexing health problem with lifelong negative health consequences, has dropped significantly over the past decade by 43%, from 14% to 8%. These kinds of health gains coupled with large reductions in overall health care costs are connected with wellness and prevention initiatives (Roizen, 2014).

Wellness and prevention also are enhanced through legislative action (see chapter 8 for more on this subject). For instance, the Patient Protection and Affordable Care Act (Health and Human Services, 2014) holds promise for promoting wellness and prevention and for saving money. Among the act's benefits are (a) evidence-based prevention screening services, (b) free Medicare wellness visits, (c) screening and counseling for interpersonal and domestic violence, and (d) mental health and substance abuse parity (Jaffe & Frieden, 2014). Representing the greatest change to American health care policy since the 1960s, the act will increase health coverage of an additional 25 million Americans by 2019 (Shaw, Asomugha, Conway, & Rein, 2014).

Yes, there remains much to do. But wellness and prevention provide a route to human and societal healthfulness that gives reason for optimism.

Issues for Reflection and Discussion

1. References were made to the important concept of "incidence reduction." Define it and indicate why it is so important for wellness and prevention in mental health.
2. Suppose you were asked to give a short speech on mental health to the Rotary Club in your community. You decide to focus on underscoring the importance of wellness and prevention in mental health. Develop an outline for a 15-minute talk that contains key points you would like to make.
3. Lifestyle is of central importance to being healthy. What are some key aspects of a healthy lifestyle?
4. This chapter maintains that wellness is more than the absence of disease and illness. Explain this point of view to a partner.
5. The rest of the book focuses on how counselors and other helpers can draw from wellness and prevention to guide their work. What early ideas might you have about this topic, even before you have read other chapters? Jot down some thoughts. Keep track of them as you read on. See what is confirmed, what you might not have thought of yet, what ideas might change—and then note what I may be missing that is important!

References

Albee, G.W. (1982). Preventing psychopathology and promoting human potential. *American Psychologist, 37*, 1043–1050. doi:10.1037/0003-066X.37.9.1043

Albee, G. (1985). The argument for primary prevention. *Journal of Primary Prevention, 5*, 213–219.

Albee, G. (1986). Toward a just society: Lessons from observations on the primary prevention of psychopathology. *American Psychologist, 41*, 891–898. doi:10.1037/0003-066X.41.8.891

American Psychological Association. (2014). Guidelines for prevention in psychology. *American Psychologist, 69*(3), 285–296. doi:10.1037/a0034569

Baicker, K., Cutler, D., & Song, Z. (2010). Workplace programs can generate savings. *Health Affairs, 29*, 304–311.

Bauer, U., Briss, P., Goodman, R., & Bowman, B. (2014). Prevention of chronic diseases in the 21st century: Elimination of the leading preventable causes of premature death and disability in the USA. *The Lancet, 384*(9937), 45–72. doi:10.1016/S0140-6736(14)60648-6

Conyne, R. K. (2004). *Preventive counseling: Helping people to become empowered in systems and settings* (2nd ed.). New York, NY: Brunner-Routledge. doi:10.4324/9780203336052

Conyne, R.K., Horne, A. M., & Raczynski, K. (2013). *Prevention in psychology: An introduction to the prevention practice kit*. Thousand Oaks, CA: Sage. doi: 10.4135/9781452275574

Ford, E. S., Bergmann, M. M., Kroger, J., Schienkiewitz, A., Weikert, C., & Boeing, H. (2009). Healthy living is the best revenge: Findings from the European prospective investigation into cancer and nutrition—Potsdam study. *Archives of Internal Medicine, 169*, 1355–1362. doi:10.1001/archinternmed.2009.237

Hage, S. M., & Kenny, M. E. (2009). Promoting a social justice approach to prevention: Future directions for training, practice, and research. *Journal of Primary Prevention, 30*, 75–87. doi:10.1007/s10935-008-0165-5

Hage, S. M., Schwartz, J., & Murray, M. (2012). Best practice guidelines on prevention: Improving the well-being of individuals, families, and communities. In E. M. Vera (Ed.), *The Oxford handbook of prevention in counseling psychology* (pp. 51–75). New York, NY: Oxford University Press. doi:10.1093/oxfordhb/9780195396423.001.0001

Health and Human Services. (2014, April 29). *HHS.gov/HealthCare*. Retrieved from http://www.hhs.gov/healthcare/prevention/index.html

Healthfinder.gov. (2014, October 8). U.S. life expectancy hits record high of nearly 79 years: CDC. *HealthDayNews*. Retrieved from http://www.healthfinder.gov/News/Article.aspx?id=692497&source=govdelivery&utm_

Healthy People.gov. (2014). *Social determinants of health*. Retrieved from http://www.healthypeople.gov/2020/topics-objectives/topic/social-determinants-health

Ivey, A. (2012). *Therapeutic lifestyle changes (TLC): Increasing daily neurogenesis and the "take rate" for maintenance of new neurons and neural connections*. Unpublished manuscript.

Jaffe, H., & Frieden, T. (2014). Improving health in the USA: Progress and challenges. *The Lancet, 384*(9937), 3–5. doi:10.1016/S0140-6736(14)61032-1

Katz, D. L. (2013). Disease proof. New York, NY: Hudson Street Press.

Kenney, M. E., Horne, A. M., Orpinas, P., & Reese, L. E. (Eds.). (2009). *Realizing social justice: The challenge of preventive interventions*. Washington, DC: American Psychological Association. doi:10.1037/11870-000

Keyes, C., & Lopez, S. (2002). Toward a science of mental health: Positive directions in diagnosis and treatment. In C. Snyder & S. Lopez (Eds.), *The handbook of positive psychology* (pp. 45–59). New York, NY: Oxford University Press.

Matthews, A. (2011, December 12). U.S. health care's future. *Wall Street Journal*, B4.

Myers, J., & Sweeney, T. (2005). *Counseling for wellness: Theory, research, and practice*. Alexandria, VA: American Counseling Association.

Myers, J., & Sweeney, T. (2008). Wellness counseling: The evidence base for practice. *Journal of Counseling and Development*, 86, 482–494.

O'Connell, M.E., Boat, T.F., & Warner, K.E. (2009). *Preventing mental, emotional, and behavioral disorders among young people: Progress and possibilities.* Washington, DC: National Academies. Retrieved from https://www.ncbi.nlm.nih.gov/books/NBK32775/

Prilleltensky, I., Dokecki, P., Frieden, G., & Wang, V. O. (2007). Counseling for wellness and justice: Foundations and ethical dilemmas. In E. Aldarondo (Ed.), *Advancing social justice through clinical practice* (pp. 19–42). Mahwah, NJ: Erlbaum. doi:10.4324/9780203936689

Ratts, M.J. (2009). Social justice counseling: Toward the development of a "fifth force" among counseling paradigms. *Journal of Humanistic Counseling, Education, and Development, 48*, 160–172. doi:10.1002/j.2161-1939.2009.tb00076.x

Roizen, M. (2014, March 3). How wellness is pushing the U.S. to prosperity. *U.S. News & World Report: HEALTH* Retrieved from http://health.usnews.com/health-news/blogs/eat-run/2014/03/03/how-wellness-is-pushing-the-us-to-prosperity

Romano, J. (2014). *Prevention psychology: Enhancing personal and social well-being.* Washington, DC: American Psychological Association.

Romano, J., & Hage, S. (2000). Prevention and counseling psychology: Revitalizing commitments for the 21st century. *Counseling Psychologist, 28*, 733–763. doi:10.1177/0011000000286001

Shaw, F., Asomugha, C., Conway, P., & Rein, A. (2014). The Patient Protection and Affordable Care Act: Opportunities for prevention and public health. *The Lancet, 384*(9937), 75–82. doi:10.1016/S0140-6736(14)60259-2

Shriberg, D., Song, S., Miranda, A. H., & Radliff, K. (Eds.). (2013). *School psychology and social justice.* New York, NY: Routledge.

Society of Counseling Psychology. (2011). *Prevention Section: A section of the division of counseling psychology (17) of the American Psychological Association.* Retrieved from http://www.div17.org/preventionsection/default.htm

Substance Abuse and Mental Health Administration (SAMHSA). (2011). *A behavioral health lens for prevention.* Retrieved from http://captus.samhsa.gov/prevention-practice/prevention-and-behavioral-health/behavioral-health-lens-prevention/1

Vera, E., & Kenny, M. E. (2013). *Social justice and culturally relevant prevention.* Thousand Oaks, CA: Sage. doi:10.4135/9781452275598

Vera, E.M., & Speight, S.L. (2007). *Advocacy, outreach, and prevention*: Integrating social action roles into professional training. In E. Aldarondo (Ed.), *Advancing social justice through clinical practice* (pp. 373–389). Mahwah, NJ: Erlbaum. doi:10.1080/01609510801960957

Walsh, R. (2011). Lifestyle and mental health. *American Psychologist, 66*, 579–592.

2

EVERYDAY WELLNESS AND PREVENTION

A Foundation of Positive Practices for People, Settings, and Systems

The best six doctors anywhere
And no one can deny it
Are sunshine, water, rest, and air
Exercise and diet.
These six will gladly you attend
If only you are willing
Your mind they'll ease
Your will they'll mend
And charge you not a shilling.

—Nursery rhyme quoted by Wayne Fields, *What the River Knows*, 1990

Lives are lived day by day, one day at a time, from day to day, day after day, day in and day out. Lives as we experience them are inherently quotidian.

—Craik (1991, p. 1)

Each individual has a universal responsibility to shape institutions to serve human needs.

—The Dalai Lama

Introduction

How we think and feel and what we do matter significantly for our own levels of wellness and for the health of our planet. This chapter focuses on *everyday wellness and prevention*, a foundational concept for wellness and prevention that points to the value of daily healthful practices, and roles counselors can play in facilitating client adoption of this approach.

The underpinning premises are that we humans can do much ourselves—every day—to promote our own wellness and to stave off future disorders, and that we each hold a responsibility to contribute to the wellness of others and of the world in which we live. Much of what we can do is embedded in practicing sound wellness and prevention behaviors every day or, at least, more regularly than not. In addition, counselors and other mental health providers can and should encourage and guide their clients to pursue everyday wellness and prevention steps in their lives as an adjunct to the therapy process.

Everyday Practice of Wellness and Prevention Is Possible and Important

Counselors, psychologists, social workers, and other mental health professionals are familiar with "best practices" in their fields; these generally apply to training, research, and practice and are intimately connected with ethics. What we will be considering in this chapter are a kind of "best practices in everyday wellness and prevention," those attitudes and behaviors that have a track record for contributing positively to a quality lifestyle, and that individuals can apply in their own lives. This material also is important to draw from by helping professionals in their wellness and prevention work with clients and their training and consulting activities within organizations and communities.

As the nursery rhyme introducing this chapter suggests, if we are willing (note, though, that readiness and supportive conditions also are very important), we can set ourselves on a healthy life course through consistently applying wellness and prevention practices that cost little or nothing. Getting out in nature, eating well, exercising regularly, resting, and relaxing can benefit our personal wellness. Becoming situationally aware with skills allowing use to be alert and available to stand up for others can help us to create positive change in the world. Note, however, the admonition tucked into the rhyme: We need to first of all be willing. Conscious choice and willing practice of positive attitudes and behaviors hold the keys to living in a healthful and responsible way.

What Is "Everyday Wellness and Prevention"?

I define everyday wellness and prevention, as follows:

> Everyday wellness and prevention refers to people enacting daily life best practices in context to enhance their personal wellness and to avert significant problems, while contributing to the health and well-being of others.

A chief role for counselors and other professional helpers is to help people incorporate everyday wellness and prevention within their lives on a daily basis. This role can be carried out in three ways: (a) by brokering proven everyday wellness and prevention practices to people, (b) by creating and delivering good everyday wellness and prevention practices, and (c) by infusing everyday wellness and prevention within all aspects of wellness and prevention counseling, programs, and initiatives.

Everyday wellness and prevention is a strand within the fabric of autonomous health care and education. It is a means for personal empowerment, based on the view that people can take fuller charge of their own lives in context. One way to think of these daily best practices is captured by Danish (2013, p. 395): "Work well, play well, love well, think well, serve well, and be well."

It also is a strand within social justice. The quote by the Dalai Lama at this chapter's beginning points us to our personal role in promoting positive social change through standing up and advocating not just for our own self-interests and betterment but also for the rights and liberties of those around us.

The Emergence of Wellness and Prevention in Everyday Life

This perspective combines both positive psychology and social justice, with application to ordinary and everyday circumstances. "Everyday wellness and prevention" is within the reach of people and counselors, and other practitioners can intentionally work with clients and client systems to develop it. Everyday wellness and prevention also should infuse and guide the work of all helping professionals.

The American population has moved beyond being passive recipients of expert-provided care to assume a much more personal responsibility for their own health and mental health care needs. People, including children, now are viewed as active decision makers. They select from available choices and preferences in nutrition, exercise, and stress management, and they participate in shaping their environments to become more habitable, usable, and sustainable. As well, many have begun to assume greater initiative and responsibility for the direction for education and schools—such as increasing parental participation in local school decision-making committees and educating themselves through e-learning and social media approaches. This active involvement in health care and education is becoming a dominant theme for the 21st century.

Professionals and professional training programs are beginning to respond to this significant change in personal orientation and responsibility. For instance, training programs in integrative medicine have appeared (e.g., at Duke University, the University of Arizona), where the primary goal is to assist people to experience optimal vitality and wellness, integrating mind, body, and spirit as well as allopathic, alternative, and complementary medical approaches. Counseling and counseling psychology programs, which have historically been founded on the prin-ciples of wellness and prevention only to depart into an emphasis on treatment, are beginning to readdress wellness and prevention more directly through course work, training experiences, and accreditation standards. Health care plans are being created that are comprehensive and dynamic, geared to promoting optimal well-being. And, of course, the nation is deep in discussion (and argument) about how to implement the Patient Protection and Affordable Care Act, discussed briefly in chapter 1 and periodically throughout this book, which contains several provisions supportive of wellness and prevention.

But, of course, millions of Americans are not waiting for the health care and education establishments to alter themselves in the direction of increased integration and variety. As I mentioned, many are experimenting with their own choices. They research, read, surf the internet, learn from one another directly and through social media, meet in small groups, and test out various combinations of exercise, diet, herbs and vitamins, spiritual practice, social support, and alternative treatments to find what works for them. Much of this experimentation is proceeding without external expert monitoring, and may be risky to health, in some degree. Conversely, countless millions are organizing for themselves what they view as healthy practices that seem to be yielding improved vitality and more satisfying lifestyles.

In short, all of this activity is a virtual wellspring of wellness and prevention, occurring at all levels in our society. Our "cultural blueprint" is being rewritten at the macro-level and put into practice by individuals and groups to say, in effect, "We are empowered." Organizations and systems tend to be slower to adapt because they have traditions, regulations, policies, revenue streams, and other forces and elements that require longer to turn around—sort of like turning around the *Titanic*. But, they are beginning to revise and reinvent themselves, too, witness the increasing number of programs and initiatives that take a wellness, health-promoting orientation. Counselors and other professional helpers have a role in assisting systems to transformatively change to benefit all members of our society.

The areas discussed in the following suggest actions that can be taken daily by people to enhance their wellness and stave off dysfunction and for counselors to encourage of clients in therapy sessions. This information is organized into person-centered and system-centered dimensions.

You will note the relative imbalance in length of coverage of person- and system-centered approaches, favoring the former. This imbalance reflects reality, with psychological research and practice in the United States reflecting a Western philosophy focused much more on the individual than on society. While a whole other topic, suffice it to suggest that this imbalance needs correcting.

Person-Centered and System-Centered: Two Avenues for Daily Practice

Person-Centered Avenues

As we shall see, the daily practice of wellness and prevention needs to occur in two broad categories: (a) person-centered practices and (b) setting- and system-centered practices. Each of these areas is discussed in this chapter.

The behaviors mentioned in the nursery rhyme that helped introduce this chapter fall under person-centered practices. These involve people taking charge of what they directly control, more or less: how we spend our time; what we ingest; how we think about our life situations; if and how we exercise; the involvements we seek to have with friends and family; our contributions to others.

Solid research bases exist to support the personal pursuit of everyday wellness and prevention. For instance, the American Psychological Association (APA) maintains a Research in Action section on its Web site (American Psychological Association, 2014), which contains a Web-based organization of evidence-based research that connects with our everyday lives. Example topics include decision making, health and well-being, parenting, violence prevention, and the workplace. The work of the Heroic Imagination Project (2013), following the lead of Philip Zimbardo (see his YouTube TED presentation on August 20, 2011), demonstrates how ordinary individuals living everyday lives can learn how to do extraordinary things to benefit others. They can learn to develop the mindset (Dweck, 2006) and skills necessary to create lasting positive change in psychological processes, allowing them to make effective decisions in challenging situations, such as bullying, negative conformity, and mindless obedience. The project seeks to help transform an egocentric "me" orientation to a sociocentric "we" orientation. In short, as the project intends, they can learn how to stand up, speak out, and change the world.

Settings- and System-Centered Avenues

The second avenue for practicing wellness and prevention involves the settings and systems in which we live, work, and play. Settings are the concrete contexts of our lives: family, work, neighborhood and community agencies, recreational facilities, faith centers, and so on. They are the stage upon which we perform. In turn, settings include a number of systems that are characterized by interactive properties and processes, such as policies, procedures, and roles. Much of our quality of life is a function of how able we are to cope with these settings and systems and the kinds of daily contributions we make to the benefit others. A key component in this domain is behaving in such a way as to contribute to settings and systems that are socially just (Aldarondo, 2007).

Person-Centered Everyday Wellness and Prevention Practice Areas

Be Positive

Research is beginning to accumulate around the concept of *positive psychology*, or moving away from a focus on psychopathology to one of building positive qualities. The popular song of several years ago, "Don't Worry, Be Happy," expressed in a nutshell a key concept in positive psychology: to develop a sense of optimism.

This, and other human strengths, such as courage, interpersonal skill, future mindedness, faith, hope, work ethic, perseverance, honesty, and the capacity to achieve flow and insight, can act as buffers against malaise, dysfunction, and mental illness.

Human strengths, such as optimism, are not enough, of course. A positive psychology seems to depend, also, on cultivating experiences that are associated with happiness and subjective well-being, the capacity to adapt and organize to successfully meet changing conditions, and with interactions that occur within positive social contexts (Seligman & Csikszentmihalyi, 2000).

Cultivate Resilience

Viktor Frankl (1962) poignantly described how searching for meaning, a quality of resilience, allowed him to persevere in the extraordinary situation of Nazi concentration camps during World War II. Hillenbrand (2010) provides a harrowing account of resilience demonstrated by U.S. POWs in the Pacific theater of the same war.

Resilience more often occurs in every day circumstances. For instance, Masten (2001), in discussing resilience in children, emphasized "the power of the ordinary" (p. 235). Based on a review of resilience studies involving children, Masten observed:

> Resilience does not come from rare and special qualities, but from the everyday magic of ordinary, normative human resources in the minds, brains, and bodies of children, in their families and relationships, and in their communities. (Masten, 2001, p. 235)

In another look at resilience in terms of its ordinary nature, the American Psychological Association's Practice Directorate developed a public education campaign following the September 11, 2001, attacks. Called the "Road to Resilience," the campaign's principles include the following: (a) Resilience is a set of learned behaviors that are not-automatic; (b) it is a personal journey that is involved with others; (c) it is an ordinary, not an extraordinary, experience; and (d) resilience demands improvement be accomplished through small, persistent steps (Murray, 2003).

Assess Your Positive Psychology Strengths to Assist in Leading the "Good Life"

Positive psychology, which I referred to earlier, appears frequently in the popular press as well as in professional/scientific outlets. This work is becoming part of mainstream America, increasingly available to the public and to counselors for their use with clients. It is an excellent example of everyday wellness and prevention.

Within the context of positive psychology, Seligman (2002) and others wonder about the following question: What is the "good life"? As Prilleltensky (1997) emphasizes in his emancipatory communitarian (EC) approach, and as others have advanced (e.g., McWhirter & McWhirter, 2007), the good life depends as much on attending to collective interests as it does to individual well-being. In many ways, the "good life" is synonymous with meaningfulness and with the "good society."

Seligman (1998) suggested that what positive psychology needs is a taxonomy for the good life, the main purpose of which would be to guide the formulation and building of the "good life." This kind of taxonomy could be a source for people to refer to in seeking their own wellness and that counselors could draw from to assist in client growth efforts. He observed that psychological science has been able to produce an exhaustive (and exhausting) compendium to describe and diagnose and ever expanding range of human dysfunction and psychopathology (American Psychiatric Association, 2013) but that there is no companion product to describe and prescribe human health and positive functioning. His later compendium (Peterson & Seligman, 2004) sought to respond with a handbook and classification of character strengths and virtues.

Happiness is an area associated with the good life that is being intensely studied. For instance, the moment-to-moment happiness of 18,420 people across the world has been studied, yielding a mathematical equation. A key element found is the ratio calculating how events actually occur in relation to the expectations for those very events, with happiness arising from a positive residual (Rutledge, Skandali, Dayan, & Dolan, 2014). Thus, if our outcomes exceed expectations for an event (say, for a date, or for a restaurant meal), then we may feel at least momentary happiness.

Seligman (2002) is interested in a more enduring kind of happiness, connected with the concept of the good life. For him, this is a life imbued with authenticity. Visit the Web site http://www.authentichappiness.org to peruse some of this work, which includes a variety of questionnaires and assessments (e.g., Fordyce Emotions Questionnaire, PANAS Questionnaire, General Happiness Scale, Satisfaction With Life Scale, and VIA Signature Strengths Survey).

The Values in Action (VIA) Signature Strengths questionnaire seeks to assess 24 "signature strengths" that are associated with authentic happiness. The VIA questionnaire was developed by the Values-In-Action Institute. It is copyrighted by the institute. The questionnaire is obtainable on the preceding Web site. It is an example of a research-based source that people can access easily to learn about (or confirm) their strengths and to explore how to draw from them in their lives.

The 24 signature strengths are organized into broader categories, as follows:

1. Wisdom and Knowledge: Five cognitive strengths involving the acquisition and use of knowledge, including creativity, curiosity, open-mindedness, love of learning, and perspective taking.

2. Courage: Four emotional strengths involving the will toward goal accomplishment even when there is internal or external opposition, including bravery, industry/perseverance, authenticity, and zest.
3. Love: Three interpersonal strengths that include supporting and caring for others, including intimacy, kindness, and social intelligence.
4. Justice: Three strengths that undergird healthy communities, including citizenship/teamwork, fairness, and leadership. (A personal comment: This area of Justice needs more emphasis because of the powerful effects that noxious settings and systems exert on human activity, a point I make throughout this book.)
5. Temperance: Four strengths that moderate and protect against excessiveness, including forgiveness/mercy, modesty/humility, prudence, and self-control/self-regulation.
6. Transcendence: Five strengths that help to connect with the universe and provide meaning, including awe/appreciation of beauty and excellence, gratitude, hope, playfulness and spirituality.

Seligman (2002) indicates that everyone possesses many signature strengths. He suggests that individuals complete and score the VIA, examine their top strengths, and apply a set of nine criteria to each one of the top strengths. As examples, three of these nine criteria are that a strength engenders: a sense of ownership and authenticity, a feeling of excitement while displaying it, and a rapid learning curve as it is first practiced. If a strength is matched by one or more of these criteria, he suggests that it is a *signature* strength and should be used frequently and across many settings and situations, such as in work, relationships, raising children, and finding a sense of meaning and purpose in life.

Strengths-Finder 2.0 (Rath, 2007) is another popular and useful strengths-based resource. Along with related sources, it is based on the work of Donald Clifton, awarded in 2002 by the American Psychological Association as the "Father of Strengths-Based Psychology." It contains a self-assessment tool that can be used to help identify which of 34 *talent themes* might best characterize a person. These themes range from "Achiever" through "Includer" to the final theme of "Woo." (A word about Woo (my personal "favorite" term), one which may not be self-explanatory: People strong in Woo are said to love the challenge of meeting people new to them and then winning them over.) Strengths-Finder 2.0 is another research-based source that is easily available for use by the general public in helping to advance their level of personal wellness.

Practice Wellness

As we know, lifestyles matter. Let's go over some of these points again, because they are so important. Making positive, consistent lifestyle choices are the most important single action people can make for a healthy life. Counselors can assist clients to make these changes.

As you have read, lifestyle factors account for 75%–80% of the incidence of cardiovascular disease (CVD). For many, therefore, CVD can be preventable, yet in 2010 some 600,000 Americans died of this disease, with costs amounting to $109 billion in health care services, medications, and lost wages (Centers for Disease Control and Prevention, 2014a; Murphy, Xu, & Kochanek, 2013). Such specific lifestyle behaviors as cigarette smoking, being overweight, high cholesterol, unbuffered stress, untreated diabetes, and weakened social supports contribute to the onset of cardiovascular disease.

Wellness is a health-promoting perspective rooted in positive lifestyle choices that are made on a daily basis. Making healthy lifestyle choices each day is important to what I mean by everyday wellness and prevention (AHRQ, 2014). Wellness reflects a concern with optimum human functioning, and it draws from holistic, developmental, and preventive sources (Myers, 1992). As I've already emphasized, wellness is not the absence of illness but a lifestyle, a way of being, that reflects positive choices aimed at optimizing daily living and serving to prevent disease and illness.

There are a number of evidence-based daily personal practices that individuals can use to increase their level of wellness and that mental health providers can incorporate within their wellness and prevention practice. These kinds of changes, such as getting outdoors and moving more each day, are relatively simple to do and inexpensive, too. All of these recommended personal best practices also can be integrated within wellness and prevention counseling initiatives.

Following are four of these evidence-based regimens for personal wellness. The first two target general life conditions, whereas the second two address heart and cancer issues specifically. Note the general commonalities of these different approaches, reflecting the solid evidence upon which they are built.

Apply therapeutic life changes. An important set of evidence-based positive practices that one can engage in are called *therapeutic life changes* (TLCs; Walsh, 2011). Counselors and therapists also can encourage their clients to engage appropriately in these kinds of behaviors, and wellness and prevention programs can intentionally include them, as well. I will refer to TLCs at various points throughout the book.

TLCs have been identified through accumulated research. They reiterate, also, previous research that yielded behavior associated with a positive quality of life and with longevity. Cross-cultural common factors associated with longevity are (a) heredity, or genetics; (b) diet and nutrition; (c) physical and mental activity; (d) alcohol abstinence or moderation; (e) satisfaction with work; (f) remaining productively involved in family and community; (g) holding positive religious or philosophical attitudes; and (h) maintaining an indelible sense of life purpose and meaning (Granello, 2013).

Walsh (2011) advocated for mental health professionals to more fully appreciate the significantly potent role that lifestyle factors play in determining physical and mental health. Because lifestyle changes, through such an approach as TLC, offer significant and low-cost therapeutic advantages for patients, therapists, and societies, Walsh urged their increased use. Here are but two "low-flying fruits" to pick that he identifies: (a) fish oils to prevent psychosis in high-risk youth, which may be as effective as pharmacotherapy or psychotherapy, and (b) exercise to prevent depression (Dowd, Vickers, & Krahn, 2004).

Some scientists (e.g., Ratey and Hagerman, 2013) have strongly suggested that practitioners who do not recommend exercise to clients who are struggling with life issues are behaving unethically. This sentiment might apply, too, to other evidence-based wellness practices, such as not smoking, good nutrition, and having friends.

Therapeutic Life Changes

Exercise
Nutrition and diet
Time in nature
Relationships
Recreation
Relaxation and stress management
Religious or spiritual involvement
Service to others

Do "10 simple things." Cooper (2013) collated 10 "simple things," supported by research, that people can do to enhance their happiness: (a) Exercise more; (b) sleep more; (c) move closer to work; (d) spend more time with friends and family; (e) go outside (happiness is maximized at 13.9 degrees Celsius/57 degrees Fahrenheit (Tsutsui, 2013)); (f) help others, with about a 100-hours-a-year threshold (Lum & Lightfoot, 2005); (g) practice smiling; (h) plan trips (don't necessarily take them); (i) meditate; and (j) practice gratitude.

Follow a heart-healthy lifestyle. The American Psychological Association Practice Central (2014) encourages taking the following steps: (a) Get active, (b) eat well, (c) manage stress, (d) recognize how emotion is dealt with, (e) accept support, and (f) avoid burnout.

Incorporate steps of the European Code Against Cancer. The European Code Against Cancer (International Agency for Research on Cancer, 2014) focuses on individual actions that can be taken to prevent cancer. As well, the code indicates that these individual actions must be supported by governmental policies and actions.

The recommended actions of the European Code are as follows: (a) Do not smoke or use any form of tobacco; (b) make your home smoke free and support smoke-free workplace policies; (c) maintain a healthy body weight; (d) follow a healthy diet; (e) if you drink alcohol of any kind, limit the intake (not drinking alcohol is recommended for cancer prevention); (f) avoid too much sun, especially for children, and use sun screen; (g) follow workplace health and safety instructions; (h) reduce high radon levels in the home; (i) for women, breast-feed and be aware that hormone replacement therapy increases the risk of certain cancers; (j) follow prescribed vaccination programs; and (k) participate in organized cancer screening programs.

Become Involved in the Wellness Domains

There are different ways to conceptualize what comprises wellness (e.g., models by Myers and Sweeney, 2005, and Granello, 2013, will be considered in chapter 4). As Greenberg (1985) described it, wellness involves the integration of the major components of health, physical, social, mental, emotional, and spiritual, with "high-level wellness" resulting when these integrated components are also in balance. Zimpher (1992) created a wellness model based on his work with cancer patients, containing seven components: (a) medical health, (b) immune function, (c) lifestyle management, (d) spiritual beliefs and attitudes, (e) psychodynamics, (f) energy forces, and (g) interpersonal relations. It is tailored for working with people already diagnosed. It raises attention to the importance of meaning-in-life issues as they relate to being well.

Hettler (1991) extended the conception of wellness, focused largely on the university student population, to include the domains of occupational and of intellectual wellness. The six dimensions comprising his model, still salient today, are highlighted next and will provide a framework to further explore wellness.

Six Dimensions of Hettler's Hexagonal Model of Wellness

Social
Physical
Occupational
Spiritual
Intellectual
Emotional

Develop social wellness. Being with positive people is good for us. Reaching out to others also is good for us. Social wellness comprises capacities to build personal connections with others, to manage conflict effectively, and to be a part of a positive network of people. Therefore, wellness and prevention education and choice making address improving relationships, support networks, connections with the community, and general involvement with others. Applications might involve becoming involved in a support group, serving in a soup kitchen, and standing up for others who are oppressed, among many others.

Connecting with others activates the therapeutic factor of altruism (Yalom, 1995) and is socially supportive (Pearson, 1990). It can aid one's development in multiple ways. For instance, the "helping connection" is discovered by helpers when they engage in regular, helping contact of a face-to-face variety with people they do not know for at least one hour per week. These volunteer activities can include tutoring, cleaning up the environment, delivering toys or food to needy families, raking leaves for senior citizens, raising money to support surgery, and countless other projects (for an especially dense concentration of such involvements, note events on "Make a Difference Day," occurring during National Volunteer Week in April).

Social connection is vitally important to health, and there is considerable supportive research. Research (World Health Organization, 2014) indicates that those who are disconnected from others are at higher risk for experiencing life-threatening illnesses and for generally experiencing a lower quality of life.

Social wellness, or social well-being, comprises five components (Snyder & Lopez, 2007): (a) social acceptance, or holding and expressing positive attitudes toward other people; (b) social actualization, or caring about society and its positive evolution; (c) social contribution, or a sense that one has something valuable to give to others and the community; (d) social coherence, or perceiving a world that is based on some sense of order and predictability; and (e) social integration, or feeling that one belongs, feels supported, and is part of a community.

I learned a lot about social wellness, especially its elements of connection and support, from our elderly neighbors, Ruby and Oren. They told me one day that they had missed their Saturday card game with friends but maybe three times over the last 35 years—two of those misses were due to funerals and one to a huge ice storm when no one was allowed to use the roads. I was astounded, especially for someone who can find absolutely no value in playing cards! How could this possibly be?

Of course, it turns out that playing cards had very little to do with it. Ruby and Oren said that card playing provided a chance for them to get together with lifelong friends at least once a week to spend time, catch up, gripe and moan, celebrate successes, and tell stories. Now I could understand—it was their consistent way of giving and getting social support, what we know as a critically important factor in promoting health and preventing isolation and decline. I've thought of this as my own "Ruby and Oren Principle."

The direct means for social contact and interaction described through Ruby and Oren's card playing contrasts with seeking social contact through social media, which is a very popular contemporary way to connect with others. Facebook and Skype, for example, can help people to make and continue contact with others, perhaps especially valuable for those who are located at a distance. Mobile apps, such as myfamily App (healthfinder.gov, 2014), provide users with a social connection to improve and maintain their health by retrieving customized wellness and prevention information and tips for healthy living; examples include creating personal health alerts, keeping track of medical check-ups and immunizations, and learning about the services and benefits made available through the Patient Protection and Affordable Care Act. These online vehicles provide virtual outlets for developing and maintaining social contact and acquiring information that can be of much value, and they hold considerable potential for wellness and prevention when used wisely and appropriately.

But their use is not without potential drawbacks. Paying slavish attention to social media and other online sources, such as Facebook and Twitter, can yield a superficial kind of social interaction that is divorced from the realities of actual life circumstances where people interact face-to-face. Caveat emptor.

Social wellness also means that our surroundings are healthy. Workplaces, communities, schools, and families can nurture or they can toxify. Interestingly, people can become more personally well when they recursively act to benefit the common good and reach out and stand up to help those in need.

Some concrete activities people can engage in to develop their social wellness include the following:

- Balancing personal, social, and work time
- Becoming engaged with others in the community
- Developing and maintaining friendships and positive family ties
- Valuing and respecting others
- Reaching out to others and contributing to the community
- Developing ways to manage stress and conflict effectively
- Remembering to enjoy life

Develop physical wellness. Physical activity is 1 of 10 leading health indicators. It is central to the health objectives set out for the United States, captured by the initiative Healthy People 2020 (2014). Physical wellness includes, but exceeds, physical activity. Physical wellness involves making healthy lifestyle choices in physical activity, nutrition, physical safety (e.g., using seat belts), and preventive medical care as well as avoiding drug use. People can be educated and learn to make positive daily choices in such areas as losing weight, stopping smoking, and daily exercise.

Here's one example related to how exercise could be included quite naturally within a challenging lifestyle. A counselor has a client whose job requires weekly air travel across the country. The client protests that she simply cannot ever start a physical exercise program because of the constant interruptions resulting from that air travel. The counselor gently challenges this assertion by pointing out that several airports, including some the client typically travels through, now provide defined walking paths, both indoors and outdoors, for passengers to use during their down time between flight segments. These paths often include posted signs, directions, maps and brochures, mileage, number of steps, and even art positioned along the way—all of which can facilitate and support walking (Baskas, 2014). "I think I will try this out next week at Logan," says the client, "and report back next session to you about how this worked."

Developing and maintaining healthy nutrition and diet also is an essential everyday wellness and prevention best practice. As one positive effect, it helps to combat the epidemic of obesity. In the United States, for instance, more than one-third (34.9%, or 78.6 million) adults are obese. Obesity is a major concern because it is associated with lifestyle-induced (and, therefore, largely preventable) conditions such as heart disease, stroke, type 2 diabetes, and certain cancers (Centers for Disease Control and Prevention, 2014b).

The White House has actively promoted wellness and prevention programs aimed at a number of issues, including obesity reduction and exercise enhancement. For instance, the Let's Move Campaign (2014) sponsored by Michelle Obama ties together these two areas. In another case, the White House and the U.S. Department of Agriculture have promulgated School Wellness Standards (White House, Office of the First Lady, 2014). These standards follow the bipartisan Healthy, Hunger-Free Kids Act (2010) which together set guidelines for nutrition education and physical activity that need to be included within school wellness policies.

Implementing physical wellness measures clearly affects psychological and emotional health. In terms of physical exercise, the human body can benefit from three types (Mayo Clinic, 2013a): (a) *aerobic* exercise, which increases oxygen available by raising heart rates and breathing—the generally accepted guideline is about 150 minutes a week, amounting to about 30 minutes of aerobic exercise over 5 days; (b) *strength training* with resistance bands or weights, which can help stabilize and protect joints while building stronger muscles—these become increasingly important with advancing age; and (c) *stretching* to improve flexibility, reduce stiffness, and improve balance.

A number of technologies can be used to help monitor and regulate physical health and the effects of exercise. Computerized health activity fitness trackers, such as FitBit, Up24, Fuelband, Exerspy, Vivofit, Basis, and Polar Loop, are one of them. These convenient and attractive devices efficiently marry computerized technology with personalized health behavior and can be a distinct aid to wellness and prevention. They allow wearers to track and monitor a range of personal performance variables during activities, such as the number of steps taken during a day, distance traveled, the amount of calories being burned, and the quality of one's nighttime sleep.

Today's monitors also incorporate motivational components, such as social networking and electronic reminders to get up and move. Performance data can be analyzed in relation to goals set by the user. Increasingly, health and fitness centers are incorporating trackers into their training offerings and, extending further, into virtual coaching—avoiding the gym entirely while being monitored at a distance by a coach (Rubin, 2014).

Indeed, there can be no question of the potential for personal empowerment through this handy method of monitoring targeted physical signs. The ongoing personalized data captured by health and fitness trackers provide the means not only for examining evidence of ongoing functioning in important behavioral areas but, also, to guide performance aimed at increasing health. By encouraging wellness and appropriate follow-up treatment, mobile health technology may not only benefit the health of an estimated one-third of the U.S. population but also save the health care system $81 billion, the IMS Institute for Healthcare Informatics estimates (HealthDay News, 2014). At present, though, no long-term, peer-reviewed study has shown that people using activity trackers become and remain more active. As well, some company wellness programs incorporate this kind of technology, allowing employee performance to be monitored, with gains made resulting in reductions in health insurance premiums.

Develop occupational wellness. This dimension of wellness involves deriving satisfaction and personal enrichment from one's work or career. Research also shows how career development wellness and prevention programs can advance a felt sense of vocational hope among adolescents (Brown, Lamp, Telander, & Hacker, 2013).

The place of leisure in one's life also may be related to occupational wellness. Occupational values and interests, life experience and roles, aptitude, contextual supports and constraints, and other career development variables are important to consider in relation to this dimension (Super & Sverko, 1995; Wicker & August, 2000).

In a Swedish study seeking to identify important work place factors that are associated with working parents' mental well-being, stress, and engagement in work, although individual differences apply, it was found that a positive attitude toward parenthood and a flexible work situation within the work setting appear to be most beneficial for the general well-being and work engagement of working parents (Eek & Axmon, 2013).

Excessive "busy-ness" at work can contribute to overall stress. I am guilty, as are many of my colleagues, of complaining about how hard we work (of course, working hard also is a "badge of honor" for too many). There is not nearly enough time to do everything, it seems, and a perceived sense of urgency can persist. In fact, we may be out of balance in this domain. Examining why this may be is important. For instance, if one reason is choice—that is, I choose rather than am told to take on all those responsibilities—then there may be something that I can do to reduce the stress being experienced. If demands are out of our control, then changes in the work setting climate and in expectations for employee production may need to be made.

Employee health programs are available that tie achieving certain performance goals to reduced health care costs. In one university program example, if at least

1,000 points are earned across 10 months, enrollment in the company health care benefit plan for the next coverage year is at the lowest available rate, meaning a savings of $10 to $30 per month, depending on pay. Here are three examples of point-based performance:

- Complete or retake your health assessment: 500 points
- Do 30 minutes of activity on at least 4 separate days: 10 points/week
- Drink water—five glasses of water on at least 5 separate days each week: 5 points/week

This kind of workplace wellness linkage can incentivize participation in wellness and prevention programs, making consistent participation in them more likely. Some critics worry, though, that employers possessing such employee personal performance data could potentially use it against them, and they raise cautions, perhaps eerily reminiscent of George Orwell's "Big Brother." For more about workplace wellness and prevention, see chapter 8.

Develop spiritual wellness. This wellness dimension centers on seeking and finding meaning in daily life and discovering meaning and purpose in one's overall existence (Heintzelman & King, 2014; Reker & Chamberlain, 2000). This exploration may be driven by spiritual and/or religious motivation (e.g., Burke & Miranti, 1995), or it may be secular (Frankl, 1962); considerable scholarly work is under way today exploring both approaches.

Counseling from an existential theoretical base has always illuminated issues of meaning with clients. Other approaches may include those from an Eastern perspective, such as meditation and yoga. Still others may be focused on values clarification and choice-making through workshops and groups. Connections between religious practice may be explored with clients by counselors who are comfortable with this domain, referrals can be made to pastoral counselors or to clerics, and program collaboration between counselors and religious organizations (i.e., churches, synagogues, mosques, temples) are occurring with increased frequency.

Develop intellectual wellness. This domain of wellness focuses on knowledge, on enhancing one's mental acuity, and on appraising events in an accurate and healthy manner (e.g., Beck, 1991; Neimeyer, 1993). Mental stimulation and growth can be nudged through active involvement with tasks, such as crossword puzzles, reading books, surfing the Internet, learning a new language, and tutoring others, and generally to being active with challenging problems. Internet sites such as Lumosity (Lumos Labs, 2014) and Posit Science (2014) provide a variety of ways, guided by research, to cognitively challenge and train the brain; as with physical exercise, it is necessary for continued practice with the experiments to advance capacities. The overall evidence for improving working memory presently is slight but promising (Weir, 2014).

Intellectual wellness also can be enhanced through being socially engaged, that is, getting together with friends and family and the sharing of private thoughts and concerns. Ybarra studied the relationship between social engagement and cognitive functioning both in the United States and in Middle Eastern counties. Conclusions demonstrated a positive correlation between higher levels of social engagement and lower levels of impaired cognitive functioning (Daly, 2011).

Remaining intellectually engaged is important at all ages and is uniquely significant as one matures into "senior status." Although much emphasis is placed on important lifestyle practices, such as exercise and diet, in "staying younger," intellectual activity seems to get relatively short shrift. A significant marker for long life and the prevention of Alzheimer's disease is found in mental involvement. Studies with people having dementia, for example, have found that those who engaged regularly in mind-stimulation activities (watching television, playing cards and other games, visiting museums) realized a decreased incidence of Alzheimer's disease compared with those in a control group situation.

Develop emotional wellness. Both emotional awareness and emotional management are aspects of this wellness domain. To be functioning well, people need to be aware of their thoughts and feelings, and how to monitor and manage them effectively and appropriately. It contains elements of positive affect, absence of negative affect, a sense of contentment or life satisfaction, and happiness (Snyder & Lopez, 2007).

Emotional wellness has been the domain most attended to by counselors and other helpers, especially in terms of remediation (e.g., see counseling theory texts), but also with skill-building programs for those functioning without major dysfunction (e.g., see Lewis, Lewis, Daniels, & D'Andrea, 2010). Moreover, counselor educators and counseling psychologists have developed effective skill training programs to help graduate-level trainees in their work with clients (e.g., Cormier, Nurius, & Osborn, 2009; Hill, 2009; Ivey, Ivey, & Zalaquett, 2013). Research by Kawamichi et al. (2014) shows the neuro benefits emerging from positive listening skills. Developing insight skills in undergraduate students also is garnering increased research and practical interest and was the subject of a major contribution in *The Counseling Psychologist* (Hill, Spanger, Chui, & Jackson, 2014).

Counselors can draw from a vast reservoir of activities to assist people to develop an enhanced emotional wellness (e.g., Kraus, 2003). Communication skills, guided imagery, psychoeducation groups, and other vehicles for personal growth are frequently used. For instance, stress management can be approached from three directions (Mayo Clinic, 2013b): (a) *proactive reducing or eliminating stress-causing events and situations* by simplifying one's daily schedule or learning to say no to new demands or opportunities; (b) *improving overall resiliency* by eating nutritiously, getting good sleep, and exercising; and (c) *monitoring and managing reactions to stressors* by learning how to relax and participating in calming activities such as yoga.

Mutual interaction of the wellness dimensions. These six dimensions of wellness are not independent, even though I have described each as if it were. That is more a matter of communication convenience. In reality, these dimensions mutually interact.

Humans are not compartmentalized into separate domains where the mind exists separate from the body, for example. Wellness enhancements to develop mental functioning can benefit physical functioning, and the reverse. Becoming more physically fit can elevate mood, for instance. Enhancements in the social domain very well may affect the spiritual domain, and vice versa. Becoming more connected with others may evolve a deeper sense of connection with nature. So, it is proper to think in terms of the "human system," where people incorporate interactive combinations of these and other domains, and in relation to larger systems, such as family, school, work, and community, in which they are embedded. Ryff and Keyes (1995) found in their analysis of wellness models that a multidimensional approach was better than one focused on a single factor.

Optimum human development is the goal of wellness initiatives, whatever the domains of interest. This goal is completely consistent with "everyday wellness and prevention." Helping people at any of multiple levels of intervention (e.g., individual to population) to become all that they can be in as many wellness domains as possible—each and every day—is a worthy goal for all counselors.

Develop and Use Life Skills

Life skills are organized and specific tools that people can learn and apply in everyday prevention. The United Nations International Children's Emergency Fund (UNICEF), the World Health Organization (WHO), and several training programs (e.g., Botvin's; discussed in chapter 6) have focused on a related construct: life skills. In each source, a start has begun on identifying sets of life skills that seem generally important in boosting children and adolescents' self-confidence, self-esteem, self-control, and autonomy, as well as to be more able to resist or avoid potential problems, such as substance abuse.

UNICEF (2005), in its *Talking Points for Teachers* document, identified 15 guidelines for the life skills approach. In this context, life skills are psychosocial and interpersonal ones, such as those in communication, decision making, creative thinking, coping, and self-awareness. Five of the life skills guidelines address their purpose, components, methods, settings for use, and process and outcome evaluation.

Danish (2013) reported on a number of strengths-based life skills wellness and prevention programs he has created over the decades. The latest of these programs targets returning service members and their families. These intentional efforts seek to advance participants' skills across socio/interpersonal, personal, emotional, cognitive, physical, and spiritual life domains.

As people advance their life skills, they can negotiate life more successfully and attain higher levels of satisfaction. Notably, because unmanaged stress is one of the biggest challenges of the day, the life skills can prove to be very helpful in lessening and managing stress. They are skills that people can develop and incorporate into their lives (Department of Mental Health, 1999). Moreover, as with the other wellness skill areas we have been considering in this chapter, counselors can enter them into their counseling sessions, and they can be included within wellness and prevention programs.

Carefully Consider Complementary and Alternative Medicine Health Care Approaches

Personal health care is very much on the leading edge of everyday wellness and prevention, as was mentioned earlier in this chapter. Of course, the ideal strategy to adopt in this area is to consistently employ personal best practices in daily life, such as eating well and exercising, as well as teaming with health care providers.

Complementary and Alternative Medicine (CAM) approaches are being used frequently by many as part of an overall strategy for personal wellness (Barnes, Bloom, & Nahin, 2007). According to national survey results (Barnes, Bloom, & Nahin, 2007), 38% of adults and 12% of children in the United States use Complementary and Alternative Medicine (CAM) health approaches as part of an overall strategy for personal wellness. The most commonly employed are non-vitamin and non-mineral natural products and therapeutic approaches such as meditation, massage, and yoga. It is estimated that $34 billion per year is spent on these approaches in the United States, amounting to 11% of out-of-pocket total spending on health care.

Many easily accessible sites addressing overall health and Complementary and Alternative Medicine are available to the public. A long-standing example includes *Psychology Today* (Sussex, 2014), which has addressed mental health issues for the public for decades. Another popular publication with a long history that translates scientific information to the consumer is the magazine *Prevention* (Rodale, 2014). The following "Message to Readers" appears in each issue of that magazine: "Every month *Prevention* brings you up-to-date health information that's thoroughly researched and fact-checked. Our aim is not to replace your medical caregiver but to help you achieve a healthy lifestyle." My aim is not to promote these magazines or Web sites but to offer them as illustrations of how good, personal health care information is available to the average consumer today.

Perhaps located at a step between the popular press and professional scientific journals are reputable newsletters on health, wellness, and prevention. Some of these resources and their accompanying Web sites follow:

About.com StressManagement, http://stress.about.com/od/understanding-stress /u/effects_of_stress.htm?nl=1

Big Think Newsletter, http://www.bigthink.com/

Mayo Clinic Health Letter: Reliable Information for a Healthier Life, http://healthletter.mayoclinic.com/

Harvard Health Letter, http://www.health.harvard/edu

"Today's Headlines" of the Office of Disease Prevention and Health Promotion, http://healthfinder.gov/news/Default.aspx

Johns Hopkins *Health After 50* newsletter, http://www.hopkinsafter50.com/

TED Talks, http://www.ted.com/

University of California, Berkeley *Wellness Letter*, http://www.berkeleywellness.com/

Work Life Nation: Transforming Work Stress, Cultivating Resilience, http://www.worklifenation.com

Prevention Matters, http://www.surgeongeneral.gov/index.html

Public Health Law News, http://www.cdc.gov/phlp/news/current.html

Agency for Healthcare Research and Quality (AHRQ, 2014). Four *Stay Healthy* brochures, based on U.S. Preventive Services Task Force recommendations, are available on the AHRQ Web site, http://www.ahrq.gov/patients-consumers/prevention/lifestyle/index.html: *Men: Stay Healthy at Any Age, Men: Stay Healthy at 50+, Women: Stay Healthy at Any Age*, and *Women: Stay Healthy at 50+*.

These sources, again through hard copy or via the Internet, provide consumers with regular, direct, and salient scientifically valid information about a range of wellness and lifestyle issues. Mental health workers may find introducing wellness and prevention concepts and activities to clients through referral to these resources to be a low-threat and acceptable avenue.

The federal government also has formally recognized the wide attention to and participation in personal health care practices. The venerable National Institutes of Health has established and funded its National Center for Complementary and Alternative Medicine (NCCAM). Complementary and Alternative Medicine (CAM) is defined by NCCAM as a group of medical and health care systems, practices, and products that are not currently included within conventional medicine. Complementary medicine is used together with conventional medicine, while alternative medicine is used in place of conventional medicine.

In general, wellness and prevention counseling can take advantage of CAM approaches, and doing so is consistent with a belief that many individuals can and should assume increased personal responsibility for creating and maintaining a positive lifestyle and for being proactive in their own health care. Engaging in yoga and practicing meditation are two excellent examples that are increasingly being used and being made more widely available to the public, as I have cited. For instance, I found the simple instructions for preparing to meditate that I've adapted, below, posted on a telephone pole in Seattle's International District (November 11, 2013):

Simple Meditation Instruction: Tame the Monkey Mind, Calm the Unsettled Heart

Choose a suitable time to meditate. Sit with a solid straight back, tip of tongue slightly curled up and touch your upper gums. Place right hand on top of left and two thumbs slightly touched and place comfortably on your lap for energy circulation. Sit in full lotus position with two legs crossed over each other or in half lotus with right leg crossed over the left. Individuals with physical limitations may use a chair or back support. Do not flex or restrain your muscles while meditating; it must be in a relaxed and tension free posture. . .

(Adapted, No Source)

Meditation and the other various everyday wellness and prevention practices discussed in this chapter, when used wisely, can contribute to a better and more fulfilling life—for clients and practitioners alike.

Settings- and System-Centered Everyday Wellness and Prevention Practice Areas

As powerful as person-centered approaches can be, everyday wellness and prevention cannot be fully accomplished exclusively through implementing person-centered best practices, as I have asserted. *The person-centered perspective must be balanced with a settings- and system-centered one.* People live their lives in context and in systems, and each is mutually influencing. This is an ecological perspective (Conyne & Cook, 2004; Cook, 2012), and it is central to wellness and prevention, in general.

Based on organizational ecology, there are five key criteria for organizational health that can illustrate everyday prevention from a system-centered perspective: (a) A sense of personal and work identity is fostered, (b) reality testing is provided so members can get feedback, (c) task accomplishment is realized, (d) problem solving and adaptability are supported, and (e) energy flow is fostered from members connecting, collaborating, and generating together.

Another example of this ecological perspective is captured by the notion "habitats of the heart" (Little, 2000); that is, people link with environments and tend to value those special places and personal niches (Willi, 1999) where they can be themselves, pursue fundamentally important projects, communicate deeply, and realize interpersonal effectiveness. Incidentally, recall that there is no broadly accessible taxonomy of situations or environments that promotes or disturbs human functioning (Hogan & Roberts, 2000), although certain initiatives are gaining steam, such as the range of scientific and practical explorations of positive psychology occurring (e.g., those reported in Snyder & Lopez, 2007) and the Heroic Imagination Project of Zimbardo and associates (2011). This deficit also needs correcting so that wellness and prevention can proceed more clearly: Taxonomies for the "good life" and guidelines for positively changing situations that foster human growth both are awaiting further development and expansion.

Perhaps we can make a start by identifying what would appear to be some important ways everyday wellness and prevention occur within major systems of our lives. I draw from an adaptation of Maton (2000) to Bronfenbrenner's classic conception of ecosystem levels (i.e., microsystem, mesosystem, exosystem, and macrosystem).

Maton envisioned a person interacting within and across settings (family, neighborhood, workplace, school). These settings, in turn, are embedded within an ever-enlarging set of mutually influencing systems or levels (community, society, world). This model provides a way to conceptualize people within environments using concepts (e.g., settings and systems/levels) that are common to our experience. It shows how people interact within and across settings that are embedded within increasingly complex systems, explicating one way to view everyday wellness and prevention from a system-centered perspective. People will not become successful wellness and preventive agents in their own lives by seeking person change only. These efforts must be contextualized. A sense of "we" must counterbalance that of "me."

Thirteen System-Centered Strategies for Everyday Wellness and Prevention

Needed is a set of system-centered actions or best practices, comparable to the various sets of person-centered best practices that you read about earlier in this chapter. The operable questions are as follows: (a) What can people do within settings and systems to improve their own health and that of others? and (b) How can counselors and other mental health practitioners augment their practice to include these actions?

Some useful directions can be found in the counselor social advocacy literature (e.g., Aldarondo, 2007; Kenny, Horne, Orpinas, & Reese, 2009; Ratts, 2009) and in the novel work of the Heroic Imagination Project (Zimbardo, 2011) referred to earlier. However, much more needs to be accomplished to help people practice everyday wellness and prevention through system-centered involvement—and to show counselors and other helpers how they can support those efforts.

Guided by the setting-level analysis of Maton (2000) described earlier, and others cited, here are a baker's dozen of system-centered actions that people can take for improving their wellness and that of the settings and systems of which they are a part. These actions also can be supported and encouraged by mental health professionals with their clients and be included within wellness and prevention programs:

1. Develop relationships and support (Reblin & Uchino, 2008) within and across settings because it is through human relationships that people feel validated and supported.
2. Connect with the natural environment (Capra, 1996; Taylor, Segal, & Harper, 2010), because people and societies are embedded in and dependent on the cyclical processes of nature.

3. View yourself as an active participant in and across settings: family, work, school, neighborhood/community (Prilleltensky, Dokecki, Frieden, & Wang, 2007), because passive acceptance or ignorance of events and conditions fosters dysfunction while active participation can empower change. The value of volunteering ("helping connection") to help others is a powerful means.
4. Collaborate with others on responsible change efforts in and across settings (Dougherty, 2013), as collaboration with others provides a necessary and powerful means for effecting social improvement.
5. Empower yourself and others toward greater opportunity, mastery, and collective efficacy, and with the ability to become an "everyday hero" (Bandura, 1997; McWhirter, 1994; McWhirter & McWhirter, 2007; Zimbardo, 2011). Empowerment in context is the guiding frame of reference for building genuine mastery.
6. Work with others to create positive settings (Eccles & Gootman, 2002). These kinds of settings are characterized by being physically and psychologically safe; appropriately structured, flexible, and orderly; supportive and challenging; provide opportunities to belong; possess positive social norms; provide support for efficacy and mattering; generate opportunities for autonomy and skill building; and that integrate efforts across family, school, work, and community.
7. Become more aware of how distal forces (e.g., world economic, political, and educational policies; media and advertising messages) affect self and others (Bronfenbrenner, 1979). Our everyday life experience is influenced by local and remote (to us) forces. Events occurring on the other side of the globe from us, such as the Arab Spring or economic changes in the Chinese economy, ripple around the world and ultimately influence life here.
8. Develop the powerful resource of resilience (Kumpfer & Summerhays, 2006; Masten & Reed, 2002) or the capacity for positive adaptation under extenuating circumstances. People cannot control events and experiences, but they can learn how to cope well in response to surprises and challenges.
9. Develop social well-being (Keyes, 1998; Keyes & Lopez, 2002), including social acceptance, social actualization, social contribution, social coherence, and social integration (see discussion earlier in this chapter about social wellness).
10. Develop environmental competence (Steele, 1980) and ecological concordance (Conyne & Cook, 2004), or the ability to be aware of one's environment and its impact—and of one's impact on the environment—and to use or change it to provide a more optimal fit.
11. Develop cultural competence, by becoming aware of one's own identity and culture and that of other groups of people, by developing skills to interact positively and effectively with those who are culturally different, and becoming able to advocate for social justice competence (Association for Specialists in Group Work, 2012; Sue & Sue, 2012).
12. Seek social justice by directly participating in actions aimed at broadening equity and access and by helping willing clients to challenge social pathologies such as oppression, privilege, racism, inequity, and lack of access to resources and

power (Albee, 1986; Crethar, Rivera, & Nash, 2008; Kenny et al., 2009; Ratts, 2009).

13. Build social justice interventions into your practice but also within counselor training, including such areas as advocacy, outreach, influencing public policy, and—of course—wellness and prevention programs (*Guidelines for Prevention in Psychology*, 2013; Hage & Kenny, 2009; Lewis, Lewis, Daniels, & D'Andrea, 2010; Pirog & Good, 2013; Vera & Kenny, 2013).

Role of the Counselor in Everyday Wellness and Prevention

Everyday wellness and prevention is conceptualized as a continuous program of involvements that people engage in directly within their life contexts. These involvements might be consistent with any of the broad array of person- and system-centered domains discussed in this chapter. A chief characteristic of everyday wellness and prevention, therefore, is the locus of change.

Everyday wellness and prevention is something that people can do to enhance their lives and protect against adverse external forces. Counselors and other health care providers and educators also can be of great assistance in helping people to intentionally include everyday wellness and prevention practices within their ongoing life contexts.

As mentioned earlier, the counselor role in everyday wellness and prevention is threefold:

- to serve as an "honest broker," linking and spreading knowledge, skills, and strategies with individual clients, groups, in organizations, communities, and across a designated population through (a) wellness and prevention programs that have demonstrated (see chapters 6 and 7 on wellness and prevention programs in family, school, community, and workplace settings and chapter 8 addressing system-level wellness and prevention), (b) sets of person-centered skills (such as in the Life Skills program, but many others as well), or (c) sets of system-centered skills, including those involved with promoting social justice, where social pathologies are targeted and sometimes directly challenged, through such interventions as taking individual action in challenging situations, policy change, advocacy, outreach, and consultation.
- to develop and/or to adapt effective wellness and prevention programs to be spread broadly through new applications

Everyday wellness and prevention is undertaken by people as they lead their lives. These people are the change agents, the decision makers, the enacters of wellness and prevention in their own lives and in the settings and systems in which they lead their lives. Counselors can assist people in reaching that goal by facilitating their adoption of everyday wellness and prevention practices. Indeed, that is the premise underlying the subtitle of this book: *Helping People Become Empowered in Systems and Settings*.

Issues for Reflection and Discussion

1. Pair up with another person and discuss how each of you is presently applying everyday wellness and prevention in your own life. (10 minutes each)
2. How can counselors assist communities and other organized environments, such as schools, enhance their collective wellness? Identify three concrete actions:

   Action A: ______________________________

   Action B: ______________________________

   Action C: ______________________________
3. What forces serve to inhibit people, and environments, from putting everyday wellness and prevention into practice? Think of an example related to one person, and another that references a neighborhood, and a third that affects a work setting. Then, again, pair up and share your thoughts. What did you find in common? What was different? (10 minutes each person)

References

Agency for Healthcare Research and Quality. (2014, May). *Living a healthy lifestyle.* Retrieved from http://www.ahrq.gov/patients-consumers/prevention/lifestyle/index.html

Albee, G. (1986). Toward a just society: Lessons from observations on the primary prevention of psychopathology. *American Psychologist, 41*, 891–898. doi:10.1037/0003-066X.41.8.891

Aldarondo, E. (Ed.). (2007). *Promoting social justice through mental health practice.* Mahwah, NJ: Erlbaum.

American Psychiatric Association. (2013). *Diagnostic and statistical manual of mental disorders* (5th ed.). Washington, DC: Author.

American Psychological Association. (2014). *Research in action.* Retrieved from http://www.apa.org/research/action/index.aspx

American Psychological Association Practice Central. (2014, October 9). *New fact sheet for psychologists and patients on maintaining a heart-healthy lifestyle: Maintaining a heart-healthy lifestyle.* Retrieved from http://www.apapracticecentral.org/update;2014/10–09/heart-healthy-lifestyle.pdf

Association for Specialists in Group Work. (2012). *Multicultural and social justice competency principles for group workers.* Retrieved from http://asgw.org/pdf/ASGW_MC_SJ_Priniciples_Final_ASGW.pdf

Bandura, A. (1997). *Self-efficacy: The exercise of control.* New York: Freeman.

Barnes, P., Bloom, B., & Nahin, R. (2007). Complementary and alternative medicine use among adults and children: United States, 2007. *National Health Statistics Reports, 12*, 1–23. doi:10.1037/e623942009-001

Baskas, H. (2014, October 20). Take a hike! (at an airport near you). *USA Today*, 7B.

Beck, A. (1991). *Cognitive therapy and the emotional disturbances.* London, England: Penguin.

Bronfenbrenner, U. (1979). *The ecology of human development: Experiments by nature and design.* Cambridge, MA: Harvard University Press.

Brown, S., Lamp, K., Telander, K., & Hacker, J. (2013). Career development as prevention: Toward a social cognitive model of vocational hope. In E. Vera (Ed.), *The Oxford handbook of prevention in counseling psychology* (pp. 374–392). New York: Oxford University Press.

Burke, M. T., & Miranti, J. G. (Eds.). (1995). *Counseling: The spiritual dimension.* Alexandria, VA: American Counseling Association.

Capra, F. (1996). *The web of life: A new scientific understanding of living systems.* New York: Anchor Books.

Centers for Disease Control and Prevention. (2014a). *Heart disease facts.* Retrieved from http://www.cdc.gov/heartdisease/facts.htm

Centers for Disease Control and Prevention. (2014b). *Overweight and obesity.* Retrieved from http://www.cdc.gov/obesity/data/adult.html

Conyne, R., & Cook, E. (Eds.). (2004). *Ecological counseling: An innovative conceptualization for person-environment interaction.* Alexandria, VA: American Counseling Association.

Cook, E. P. (Ed.). (2012). *Understanding people in context: The ecological perspective in counseling.* Alexandria, VA: American Counseling Association.

Cooper, B. B. (2013, August 6). *10 simple things you can do today that will make you happier, backed by research.* Retrieved from http://blog.bufferapp.com/10-scientifically-proven-ways-to-make-yourself- happier

Cormier, S., Nurius, P., & Osborn, C. (2009). *Interviewing and change strategies for helpers: Fundamental skills and cognitive-behavioral interventions* (6th ed.). Belmont, CA: Cengage Learning.

Craik, K. (1991). The lived day of an individual: A person-environment perspective. In W. B. Walsh, K. Craik, & R. Price (Eds.), *Person-environment psychology: New directions and perspectives* (pp. 233–266). Mahwah, NJ: Erlbaum.

Crethar, H., Rivera, E. T., & Nash, S. (2008). In search of common threads: Linking multicultural, feminist, and social justice counseling paradigms. *Journal of Counseling & Development, 86,* 269–278.

Daly, M. (2011, November). Stay connected: Friends and family can help you build brainpower, too. *Prevention.* Retrieved from http://www.prevention.com/health/brain-games/social-connection

Danish, S. (2013). A life skills, community-based approach for helping returning service members and their families In E. Vera (Ed.), *The Oxford handbook of prevention in counseling psychology* (pp. 393–408). New York, NY: Oxford University Press. doi:10.1093/oxfordhb/9780195396423.001.0001

Department of Mental Health, World Health Organization. (1999). *Mental health promotion partners in life skills education.* Retrieved from http://www.who.int/ mental_health/media/en/30.pdf

Dougherty, A. M. (2013). *Prevention and consultation.* Thousand Oaks, CA: Sage.

Dowd, S., Vickers, K. S., & Krahn, D. (2004). Exercise for depression: It really does help—here's how to get patients moving. *Current Psychiatry, 3,* 10–20.

Dweck, C.S. (2006). *Mindset: The new psychology of success.* New York, NY: Random House.

Eccles, J.S., & Gootman, J.A. (Eds.). (2002). *Community Programs to Promote Youth Development/Committee on Community-Level Programs for Youth.* Washington DC: National Academy Press.

Eek, F., & Axmon, A. (2013). *Attitude and flexibility are the most important work place factors for working parents' mental wellbeing, stress, and work engagement. Scandinavian Journal of Public Health, 41,* 692–705. doi:10.1177/1403494813491167

Frankl, V. (1962). *Man's search for meaning: An introduction to logotherapy.* New York, NY: Washington Square Press.

Granello, P.F. (2013). *Wellness counseling.* Upper Saddle River, NJ: Merrill-Pearson.

Greenberg, J. (1985). Health and wellness: A conceptual differentiation. *Journal of School Health, 55,* 403–406. doi:10.1111/j.1746-1561.1985.tb01164.x

Guidelines for Prevention in Psychology (2013). *American Psychologist, 69*, 285–269. Doi: 10.1037/a0034569

Hage, S., & Kenny, M. (2009). Promoting a social justice approach to prevention: Future directions for training, practice, and research. *Journal of Primary Prevention, 30*, 75–87.

HealthDay News. (2014, September 23). *Report identifies game changers for U.S. health care.* Retrieved from http://www.healthfinder.gov/News/Article.aspx?id=691988&source =govdelivery&utm_medium=email&utm_source=govdelivery

Healthfinder.gov. (2014, October 14). *Stay connected.* Retrieved from https://sslvpn.uc.edu/ StayConnected/,DanaInfo=www.healthfinder.gov+

Healthy, Hunger-Free Kids Act (2010). Public Law 111–296. Retrieved from https:// www.govtrack.US/Congress/bills/111/s3307

Healthy People 2020 (2014). https://www.healthypeople.gov/

Heintzelman, S., & King, L. (2014). Life is pretty meaningful. *American Psychologist, 69*, 561–574.

Heroic Imagination Project (2013). http://heroic imagination.org/

Hettler, B. (1991). Keynote speech: Wellness. Paper presented at the American Association of Counseling and Development, Reno, NV.

Hill, C. (2009). *Helping skills: Facilitating exploration, insight, and action* (4th ed.). Washington, DC: American Psychological Association.

Hill, C., Spangler, P., Chui, H., & Jackson, J. (2014). Training undergraduate students to use insight skills: Overview of the rationale, methods, and analysis for three studies. *The Counseling Psychologist, 42*, 702–728.

Hillenbrand, L. (2010). *Unbroken: A World War II story of survival, resilience, and redemption.* New York, NY: Random House.

Hogan, R., & Roberts, B. (2000). A socioanalytic analysis perspective of person-environment interaction. In W. Walsh, K. Craik, & R. Price (Eds.), *Person-environment psychology: New directions and perspectives* (pp. 1–24). Mahwah, NJ: Erlbaum.

International Agency for Research on Cancer. (2014). *European code against cancer: 12 ways to reduce your cancer risk.* Retrieved from http://cancer-code-europe.iarc.fr/index.php/en/

Ivey, A., Ivey, M. B., & Zalaquett, C. (2013). *Intentional interviewing and counseling: Facilitating client development in a multicultural society* (8th ed.). Belmont, CA: Cengage Learning.

Kawamichi, H., Yoshihara, K., Sasaki, A. T., Sugawara, S. K., Tanabe, H. C., Shinohara, R., . . . Sadato, N. (2014, September 4). Perceiving active listening activates the reward system and improves the impression of relevant experiences. *Social Neuroscience*, 1–11. doi:10.1 080/17470919.2014.954732

Kenny, M. E., Horne, A. M., Orpinas, P., & Reese, L. E. (Eds.). (2009). *Realizing social justice: The challenge of preventive interventions.* Washington, DC: American Psychological Association. doi:10.1037/11870-000

Keyes, C. (1998). Social well-being. *Social Psychology Quarterly*, 61, 121–140. doi:10.2307/ 2787065

Keyes, C., & Lopez, S. (2002). Toward a science of mental health: Positive directions in diagnosis and interventions. In C. Snyder & S. Lopez (Eds.), *Handbook of positive psychology* (pp. 45–62.). New York, NY: Oxford University Press.

Kraus, K. (2003). *Exercises in group work.* Columbus, OH: Merrill Prentice Hall.

Kumpfer, K., & Summerhays, J. (2006). Prevention approaches to enhance resilience among high-risk youth: Comments on the papers of Dishion & Connell and Greenberg. *Annals of the New York Academy of Science, 1094*, 151–163.

Let's Move Campaign (2014). *Let's Move! America's move to raise a healthier generation of kids.* Retrieved from http://www.letsmove.gov/initiatives

Lewis, J. A., Lewis, M. D., Daniels, J. A., & D'Andrea, M. J. (2010). *Community counseling: A multicultural–social justice perspective.* Belmont, CA: Brooks/Cole.

Little, B. (2000). Free traits and personal contexts: Expanding a social ecological model of well-being. In W.B. Walsh, K. Craik, & R. Price (Eds.), *Person-environment psychology: New directions and perspectives* (2nd ed., pp. 87–116). Mahwah, NJ: Erlbaum.

Lum, T.Y., & Lightfoot, E. (2005). The effects of volunteering on the physical and mental health of older people. *Research on Aging, 27*(1), 31–55.

Lumos Labs. (2014). *Lumosity: Human cognition project.* Retrieved from http://www.lumosity.com/

Masten, A. S. (2001). Ordinary magic: Resilience processes in development. *American Psychologist, 56*(3), 227–238. doi 10.1037/0003-066x.56.3.227

Masten, A., & Reed, M.-G. (2002). Resilience in development. In C. Snyder & S. Lopez (Eds.), *Handbook of positive psychology* (pp. 74–88). New York, NY: Oxford University Press.

Maton, K. (2000). Making a difference: The social ecology of social transformation. *American Journal of Community Psychology, 28*, 25–57.

Mayo Clinic. (2013a). Fitness basics. Retrieved from http://www.mayoclinic.org/healthyliving/fitness/basics/aerobic-exercise/hlv- 20049447

Mayo Clinic. (2013b). Stress management: Examine your stress reaction. Retrieved from http://www.mayoclinic.org/stress-management/art-20044289?pg=2

McWhirter, B., & McWhirter E.H. (2007). Toward an emancipator communitarian approach to the practice of psychology training. In E. Aldorando (Ed.), *Advancing social justice through clinical training* (pp. 391–416). Mahwah, NJ: Erlbaum. doi:10.4324/9780203936689

Murphy, S., Xu, J., & Kochanek, K. (2013). Deaths: Final data for 2010. *National Vital Statistics Reports, 61*(4). Retrieved from http://www.cdc.gov/nchs/data/nvsr/nvsr61/nvsr61_04.pdf

Murray, B. (2003, October). Rebounding from losses: Psychologists shared how they've applied resilience-building strategies from APA's public education campaign. *Monitor on Psychology, 34*(9). Retrieved from http://www.apa.org/monitor/

Myers, J. (1992). *Wellness throughout the lifespan* (Vol. 24). Denver, CO: Love.

Myers, J., & Sweeney, T. (2005). *Counseling for wellness: Theory, research, and practice.* Alexandria, VA: American Counseling Association.

Neimeyer, R. (1993). An appraisal of constructivist psychotherapy. *Journal of Consulting and Clinical Psychology*, 61, 221–234. doi:10.1037/0022-006x.61.2.221

Pearson, R. (1990). *Counseling and social support.* Newbury Park, CA: Sage.

Peterson, C., & Seligman, M.E.P. (2004). *Character strengths and virtues: A handbook and classification.* New York, NY: Oxford University Press.

Pirog, M., & Good, E. (2013). *Public policy and mental health: Avenues for prevention.* Thousand Oaks, CA: Sage.

Posit Science. (2014). *brainHQ.* Retrieved from http://www.positscience.com/

Prilleltensky, I. (1997). Values, assumptions, and practices: Assessing the moral implications of psychological discourse and action. *American Psychologist*, 52, 517–535. doi:10.1037/0003-066x.52.5.517

Prilleltensky, I., Dokecki, P., Frieden, G., & Wang, V. O. (2007). Counseling for wellness and justice: Foundations and ethical dilemmas. In E. Aldarondo (Ed.),

Advancing social justice through clinical practice (pp. 19–42). Mahwah, NJ: Erlbaum. doi:10.4324/9780203936689

Ratey, J.J., & Hagerman, E. (2013). *Spark: The revolutionary new science of exercise and the brain.* New York, NY: Little, Brown.

Rath, T. (2007). *Strengths Finder 2.0.* New York, NY: Gallup Press.

Ratts, M.J. (2009). Social justice counseling: Toward the development of a "fifth force" among counseling paradigms. *Journal of Humanistic Counseling, Education, and Development, 48,* 160–172. doi:10.1002/j.2161-1939.2009.tb00076.x

Reblin, M., & Uchino, B. (2008). Social and emotional support and its implication for health. *Current Opinion in Psychiatry, 21,* 201–205. doi:10.1097/2FYCO.0b013e3282f3ad89

Reker, G., & Chamberlain, K. (Eds.). (2000). *Exploring existential meaning: Optimizing human development across the life span.* Thousand Oaks, CA: Sage. doi:10.4135/9781452233703

Rodale. (2014). *Prevention magazine.* Retrieved from http://www.rodaleinc.com/brand/prevention

Rubin, C. (2014, April 16). Your trainer saw that. *New York Times.* Retrieved from http://www.nytimes.com/2014/04/17/fashion/devices-like-fitbit-and-up24-being-used-by-gyms-to-track-clients-fitness-activity.html

Rutledge, R., Skandali, N., Dayan P., & Dolan, R. (2014). A computational and neural model of momentary subjective well-being. *Proceedings of the National Academy of Sciences of the United States of America, 111,* 12252–12257. doi:10.1073/pnas.1407535111

Ryff, C., & Keyes, C. (1995). The structure of psychological well-being revisited. *Journal of Personality and Social Psychology, 69,* 719–727. doi:10.1037/0022-3514.69.4.719

Seligman, M. (1998). What is the "good life"? *Monitor on Psychology, 29*(10), 1–3.

Seligman, M. (2002). *Using the new psychology to realize your potential for lasting fulfillment.* New York, NY: Simon & Schuster.

Seligman, M. E. P., & Csikszentmihalyi, M. (2000). Positive psychology: An introduction. *American Psychologist, 55,* 5–14. doi:10.1037/0003-066x.55.1.5

Snyder, C., & Lopez, S. (2007). *Positive psychology: The scientific and practical explorations of human strengths.* Thousand Oaks, CA: Sage.

Steele, F. (1980). Defining and developing environmental competence. In C. P. Alderfer & C. L. Cooper (Eds.), *Advances in experiential social processes* (Vol. 2, pp. 225–244). New York, NY: John Wiley.

Sue, D. W., & Sue, D. (2012). *Counseling the culturally different* (6th ed.). New York, NY: John Wiley.

Super, D., & Sverko, B. (Eds.). (1995). *Life roles, values, and careers: International findings of the work impact study.* San Francisco, CA: Jossey-Bass.

Sussex. (2014). *Psychology today.* Retrieved from http://www.psychologytoday.com/aboutcontact

Taylor, D., Segal, D., & Harper, N. (2010). The ecology of adventure therapy: An integral systems approach to therapeutic change. *Ecopsychology, 2,* 77–83. doi:10.1089/eco.2010.0002.

Tsutsui, Y. (2013). Weather and individual happiness. *Weather, Climate and Society, 5,* 70–82. doi:10.1175/WCAS-D-11-00052.1

UNICEF. (2005, January). *Teachers talking about learning.* Retrieved from http://www.unicef.org/teachers

Vera, E., & Kenny, M. E. (2013). *Social justice and culturally relevant prevention.* Thousand Oaks, CA: Sage. doi:10.4135/9781452275598

Walsh, R. (2011). Lifestyle and mental health. *American Psychologist, 66,* 579–592.

Walsh, W., Craik, K., & Price, R. (Eds.). (2000). *Person-environment psychology: New directions*. Mahwah, NJ: Erlbaum.

Weir, K. (2014). Mind games: Can brain-training games keep your mind young? *Monitor on Psychology, 45*(9), 43–46.

White House, Office of the First Lady. (2014, February 25). *The White House and USDA announce School Wellness Standards*. Retrieved from http://www.letsmove.gov/initiatives

Wicker, A.W., & August, R.A. (2000). Working lives in context: Engaging the views of participants and analysts. In W.B. Walsh, K.H. Craik, & R.H. Price (Eds.), *Person-environment psychology: New directions and perspectives* (2nd ed., pp. 197–232). Hillsdale, NJ: Erlbaum. doi:10.4324/9781410605771

Willi, J. (1999). *Ecological psychotherapy: Developing by shaping the personal niche*. Seattle, WA: Hogrefe & Huber.

World Health Organization. (2014). *Social determinants of health*. Retrieved from http://www.who.int/social_determinants/en/

Yalom, I. (1995). *The theory and practice of group psychotherapy*. New York, NY: Basic Books.

Zimbardo, P. (2011, August 20). *The heroic imagination project* [Video]. Retrieved from https://www.youtube.com/watch?v=mWQq0E8ENSc

Zimpher, D. G. (1992). Psychosocial treatment of life-threatening disease: *A wellness model. Journal of Counseling and Development, 71*(2), 203–209. doi:10.1002/j.1556-6676.1992.tb02201.x

3

WELLNESS AND PREVENTION STRATEGIES IN MENTAL HEALTH

> How great it will be when the Wellness & Prevention Paradigm is the foundation of healthcare and so much of the tragic suffering and death are prevented. This is not a pipe dream. This is an evidence-based goal and it is an achievable goal.
>
> —Chestnut (2011, p. 218)

Introduction

What are the fundamental strategies that support wellness and prevention? This chapter begins by examining the public health and medical health models in relation to wellness and prevention. The place of wellness and prevention within the counseling profession is considered historically. The majority of the chapter is then devoted to discussing major seven broad strategies in wellness and prevention: (a) education, (b) social competency facilitation, (c) natural caregiving connection, (d) community organization and system intervention (COSI), (e) environmental redesign, (f) assisting developmental transitions, and (g) encouraging everyday wellness and prevention.

Public Health and the Medical Model in Relation to Wellness and Prevention

Two classic health models anchor what essentially are polar opposites on the health continuum. Each one historically has generated unique and significant contributions to fight illness and dysfunction and to support healthier functioning. But each also goes about the task differently. One result is that wellness and prevention is directly supported by one model but only indirectly so (some might argue, blocked) by the other one. These models are public health and the medical model.

Public Health Model: Direct Support for Wellness and Prevention in Mental Health

Wellness and prevention are the products of several disciplines. However, the clearest and strongest contributor is public health. Itself containing several subdisciplines, public health is the science and art of preventing disease, promoting health, and prolonging life. It adopts an incidence reduction approach aimed at an entire population. It is focused on eradicating known environmental causes of an infectious disease (such as draining swamps in relation to malaria), removing agents of transmission (such as mosquitoes) or sometimes quarantining those already infected or at risk of having been infected, and strengthening the resistance of the host to the disease (e.g., through inoculation or improved daily health practices).

This public health model has been dramatically effective in preventing a number of illnesses and diseases. For instance, the scourge of small pox has been stamped out, and malaria has been eliminated in 111 countries with active eradication programs underway in the remaining 98 where malaria still has a pernicious presence (Liu, Modrek, Gosling, & Feachem, 2013). Considerable progress is being made with reducing the spread of HIV/AIDS through public health and other behavioral interventions (Centers for Disease Control and Prevention, 2013). Currently, the public health model is being employed against the deadly Ebola virus epidemic emanating from West Africa and with enterovirus D68, a flulike virus disease that is infecting children throughout the United States (Kluger, 2014).

Embedded in the public health model are six significant strategies (see the following box).

Public Health Model

Incidence reduction
Population focus
Environmental changes
Breaking the transmittal process
Managing fear
Strengthening the host

Medical Model: Indirect Support for Wellness and Prevention in Mental Health

The medical model provides direct support for traditional reactive practice in addressing existing physical and mental illness and dysfunction. It is the basis of what Chestnut (2011) refers to as the "sickness and treatment" approach. Its hallmarks are to cure an existing disease or dysfunction or, if that is not possible, to relieve suffering. It is marked by after-the-fact remediation typically delivered to one person (the client) by a professional practitioner (counselor, social worker, psychologist) to correct an identified dysfunction so that the client can return to usual functioning.

Although much more complicated, major mechanisms of the medical model treatment approach typically involve the following. A person seeks medical or psychological aid for distress being currently experienced, chronically or acutely, from a licensed practitioner. In mental health, let's use the example of depression. That person now becomes a client or patient of the practitioner, who establishes a positive working relationship and assesses the client's situation using interview and possibly testing. A diagnosis is sought by the practitioner, which then is tied to a particular treatment or set of treatment options, such as cognitive therapy, that may include referral for prescriptive medication (e.g., one of the selective serotonin reuptake inhibitors, SSRIs, such as Paxil). When the treatment is followed by the client under the guidance and supervision of the practitioner, the intention is to relieve or remove symptoms, restoring the client to a state of homeostasis, being more or less free from depression.

A secondary intention in the medical model is for the client to gain knowledge and skills that might apply in coping effectively with future situations (e.g., helping a client learn how problem-solving skills learned now can be used to better manage events in the future), or to give specific concern to others in a client's world who are impacted by the client's situation (e.g., suggesting that family members might join counseling with the client). These represent very important opportunities for wellness and prevention. Counselors who function with clients in this way can be thought of as engaging in "prevention-minded treatment" (Mrazek & Ritchie, 2012).

Major steps involved in the medical model are summarized in the following box.

Medical Model

Establish positive working relationship
Assess
Diagnose
Develop a treatment plan
Client follows the plan
Problem correction or cure is achieved
Secondarily, apply learning to future situations

Preventive effects within the medical model: Being "prevention-minded." The secondary intention of working in a remedial fashion with clients clearly is preventive and its importance should not be underestimated. So, even within the medical model of suffering and treatment it is very possible to exert a preventive effect in several ways. Chapter 5 addresses this topic in detail, but five important ways are addressed next:

1. Intrapersonal focus: The counselor teaches clients intrapersonal skills that can be used not only in relation to correcting the current problem being addressed (say, anxiety) but which clients can apply and perhaps generalize for future benefit in similar and other aspects of their lives. That means wellness and prevention. An example of such a set of skills is found in learning stress management strategies, such as practicing deep breathing, to more productively handle future life demands. Referral to other health providers possessing expertise in areas of wellness can be very appropriate, also, such as to a nutritionist, then processing and monitoring behavior trials in ongoing counseling.
2. Relationship focus: Here the counselor helps clients to learn and apply in future situations more effective ways of perceiving and acting on their relationships with others. The presenting problem might revolve around communication challenges involved with one's life partner. Counselors can help individual clients modify, as necessary, and generalize skills they learned in how to better communicate with their partner to other situations, as well, such as to communication issues that may be occurring at work.

   A relationship focus also invites direct counseling methods that capitalize on interpersonal interactions and processes. The two main interpersonal interventions are group work and family counseling. Group work (ASGW, 2000) is a comprehensive interpersonal process approach with four main types: (a) task facilitation groups, such as committees and classrooms; (b) psychoeducation groups, which typically are the group type most often included in wellness and prevention programs because of their emphasis on competency enhancement; (c) counseling groups, which approach problems of daily living through interpersonal problem solving; and (d) psychotherapy groups, which are geared toward alleviating dysfunction through group interaction. Family counseling aims to produce therapeutic benefit by focusing on the relationships existing among members of a family system.
3. External systems focus: Counselors frequently help clients who come to them with problems that express themselves in a particular setting, such as at work or school. One stance, a fairly typical one unfortunately, is to help these clients to adapt to the environment. The underlying assumption is that the environment is healthy and the client is not. An opposed stance is for counselors to assist clients to more proactively interact within the environment, learning how to take action steps toward shaping their environment or, perhaps, in making a choice to select another more positive one. The assumption here is that the client is healthy while the particular environment is not.

   In a related way, counselors also can become advocates for changing negative social systems and noxious aspects of the environment. Advocacy is an indirect means of assisting client issues and promoting healthier environments and it is a core approach in social justice. Advocacy can take the form of consulting aimed at system change, participating in collaborative action research projects aimed at improving systems through using data and working hand-in-hand with other professionals and with representatives of the community involved, of testifying before lawmakers about a grievous mental health issue, of collaborating with others to influence or even create needed legislation reform, of serving as an expert media commentator on important educational or mental health matters, or even participating in more active stances such as supporting or participating in protests, and civil disobedience causes.

4. Connecting with community resources focus for social competence–facilitation. Clients can be connected with existing community resources that serve to extend or to deepen ongoing counseling, which itself can continue to address similar or other issues and to monitor outcomes of the connection. For instance, a client who feels isolated from others and without value to them or the world might be linked with a local homelessness project or with a group such as Habitat for Humanity—depending on the client's readiness and talents, interests, and politics. Or, perhaps a book club at the library might speak more directly to a particular client. Counselors need to be aware of community resources such as these and how they might be used to augment ongoing counseling itself by providing avenues to promote social competence.
5. Ripple effect: Picture how a stone thrown into a lake sends out concentric circles of ripples that continue long after being initiated by that stone hitting the water. Imagine a client in counseling who corrects a dysfunctional behavior, such as continually ignoring others, and learns how to behave more graciously with them. It's not unlikely that these others are themselves positively affected by the new and positive behavior, the effect of which can ripple to enhance their own involvements with others.

The Counseling Profession in Relation to the Two Models

History of Counseling and Counselor Education

The historical evolution of counseling as a profession has its roots in wellness and prevention. These same roots gave rise to counseling psychology (for a review of counseling psychology's evolution, see Altmaier & Hansen, 2012). Most historians in the profession trace counseling's origins to the work of Frank Parsons (1884, 1909) and Jesse B. Davis (see Gladding, 2006) in vocational guidance and to Clifford Beers's (1908) book, *A Mind That Found Itself*, that gave impetus to mental hygiene and mental health.

What was to become school counseling (and to evolve, also, into community and then clinical mental health counseling, as well as additional forms, see later) began in the early 1900s as vocational guidance, focused to a large extent on the large immigrant population that had settled in Boston and on establishing a systematic school vocational guidance program. Parsons himself was an attorney and a social reformer when he became involved with guidance activities for selecting vocations. His formula for working with people then was prescient: (a) know yourself, (b) learn about various work opportunities, and (c) use "true reasoning" to arrive at a good choice and direction. See Zytowski (2008) for an interesting summary of these early initiatives. Parson's tripartite approach, then, was an early foray into a vocationally based ecological approach, where a match between persons and environment was sought.

Guidance and counseling evolved, later to become known as counselor education, or sometimes, counseling programs. Until the late 1960s these training programs were focused on preparing school guidance and counseling personnel at the elementary and secondary levels. Some programs also educated students in student personnel work in higher education. The clear emphasis of all this training was on the growth and development of students in schools.

Much changed after the former Union of Soviet Socialist Republics (USSR) launched its automatic scientific laboratory space rocket, Sputnik, in 1957. The National Defense Education Act was passed in 1957 to provide resources to educate high school students in science and math (we were, all of a sudden, in a race with the USSR). Also, funds were provided to fund students to attend counselor education programs, as new counselors would be needed to assist in vocational development and choice and to teach these courses at the university level.

The 1960s were a time of unrest and foment, marked by demonstrations of college students against America's participation in the Vietnam War, and by various expressions of a counter-culture movement. The 1960s and 1970s also were a period of much change within the country, with gains made—not without bloodshed and considerable courage exhibited—in civil rights. Moreover, experiments were taking place within mental health, with the community mental health movement introducing a prevention component to mental health center service and the initiative to deinstitutionalize patients back into the community from hospitals. Group methods began to assume a higher profile for both practitioners and the general public, marked by experimentation with T-groups on the East Coast and encounter groups on the West.

Focusing on counselor education: Credentialing frameworks. Counselor education training programs prepare master's-level counseling practitioners and doctoral-level faculty, researchers, and practitioners. These training programs also were involved in the mix of change discussed previously.

Community counseling became a new offering in the 1970s, followed by mental health counseling in the 1990s. Current specialties covered by accreditation by the Council for the Accreditation of Counseling and Related Educational programs (CACREP, 2009) now include Addiction Counseling; Career Counseling; Clinical Mental Health Counseling; Marriage, Couple, and Family Counseling; School Counseling; Student Affairs and College Counseling; and Counselor Education and Supervision (doctoral level). Note that the discussion of counseling accreditation in this section is limited to CACREP, although the master's degree in psychology and counseling (MPAC, 2013) offers an alternative being explored by some programs, including counseling psychology.

Counselor licensure and counseling program accreditation were established and spread across every state in the nation. The American School Counseling Association (ASCA; 2005) National Model for training school counselors was created. Among other facets, the ASCA model charted four central behaviors for the 21st-century school counselor: (a) advocacy, (b) leadership, (c) collaboration, and (d) system change. Note that all four of these behaviors are fundamental to doing prevention.

With all these (and many other) changes occurring through the last half-century, or so, counselor education expanded to now also include a strong emphasis on remedial, treatment-oriented training. As many new counselors moved into employment within the community mental health system or in private practice, it became imperative for them to become conversant with the dominant language used and trained in its application. That language revolved—and still does—around the lexicon of sickness and treatment, with a parenthetical phrase or two connected to wellness and prevention.

It is important to note that the obvious components of most counselor education training programs, as well as the preponderance of CACREP accreditation give only occasional attention to wellness and prevention. The same holds for state licensure laws. The main exception, perhaps, is in School Counseling accreditation standards, influenced by its National Plan, which gives relatively more attention in both training and in accreditation standards to wellness and prevention.

However, two of the clearest statements contained in the CACREP (2009) standards supporting wellness and prevention are found under the Clinical Mental Health Counseling specialty, and in the common core curriculum standards within Human Growth and Development. One of the skills and practices for Clinical Mental Health Counseling (section D-3) reads, "Promotes optimal human development, wellness, and mental health through prevention, education and advocacy activities." One of the standards for Human Growth and Development reads, "Theories for facilitating optimal development and wellness over the life span" (G3-h). In addition, in all the specialties a section is included that is labeled, "Counseling, Prevention, and Intervention," and another one labeled, "Diversity and Advocacy." At the doctoral-level standards, "Leadership and Advocacy" are specially indicated. The School Counseling specialty standards also include "Collaboration" and another on "Leadership."

Sprinkled sporadically through the eight common core curricular standards is the occasional reference to wellness and prevention. For instance, under Professional Orientation and Ethical Practice can be found "advocacy processes needed to address institutional and social barriers that impede access, equity, and success for clients" (G-1.i). The Social and Cultural Diversity core section finds two statements especially supportive of prevention, with statements emphasizing advocacy, community-level strategies, eliminating intentional and unintentional oppression and discrimination, and social justice. The presence of these supportive statements typically is not mirrored by required coursework in wellness and prevention within counselor education, although it can be found in elective courses or being infused within other core courses in the curriculum, such as Theories of Counseling or Internship.

Discrepancy: Endorsement versus application. It is useful to remember that wellness and prevention are at the root of both the counseling profession and of counseling psychology. They remain clearly included today in the philosophy and mission of these two professions. A case in point is the counseling definition developed by the American Counseling Association (2014) in its 20/20 Vision document:

> Counseling is a professional relationship that empowers diverse individuals, families, and groups to accomplish mental health, wellness, education, and career goals.

However, a gap exists between history and philosophical endorsement of wellness and prevention concepts and applications realized through accreditation, licensure, and counselor education curricula. It is clear that revision is needed in both counseling and mental health training to close this discrepancy.

Remedial treatment is needed, in fact, it needs to be expanded and made more accessible and affordable. More practitioners providing therapy need to be available. But we have seen how a reliance on treatment and remediation at the expense of wellness and prevention is not a proper balance. Better proportionately is needed, where resources expended on wellness and prevention are at least the equivalent of those assigned to sickness and treatment.

As Walsh (2011) stated with regard to TLCs specifically, "given the enormous mental, physical, social and economic cost of contemporary lifestyles, such interventions may be essential. In the 21st century, therapeutic lifestyles may need to be a central focus of mental, mental, and public health" (p. 589).

The healthcare system in the United States is evolving an increased emphasis on wellness and prevention. The prevention component of the Patient Protection and Affordable Care Act illustrates this point, as I discussed in chapter 1. This movement, in turn, will cause counseling training programs to expand their training in these vital areas. Opportunities can be expected to increase for counselors and other health care professionals who are able to deliver wellness and prevention services.

Seven General Strategies of Wellness and Prevention

Let's now move to examine general strategies in wellness and prevention. A discussion of five major prevention strategies was provided in the voluminous prevention volume edited by Gullotta and Bloom (2003), from which I will principally draw. To this set of five general strategies, I add two more: assisting developmental transitions and encouraging everyday wellness and prevention.

In addition to Gullotta and Bloom (2003), other contributing resources to understanding strategies include the spectrum model of prevention (Rattray, Brunner, & Freestone, 2002), the dimensions of counselor functioning cube (Morrill, Oetting, & Hurst, 1974), the community counseling model (Lewis, Lewis, Daniels, & D'Andrea, 2010), the comprehensive mental health counseling model (Gerig, 2007), the preventive counseling model (Conyne, 1987, 2004), the ecological model (Bronfenbrenner, 1979), and the counseling model (Conyne & Cook, 2004; Cook, 2012), the counseling for wellness model, the counseling for wellness and justice perspective (Prilleltensky, Dokecki, Frieden, & Wang, 2007), and the counseling model for positive behavioral change (Granello, 2013). These and related models will be examined in the next chapter.

The wellness and prevention strategies to be discussed next are not exclusive, often blend, and the most effective efforts usually use some combination of them. These general wellness and prevention strategies and associated competencies are listed in the following box.

General Wellness and Prevention Strategies With Exemplary Competencies

(Note: Combinations of strategies work best.)

***Strategy Exemplary Competencies**

1. *Education: Direct and Indirect*: Teaching, training, TLCs, counseling, and more
2. *Social Competence–Facilitation*: Connecting and matching with resources
3. *Natural Caregiving Connection*: Connecting with helpful people
4. *Community Organizing and Systems Intervention (COSI)*: Consulting, advocating, outreach, influencing public policy and legislation
5. *Environmental Redesign*: Altering physical or organizational environment
6. *Assist Developmental Transitions*: Anticipating predictable needs and challenges
7. *Encourage Everyday Wellness and Prevention*: Positive practices for people, settings, and systems

   *Note: First five strategies are drawn from Gullotta and Bloom (2003).

Wellness and Prevention Strategy 1: Education, Both Direct and Indirect

The education strategy is a broad one. It includes direct approaches, such as instruction and counseling. It also contains indirect approaches, such as print and social media. It has been the forte of counselors for generations. This strategy provides the greatest counselor control in the helping endeavor and allows the professional helper to exert the most personal influence (Gullotta & Bloom, 2003; Ketterer, 1981; Ketterer, Bader, & Levy, 1980).

Individual, group, and family counseling, are essential tools of the counseling practitioner. When these familiar counseling methods are used for wellness and prevention, however, they are focused on helping clients to reverse the course of their present direction and to forestall the emergence of related negative conditions. For example, a counselor may work with a recently unemployed client to assist with plans for becoming reemployed but, also, to avoid the development of depression. Myers (2003) has shown how a wellness-oriented, strengths-based approach can be used by family counselors to help caregivers cope with stress.

However, although education is the most frequently used prevention strategy, as mentioned before education alone cannot prevent dysfunction and promote healthy functioning (Gullotta & Bloom, 2003). Education can increase knowledge and sometimes can change attitudes but very seldom can education alone change. It takes a combination of strategies to change behavior and to change it in any lasting way—education plus social competency, plus natural caregiving, for example, all organized and delivered in an intentional and appropriate way.

Direct approaches with the education strategy. Direct approaches bring the educator or counselor in face-to-face contact with the learner or client in the classic way that this strategy has been delivered. Some of the direct delivery format for education include classes, seminars, workshops, and counseling.

Gullotta and Bloom (2003) identified three education strategies (teaching, skill-based training, and counseling of individuals, groups, or families). I add two additional ones: (a) empowerment, which is an important social justice approach, and (b) anticipatory guidance, which is providing information and education to clients and the general population before the onset of disorders.

Following are short, generic definitions of each educational strategy considered from a direct service perspective:

1. Teaching involves any of a variety of intentional means that usually include some form of information transmission and exchange, where an instructor assists learners to understand and be able to apply a body of knowledge. It goes without saying that teaching is the central means used in educational institutions and training centers to educate learners. This also is the case in counseling and mental health training programs, where academic preparation is addressed through teaching. Yet, the nature of teaching is radically changing throughout all levels of education. The traditional lecture format for delivering information still exists, yet other formats are gaining increased use, including experientially-based small group approaches and online or hybrid approaches. Two notable examples include problem-based learning (PBL; Savery, 2009) and flipped learning (Bergmann & Sam, 2014), where in-class activities are focused on increasing the direct engagement of students with content applications and meaning, and with each other.

2. Skills-based training helps learners to master specific behaviors and skills that they can effectively apply. Counseling and psychology programs have long included skills training approaches in preparing counselor. A number of other disciplines and professions also use this kind of training (e.g., management, social work, teaching, medical centers), as do many customer service-oriented businesses, such as restaurants and mortuaries. In just one example drawn from a medical center, Virginia Mason Hospital in Seattle is using interpersonal skills-based training and coaching to increase the interpersonal effectiveness of physicians and other staff with patients (L. Rapin, personal communication, November 12, 2013).

Within counseling, skills training programs have centered on teaching basic interviewing, helping and counseling skills (e.g., Carkuff & Berenson, 1976; Ivey, Ivey, & Zalaquett, 2013), group microskills (Ivey, Pedersen, & Ivey, 2008), and the development of interpersonal skills. In turn, practitioners in the helping fields have created programs for clients and for the general public that have featured education and training in communication skills, social skills, and interpersonal skills. A major form of group work, psychoeducation, incorporates skills training as a core ingredient. Many wellness and prevention programs include skills building components. Examples include the bully buster prevention program of Horne, Bartolomucci, and Newman-Carlson (2003), and the multiple prevention programs of the Social Development Research Group (2012), where interpersonal problem solving and refusal skill training are key ingredients in promoting protective factors while reducing risk.

3. Individual, group, and family counseling are modes used to directly help a client or clients to grow and change in desired directions, leading to problem resolution with the potential for wellness gains and preventive applications. Several useful behavioral change and counseling models are available that are especially attuned to wellness and prevention. These approaches will be discussed in chapter 4.

Although the focus of traditional counseling typically is on remediating existing problems and concerns, the potential exists for going beyond correction to wellness enhancement and prevention, both in the context of a client session and in programs that are dedicated to wellness and prevention goals. Within sessions, counselors can introduce beneficial wellness practices that fit the presenting situation, such as encouraging a depressed client to connect with nature and to begin a modest exercise program. These initiatives can assist with lessening current depressive feelings but they also hold preventive potential for future functioning in general. Counselors also can help clients who are making progress in problem resolution to reflect on what they are doing that's helpful. This process of "taking perspective" is critically important within the therapeutic experience itself because it helps clients to develop meaning (Conyne & Cook, 2004; Cook, 2012; Lieberman, Yalom, & Miles, 1973). Even more so, taking perspective is valuable because it assists clients to identify actions and underlying principles that they can generalize and translate to avert significant future life challenges.

As counseling expands beyond the individual level to the group and family, the scope of impact for wellness and prevention is enhanced. Scope broadens because the number of people involved in the intervention is increased, obviously increasing efficiency of program delivery. Moreover, because of the associated interactive dynamics in a group the potential magnifies for gaining and applying knowledge and skills for future benefit (Marmarosh, Dunton, & Amendola, 2014). An example is found in the 19,000 or so Lean in Circles that are taking place today in more than 70 countries. Based on the concept of "Leaning In" (Sandberg, 2013) to empower women and girls to reach their goals, the common bond of these circles is found in the peer power that is transmitted through the small group experience (AARP, 2014). It may be no surprise, then, that group methods, especially psychoeducation, often are included as mainstays of wellness and prevention programs (Clanton Harpine, 2013), and there are a number of excellent projects that are geared to prevention with families (Small & Huser, 2012).

4. Empowerment is a process through which people, groups, or organizations that presently are marginalized or powerless become aware of this life situation, gain competencies allowing them to increase control over their lives or situation, which they then apply without harming others and in concord with the needs of others in the community. Five C's of empowerment have been identified: (a) collaboration, where counselor and client or community members work together, pooling their mutual expertise and experience; (b) context, where an ecological (person × environment) change model guides activities; (c) critical consciousness, where both awareness of a need for change in a system is accompanied by action to make it; (d) competence, where the main focus in the therapeutic process is on the participant's strengths and assets; and (e) community, where bonds and connections with others in a setting are enhanced (McWhirter & McWhirter, 2007). Wellness and prevention programs seek to help people to become empowered within the major settings and systems they encounter. Helping people develop proactive competencies to assert their interests and needs appropriately and effectively speaks to empowerment. Empowerment also can be aimed at the settings and systems themselves using consultation, outreach, organization change, and advocacy methods. True to an ecological perspective, empowerment efforts typically can be found in the person × environment intersection, people and their context are the subject of change.

5. Anticipatory guidance is an overall intent of the education strategy in wellness and prevention. Information or skill development about an event or condition is made available prior to its occurrence to help recipients avoid future negative consequences. For instance, a client learns how to attend as a listener in order to become more effective in future conversations. Anticipatory guidance is an important mental health prevention concept introduced by Gerald Caplan (1964) in his classic text *Principles of Preventive Psychiatry*.

Anticipatory guidance and training are related and important educational services in wellness and prevention. They are often delivered in group formats, frequently to those who are assessed to be free of the problem to be prevented. For example, anticipatory guidance can be provided in a group format to prospective retirees to help them to gain information, skills and tools to better function in their future retirement, or to high school seniors regarding expectations for college life. Training is used to equip those who will deliver helping services to do so more effectively and appropriately in the future; volunteers, for example, may work in the schools to provide tutoring to elementary school students. With self-instruction, people teach themselves (e.g., through video tapes, meditation, reading, Internet) about any number of life skills, such as relaxation, problem solving, and forming friendships, all of which can help them to anticipate and cope more effectively in the future. Traditional, remedial application of counseling also can exert an intended preventive effect, even on a one-to-one basis. A client can unlearn negative ways of being and doing now that can hold consequences for events that may occur later. For instance, the counselor can assist the same client to develop problem solving skills aimed at both resolving a current situation but, also, can be used to anticipate challenging demands that may occur later in life.

Indirect approaches with the educational strategy. Education also can occur indirectly through a number of electronic, print, social media, or telephonic means. Examples of e-learning or virtual systems include Blackboard.com and Canvass.com. Telehealth services (e-therapy, distance counseling, and telemedicine) are becoming frequent (Reinhardt, 2013). Video chats and synchronous video chats, including synchronous group work (Page, 2011) are available.

Virtual delivery of academic courses and training programs is being increasingly provided either completely online or in a hybrid form. The development of massive open online courses (MOOC, 2013), a Web site that can reach tens of thousands of participants worldwide, represents one emerging route. Online universities are common now. Some counseling programs in online institutions follow a hybrid model and have been accredited by CACREP. As with any new season, there are calm and stormy times to be experienced and resolved. Counselor education programs that deny MOOC-type technology may be proceeding at their own peril.

Public health information often is disseminated indirectly. One example of this approach includes the inclusion of public service warnings on food, medicine, cigarette, and alcoholic beverage labels. Another public health initiative underway in some locations is bringing to a vote a requirement that genetically modified/engineered foods clearly be labeled as such. In another example of the use of public health information, mass media campaigns have been used to lower the incidence of problem health behaviors and to promote healthy functioning. In the first case, reducing or stopping cigarette smoking, which I discussed in chapter 1, has been a subject of mass media projects. The Legacy TruTH campaign realized a 22% reduction in youth taking up smoking during the early 2000s. The more recent TIPS campaign of the Centers for Disease Control and Prevention (2013) yielded 1.6 million quit attempts by smokers, with 200,000 of them not smoking over the succeeding 3-month period that was measured. In the second case of promoting health, an early mass campaign project was the "Friends Can Be Good Medicine" campaign in California (Taylor, Lam, Roppel, & Barter, 1984), which produced positive results in knowledge, behavior, and attitudes extending into one year.

The indirect education strategy's use in print media, radio and television is extensive and it is exponentially increasing through electronic platforms available on the Internet, such as blogs, videos, pods, newsletters, and other social media. Refer back to chapter 2 for resources. However, when the aim is attitude and behavior change, which are goals for most wellness and prevention programs, indirectly delivered educational strategies may at best produce initial positive changes that run a distinct risk of being unsustainable (Gullotta & Bloom, 2003). This is so because enduring change in attitudes and behavior, always a high threshold to attain in any effort, is limited when learners may not be ready for the intervention presented and/or when the learning experience fails to adequately engage learners actively in the process. Generally, learners need to be engaged actively with subject material in order for it to "stick." So, for instance, the information you read contained in the "10 simple things," by itself, may be insufficient to yield change in many cases. Change that sticks is more likely if the information is supplemented by intentionally interactive experiences in which learners are open to applying any learning that is gained. You will read about the stages of change model in chapter 4, which helps explain how engagement can be enhanced based on connecting an educational strategy with a learner's level of readiness for change.

Wellness and Prevention Strategy 2: Social Competency Facilitation—Connecting With Resources

Social competency involves connecting people to existing groups and communities in viable ways through which they both make contributions and receive benefits simultaneously. One of the chief personal benefits is in their improved capacity to function with others. As examples, they are able to enhance a sense of belonging, being of value, feeling satisfied, enjoying a sense of mastery and self-efficacy, and a positive self-esteem.

After-school programs for children and adolescents are great examples of social competency-facilitation. Organized activities for participating in art, music, sports, and service groups provide kids with significant opportunities for testing their interests, gaining skills, forming friendships, expanding their horizons, and providing positive alternatives that can help immunize them from adversity and negative mental health. Unfortunately, in too many schools and communities these opportunities are unavailable or scarce due to limited resources and/or choices that are made with those resources. Counselors can advocate in schools and communities for building consensus to support these kinds of after-school programs where they do not exist. And, where they do exist, counselors can encourage children take advantage of them.

Social competency-enhancement can be an important wellness strategy for seniors, too, especially those who are retired or are intending to retire soon. I have experience working with retirees or those about to retire, helping them to anticipate and learn how to cope positively with this major life transition.

Far too many retirees, who may have been waiting for a long time for what they imagined would be a kind of utopian existence in retirement find, instead, that after a while (say, 6 months), they realize they simply do not know what to do with themselves. After a first few weeks or months of elation doing what they had long dreamed of (e.g., golf or travel), a kind of boredom can eek in that, if left unchecked, can deepen into sadness and then depression. This is so because the typical roles, responsibilities, routines, relationships, and previous assumptions about themselves and the world with which they were very familiar have vanished or, if they still try to apply them, simply do not fit their new situation (Conyne & Rapin, 2009; Schlossberg, 2004). On the positive side, lots of seniors have learned to adapt to their new life by plugging themselves in to existing community opportunities, such as volunteering with the Red Cross to assist in disaster relief, or tutoring kids in an after-school program. Getting involved in these new ways allows these seniors to tap existing skills and experience and make contributions that are valuable to others and that also provide needed meaning in their own lives.

Social competency can be fostered through such means as volunteering at a soup kitchen, reading to a blind person, or mentoring an adolescent from an impoverished environment. As was pointed out in chapter 2, the "helping connection" is a major contributor to benefits in our society, both for those helped but, also, for those providing the voluntary assistance. While any amount of helping others can contribute positively to one's own health, there seems to be a dosage threshold for making a real difference (Anchor, 2010). Engaging in helping others 100 hours a year, or about 2 hours a week, seems to be the optimal number.

Wellness and Prevention Strategy 3: Natural Caregiving—Connecting With Helpful People

This wellness and prevention strategy refers to people in their natural environment being of help and service to others, without the direct involvement of counselors or other helping professionals. We might forget from time to time that the world around us is full of people and systems that function harmoniously and effectively, and that they do so without the intervention of outside experts. In effect, they are displaying aspects of everyday wellness and prevention. Indeed, sometimes professional helpers can just get in the way of what is working well. Kellehear (2005), for instance, urges communities to reinitiate the validity of people helping people during periods of stressful and challenging times as an antidote against being dominated by professional and medical experts.

Take a census of your life context to personally examine the presence of positive resources around you. Are there groups (that you may be a part of, or not) that seem to progress in a healthy fashion? Are there families or relationships you know of that function well? Are you aware of any work settings where creativity, productivity, and employee satisfaction are evident? Do you know of any highly effectively functioning individuals? I'll bet you can answer affirmatively more than once to these questions.

Because the mindset of mental health professionals revolves around a deficit-reduction compass point where we tend to anticipate and see problems instead of strengths, it's too easy for us to miss the positive people, events and situations that are right before us all the time. This comment is not to deny the existence of far too many deeply troubling issues in our society or the extensive needs for mental health assistance that exist. Rather, I simply seek to place the strategy of natural care giving in a context: As counselors, we need to become particularly aware of what works well with people and settings, not just with what is not working. Then, we need to honor those positive situations by refraining from intrusively intervening. Role alternatives for counselors in this strategy, then, are to observe unobtrusively and to recognize successes, to leave alone what functions well, to offer support in those cases where such aid might be welcomed, and sometimes to invite collaboration in order to mutually yield a more comprehensive and culturally valid (Vera & Kenny, 2013) wellness and prevention initiative.

Gullotta and Bloom (2003) identified three forms of natural care-giving: (a) mutual self-help groups, (b) indigenous trained caregivers, and (c) indigenous caregivers with no previous training. Let's take a look at each of these forms.

(a) Mutual self-help groups comprise people of like minds and needs who come together to share, support, and help each other through life demands, such as grieving and substance abuse (see White & Madera, 2002). Related forms of these kinds of groups are developmental or task focused, including study circles, prayer groups, and training groups. The focus of the discussion here, though, is on those groups that are formed and run by members to assist in coping with difficult life challenges and passages.

Mutual self-help groups are autonomous and member-run, where phases of formation, conduct, and help giving are under the control of the members. Group support is a prime catalyst in recovery and in promoting well-being. Peers come together in mutual self-help groups to encourage and support one another. They share their personal experiences, providing a sense of universality, and they reach out to provide hope, help, and healing. They also can serve as a source of accountability, reinforcing the taking of personal responsibility for coping with life challenges. These mutual self-help groups offer a culture of caring where social support, modeling, and personal experience are joined. Professional helpers sometimes connect with these groups, at their invitation, to provide collaborative consultation (e.g., Silverman, 2004), widow-to-widow program and her work with bereavement through mutual self-help groups (Silverman, 2011); involvement such as this represents an opportunity for providing wellness and prevention. Most often, though, these groups are autonomous. The most common version of this form type of support is found in Alcoholic Anonymous, with 53,000 groups in the United States containing some 1.2 million members (Kelly & Yeterian, 2012).

(b) Indigenous caregiving is provided by those who are trained in a profession (but not in mental health) to whom others often turn for assistance, support, advice, and comfort. Examples include clergy, teachers, police, barbers, bartenders, aboriginal support programs, and increasingly, family members caring for an ill or dying relative. You've already read about how barber and beautician shops are one of the places in the community where customers may naturally exchange information about issues of the day, often obtaining and providing useful information and mutual support in the process. These sites can be thought of as "natural oases" of support and assistance. Of course, the information exchanged is typically not evidence or theory-based and some of it may not be accurate (Bergstrom, 1982), yet the connections occurring among one another cannot be denied. With permission, issues of information accuracy and of technical helping skills can be increased through the training and consultation of helping professionals (Toseland, Haigler, & Monahan, 2011), providing another avenue for wellness and prevention.

A way to leverage, with permission, a naturally occurring situation can be found in relation to the Affordable Care Act. The underlying belief is that this less costly way to obtain healthcare serves a wellness and prevention need. It can help people stay healthier (through free preventive care provisions), and certainly the ability to obtain more regular medical care is a far better option for enrollees, and for the society than in using the hospital emergency center as primary health care.

A feature of the act is to make available adequate health insurance, often to people who have never had it and know little about the intricacies of using it, at lower cost through market exchanges. Politics aside for a moment, many potential consumers are experiencing considerable unease and confusion about the options available, what they mean, and how to enroll. A wellness and prevention initiative co-sponsored by the National Association of Hispanic Nurses and the National Black Nurses Association is placing nurses in community settings where people congregate to receive service and, by the way, to schmooze about everything and anything. One such type of setting is the inner city beauty shop and barber shop, long locations for getting a haircut and for freely talking about general life issues. Many nurses, typically one of the more trusted of health care providers, are visiting these shops, with permission, to inform customers about how to enroll to receive health care, to answer questions, and to help soothe the soul about this initiative. In addition to this health care insurance issue, barber shops and beauty shops, as well as neighborhood bars and other informal settings where people may feel free to chat and share, have been the locations for other wellness and prevention efforts, too, including educating about preventing breast cancer, prostate cancer, and depression.

(c) Indigenous caregiving is provided by people with no particular training related to helping but who are instinctively sought out by others for help. Think about it. In your own life, you no doubt can identify a person or two whom others just naturally turn to because they just seem to be naturally good listeners, are caring, and are willing to take time to help. Maybe you are one of these kinds of people. These people are natural helpers.

Wellness and prevention can be well served by counselors identifying these natural helpers within families, neighborhoods, schools, workplaces, and places of formal and informal service delivery—and then finding ways to support them. Not to take them over, but to be available unobtrusively to aid and support. In chapter 2 you were introduced to the story about my older neighbors, Ruby and Oren, who found natural support through more than 35 years of weekly card playing. A task for wellness and prevention counselors is to augment without interfering or usurping.

Wellness and Prevention Strategy 4: Community Organizing and Systems Intervention

Gullotta and Bloom (2003) indicate that the COSI strategy is the most powerful one. It is geared to environmental and systemic levels where changes made contain a built-in multiplicative wellness and prevention factor that can impact many people. COSI is concerned with how a community provides opportunities and support for involving people in local activities and processes, particularly as these relate to governance and quality of life. Positive changes made at environmental and systemic levels, such as responding to a community's expressed need for exercise options by creating parks and walk paths where none had existed provide one example of how whole populations can be positively affected. In another, the First Ladies Health Initiative (2014) founded in 2008 in Chicago to network African American churches against HIV/AIDS, finds Mayor's spouses mobilizing citizens to improve targeted local health conditions, such as reducing the rate of infant mortality in Cincinnati (Saker, 2014).

COSI interventions constitute a major way that social justice can be advanced, as well. One illustration can be found in the legislative changes that have occurred in 36 states (as of this writing) to permit gay marriage. Counselors and other mental health workers can participate in COSI efforts through providing consultation to decision makers, engaging in collaborative-participative action research projects, and advocating for system changes—among other ways. This topic is considered next.

Gullotta and Bloom (2003) identified three main forms of COSI, community development, systems intervention, and legislative change. I add three more: (a) advocacy, (b) culturally relevant social justice, and (c) consulting and outreach. See the brief definitions that follow.

1. Community development engages community members in expressing their concerns and developing solutions related to important aspects of community

life (e.g., crime, recreation, politics, race relations). Community Conversations about Mental Health, a program of the Substance Abuse and Mental Health Services Administration (2013), is an exciting illustration of how a planned community-wide small-group prevention intervention can be launched and executed. Online materials include an information brief (in English and Spanish) and discussion and planning guides. Community development grants to cities from the U.S. Department of Housing and Urban Development (HUD) provide for an ongoing program, this one aimed at supporting low and moderate income individuals, families, and communities.

The Community Development Society has promulgated principles of good practice. See the following box that contains these principles, as stated on the society's official Web site.

Principles of Good Practice in Community Development

Promote active and representative participation toward enabling all community members to meaningfully influence the decisions that affect their lives.

Engage community members in learning about and understanding community issues, and the economic, social, environmental, political, psychological, and other impacts associated with alternative courses of action.

Incorporate the diverse interests and cultures of the community in the community development process; and disengage from support of any effort that is likely to adversely affect the disadvantaged members of a community.

Work actively to enhance the leadership capacity of community members, leaders, and groups within the community.

Be open to using the full range of action strategies to work toward the long-term sustainability and well-being of the community. (Community Development Society, 2014)

2. Systems intervention involves existing institutions and organizations in examining their practices, policies, and procedures to correct dysfunction and make them more effective. Parents pressing for increased influence in a school, for instance, may lead to the creation of a local school decision making committee that includes parent representation and participation. Guideline 8 of the American Psychological Association's (APA; 2013) document *Guidelines for Prevention in Psychology*, which you read about in chapter 1, specifically addresses the COSI set of interventions: "Psychologists are encouraged to engage in systemic and institutional interventions that strengthen the health of individuals, families, and communities, and prevent psychological and physical distress and disability" (p. 3).

The relationship between gender and health, for instance, affords an example. Gender is a significant determinant of health, manifested in a number of ways including differential wage gaps for males and females (favoring males), higher secondary school dropout rates (favoring girls), and applying a binary definition of gender identity (which can oppress those who do not "fit" this mold). Positively changing gender-based inequities by counselors, psychologists and other human service professionals may be a function of social transformation emerging from system change programs (Castro, 2012). Health care is inextricably intertwined not only with individual choices that are made but, also, with social conditions, culture, and politics.

3. Influencing public policy and legislation includes legislative development, its change, and judicial action afford avenues for prevention (Ackerson & Korr, 2007; Pirog & Good, 2013). Ample examples exist of legislation targeting health issues, including the areas of smoking cigarettes (e.g., the Family Smoking Prevention and Control Act of 2009); alcohol abuse (e.g., the National Minimum Drinking Age Act of 1984); suicide prevention (the Garrett Lee Smith Memorial Act of 2004, reauthorized 2013); postpartum depression (e.g., the Melanie Blocker Stokes Mothers Act of 2010); and new undocumented immigrants (the Deferred Action for Childhood Arrivals of 2012). Chapter 8 contains a useful chart summarizing a number of important public policy legislation initiatives, accompanied by an extended discussion.

We sometimes can learn from other countries about wellness and prevention. A case in point is public health legislation passed by the new government of Mexico to generate tax money to support clean water and to prevent obesity and related health issues. Mexicans consume the most soda per capita in the world. In November 2013 its Congress passed legislation placing a one peso tax per liter of soda and another 8% tax on junk food. Independent legislation is under review to invest some of the revenue gained through these taxes to install water fountains throughout the country (Prevention Institute Alert, 2013). This action is spreading and reaching the United States, with a soda tax having passed in Berkeley, California in 2014 (Ritterman, 2014). Of course, such legislation is not without its detractors who raise issues surrounding the curtailing of personal liberties.

4. Advocating for social action comprises proactive initiatives. Advocacy is a part of social action that is becoming of increasing importance for all counselors, and certainly for those committed to wellness and prevention. Vera and Speight (2007) have identified three forms of advocacy: (a) empowerment, or helping clients to advocate for themselves; (b) direct professional involvement with policy makers or with institutions; and (c) educating and training professionals who work with a targeted clientele, such as underserved. In a viewpoint of advocacy within school psychology (Briggs, 2013), advocacy can be considered occurring at four levels: (a) zero-level, aimed at laws and policies; (b) Tier 1, targeting whole-school systems and practices; (c) Tier 2, advocacy with groups of students; and (d) Tier 3, advocacy with individual students.

The American Counseling Association (ACA), the American Psychological Association (APA), the National Association of School Psychologists (NASP), and the National Association of Social Workers (NASW) have public policy and legislation advocacy programs that are intended to benefit their respective professions, professionals, and clients. As part of these programs, counselors, psychologists, school psychologists, and social workers can receive training in public policy analysis and advocacy as a means for improving their effectiveness (Pirog & Good, 2013). Advocacy competencies for counselors (Lewis, Arnold, House, & Toporek, 2002) were approved by the American Counseling Association in March, 2003. Advocacy is commonly understood as a systems intervention, but the authors indicate that it also includes the implementation of empowerment strategies in direct counseling with individuals, families, and groups.

Advocacy competencies involve counselors acting with and on behalf of clients and members of schools and communities to reach goals. As illustrations, a counselor can serve a preventive effect by confronting oppressive policies and procedures within an institution, thus intending to benefit large numbers of people, clients and nonclients, alike. That same counselor can help empower others to serve as his own advocate in seeking redress of grievances or in promoting positive work environments (Lewis et al., 2010). A key is that when external barriers to a person's development are identified counselors may choose to advocate for change (Lewis et al., 2002; Williams & Greenleaf, 2012). Vera and Speight (2007) point out a caveat related to counselor-led advocacy efforts. One needs to exercise caution when acting on behalf of others lest it reinforce a self-belief of powerlessness. Whatever is done by counselors needs to be consonant with the culture of the participants and their settings.

5. Culturally relevant social justice interventions emphasize the full and equal participation and collaboration of members in social and community processes in ways that are consistent with a community's values, beliefs, and desired outcomes (Vera & Kenny, 2013). Guideline 2 in the *Guidelines for Prevention in Psychology* (APA, 2013) document states, "Psychologists are encouraged to use culturally relevant prevention practices adapted to the specific context in which they are implemented." These interventions emerge from a societal vision where resource distribution is equitable and all members are safe and secure, both physically and psychologically (Bell, 2007). Moreover, these interventions seek to promote capacity building in participants and to strengthen the communities in which they occur. In pursuing culturally relevant social justice interventions a variety of extra-individual, community, and social systemic approaches are used; Evans, Hanlin, and Prilliltensky (2007) created the acronym, SPEC (Strengths-based, Prevention, Empowerment, and Community-focused) to capture key aspects.

6. Consulting and outreach can improve the capacity of service providers, decision makers, organizations, and communities. In consultation, the professional counselor typically is involved in a triadic effort (Borders, 2012; Conyne & O'Neil, 1992; Dougherty, 2000, 2013; Gallessich, 1982, 1985; Kurpius & Brubaker, 1976;

Sander, 2013). The consultant (Point A) works through consultees (Point B) to benefit a client system (individual, group, organization, or community; Point C). This sequence demonstrates the indirectness of the triadic process of consultation, where the consultee is presumed to gain increased competencies that are used to benefit current and future client systems. Consultation leverages resources, in effect, multiplying their effect to third parties and then beyond. Owing to its broad scope, consultation is frequently used within COSI interventions across all ecological levels to produce preventive effects individual, group, organization, and community.

One frequent way in which this triadic orientation is implemented can be found when a counselor consults with the "manager" of a situation or organization (e.g., the teacher of a classroom, the director of a corporation, or a guidance counselor working with a particular student) to enable that manager to improve his/her effectiveness in working with the situation or organization. The consultant's focus is on improving the work of the consultee (the "manager"). Through consulting with the manager the third party benefits.

Therefore, in addition to a triadic orientation to helping, consultation is also characterized by its primary focus upon professional or work problems (Bardon, 1985). This work emphasis serves to further delineate consultation from other modes of helping, especially clarifying it from the personal orientation of psychotherapy.

Outreach is one of the staples of the community counseling model (Lewis et al., 2010). They noted, "When people are forced to contend with environmental stressors that outweigh their personal resources and coping abilities, they need help that is practical, positive, and empowering" (p. 90). Oppression, marginalization, community disasters, unemployment, lacking access to health care, and many other problems whose source are located in the environment and/or beyond their control make it hard to impossible for victims to help themselves. Rather, they often can benefit from culturally-relevant and collaboratively-offered help provided through preventive outreach services.

Counselors need to get out of their offices more and into the communities where people live their lives. I mentioned earlier how helping people understand the Affordable Care Act (ACA) is being attempted through barbershops and beauty salons in the inner city. Another outreach effort in relation to the ACA is tackling the significant problem of language barriers among Asian Pacific Islanders (Dondero, 2013). The International Community Health Services and the Asian Counseling and Referral Services in Seattle are providing Asian translators in community shopping malls to assist in communicating face-to-face the key aspects of the act and how to sign up. These services are aimed at enhancing participants' self-control while empowering them to connect with opportunities to help themselves and one another. Outreach programs have helped people cope with disruptions caused by divorce (Bloom, Hodges, & Calewell, 1982), unemployment (Choi, Price, & Vinokur, 2003), and helping pregnant adolescents

(Brodsky, 1999), to list just three. Some mental health counselors provide disaster mental health services through their volunteer role in the Red Cross, being deployed early into communities that recently have been devastated by a natural disaster (e.g., hurricane or tornado) or, especially regrettably, a human-caused disaster (e.g., school shooting). They provide crisis- and strengths-based support and counseling as well as link victims with local or Federal resources (e.g., Federal Emergency Management Agency) that can provide specific daily life or healthcare assistance and follow-up.

Wellness and Prevention Strategy 5: Environmental Redesign—Altering Physical or Organizational Environment

This wellness and prevention strategy, as discussed by Gullotta and Bloom (2003), refers to how humans and built environments can coexist in such a way as to promote an ecologically sustainable future and to enhance public health. The interactions of people with environments set the dynamic stage for what can occur immediately and over time.

A significant interest in the domain of environmental redesign presently is how technology has entered into and is shaping our lives (Weir, 2013). Consider this example that Weir draws from Stokols, about the home no longer being just a refuge from the external world: "The home is now a 'hub'—a place where residents do online banking, respond to work emails and socialize on online forums" (p. 51). Opportunities exist for staying in contact and remaining productive throughout the day and night but the downsides are only beginning to be realized.

When considering the redesign of physical environments as a wellness and prevention strategy, Geller's (2003) suggestion to increase environmentally responsible behaviors (ERB), while decreasing environmentally destructive ones, represents an important goal for creating a world sustained by harmony and equilibrium among all species. Different approaches have been described for addressing the interactions of humans with built and natural environments. Steele (1973) discussed the goal of environmental competence as a highly desirable one to attain. When environmentally competent, people learn to function effectively in existing natural and built spaces and, as important, how to shape environments ethically to support healthier behavior. Ecological counseling (Conyne & Cook, 2004) outlines for counselors and other helpers how to help clients learn to enjoy and take satisfaction in their natural environment and learn how to adapt built environments better support their functioning. Sommers (2008) discussed the numbing effect that environments impervious to human touch (so-called hard architecture, exemplified by immutable seating arrangements common to many public spaces, such as are often found in airports) can exert on users. He provided a range of methods for humanizing them, emphasizing the ethic of collaborative user participation in the environmental design process. Conyne and Clack (1981) suggested a range of environmental assessment and design strategies that counselors could employ with clients, or when consulting with decision makers, to adapt built environments and their accompanying organizational culture, policies, and procedure so they might better fit people, rather than continuing to require people to fit noxious environments.

Attention to the natural environment also is increasing quickly. Communities are becoming much more conscious of the need to embrace natural habitats. I recently came across a small fenced-off space in a busy neighborhood. I noticed a sign posted there, describing a proposed "woonerf." You might wonder, as I did, about the term: What is a woonerf? Well, a woonerf is a "street where pedestrians and cyclists have legal priority over motorists. The techniques of shared spaces, traffic calming, and low speed limits are intended to improve pedestrian, bicycle, and automobile safety" (Seattle Parks & Recreation, 2014). This is an example of how a densely packed urban center can be accommodated to fit people and support lower impact people-moving.

Ecopsychology (Roszak, 1992) and EcoWellness (Reese, 2013) are concerned with the transactions of humans with their natural, nonbuilt environment. The biophilia hypothesis holds that an innate desire exists in humans to be seek out and be connected to nature. The position taken is that people can find solace, calm, and rejuvenation through being involved with nature. Research also shows that people who take a break by walking in a park performed better on memory and attention tests than did people who strolled in the city (Berman, Jonides, & Kaplan, 2008). Participation in natural environments is part of an everyday wellness and prevention approach.

Natural design is gaining force among planners, as the woonerf example shows. In industrialized countries over 90% of time is spent by people inside buildings. Psychologists are beginning to collaborate with designers to produce buildings and public spaces that enhance sustainable choices, making them easier and more automatic. For example, if it becomes safer and more convenient for workers to commute to work by bicycle (bicycle lanes and bike racks and showers at work can help), then it is more likely they will build that practice into their daily routine. If neighborhoods contain walking paths and parks that are safe, attractive, and convenient it is much more possible that residents will use them—and get healthier and more fit in the process.

Modern life can lead to people being sequestered from the nurturance and healing capacity of nature. Work life often removes employees from the outside world and encapsulates them inside offices and cubicles, usually stationed behind a computer screen while they breathe conditioned air. Leisure life, too, can find many choosing to spend time indoors, watching television, playing computer games, reading, or just "relaxing." Spending too much time divorced from nature can fracture our connection with it and it deprives us from sources of wonder and nourishment that can promote healthy functioning (Buzzell & Chalquist, 2009). Recall the "Simple Thing" step mentioned earlier of getting outside, as happiness is said to be maximized at 13.9 degrees Celsius (Tsutsui, 2013).

A lifestyle devoid of nature is associated with increased levels of stress, which can lead to a variety of negative health consequences. From an ecopsychology standpoint, the antidote to this unnatural way of existence is to re-connect with one's natural surroundings. Appreciating nature's bounty—its flowers, sunsets, ocean breezes, gentle rainfalls, and animal and fish life—can be a simple prescription for staying healthy and preventing disease.

Wellness and Prevention Strategy 6: Assist Developmental Transitions—Anticipating Predictable Needs and Challenges

Note that the five strategies discussed above are not necessarily inclusive of all important wellness and prevention strategies. Another significant strategy is to assist developmental transitions. These are anticipated changes that generally can be predicted for a particular age group as members of it pass through stages of life. These transition points also have been termed "developmental pathways" (Seidman, Aber, & French, 2004). This wellness and prevention strategy is to identify a prospective transition in a population along with the needs that most likely will be present, and then to install a preventive program that will enhance, disrupt, or modify the developmental pathways (processes, settings, and conditions) that can lead either to increased well-being or to serious dysfunction or social problems (Weissberg & Greenberg, 1998; Zittoun, Duveen, Gillespie, Ivinson, & Psaltis, 2003). Examples include couples anticipating the birth of a firstborn child, students moving from elementary to middle school or from high school to post-secondary education or training, adolescents coping with body changes and with new tasks, beginning a new job in a different city, moving toward retirement, seniors beginning to experience some loss of physical or cognitive function, and many others.

Consider one developmental transition, retirement. From January 1, 2011, for the next 19 years, 10,000 baby boomers will reach age 65 each day, and some thousands of them will retire (Pew Research Center, 2013). This is a developmentally predictable transition that needs to be faced. While many will do well without the need to seek professional assistance, too many will do poorly for any number of reasons, including neglecting to plan and prepare for the change. Retirement, then, represents one developmental transition point for prevention. This prevention strategy involves assessment as well as elements of risk reduction and of protection enhancement, focused on individual capabilities (e.g., planning for the future) and environmental contexts and forces (e.g., economic conditions, community resources available).

Because wellness and prevention strategies are intended frequently to be before the fact, their effect is more limited when applied to prevent dysfunctions that have already occurred within a person, a population, or a setting. Thus, in the assisting developmental transitions strategy, what is targeted are the unfolding processes, conditions, and settings that may give rise to the emergence of either wellness or dysfunction. Cowen (1994, 2000) had much to say about the unfolding processes that seem associated with wellness, having identified the following productive pathways: (a) promote healthy caregiver–child attachment relationships; (b) assist children to build early, stage-appropriate life competencies; (c) social engineer environments that are wellness enhancing (e.g., healthy schools and workplaces); and (d) enhance the sense of empowerment and personal control people experience in their lives. At the same, time those unfolding processes, conditions, and settings that may give rise to dysfunction need to be identified, disrupted, and modified to become more positive pathways. Examples include using social justice interventions to advocate for needed changes in the community (e.g., increasing access to mental health services) or consulting with school personnel to create positive policies and practices (e.g., establishing antibullying programs).

Wellness and Prevention Strategy 7: Encourage Everyday Wellness and Prevention—Positive Practices for People, Settings, and Systems

Everyday wellness and prevention, considered at length in chapter 2, are daily actions that individuals can take themselves, given contextual supports and constraints, to enhance their lives and the settings and systems in which they live, work, and play. These personal actions can be thought of as "Personal Best Practices," similar to the best practices that professions have developed in group work and other interventions.

Counselors and other mental health professionals need to encourage positive lifestyle choices in clients and also build them into wellness and prevention programs. The evidence is clear that lifestyle choices account for a substantial proportion of the health or dysfunction that people can experience in life and that three-fourths of health care costs are due to chronic disease and lifestyle choices (National Center for Chronic Disease Prevention and Health Promotion, 2009). The evidence also is clear about what lifestyle choices and behaviors promote wellness. The therapeutic lifestyle changes (TLCs) outlined by Walsh (2011) and the 10 Simple Things (Cooper, 2013), both reported in chapter 2, are among the sources that outline these very practical (and evidenced-based) steps.

Likewise, it is the responsibility of every person to do as much as they can, given their life context, to incorporate everyday wellness and prevention practices. Positive nutrition, exercise, friendships, involvement with nature, citizen action programs, and the others you already have read about, including cautious use of Complementary and Alternative Medicine (CAM) approaches such as yoga, meditation, tai chi, and acupuncture all qualify.

For instance, with regard to moving toward controlling eating portions, people can use a smaller plate, eat breakfast every day, drink water rather than calorie-laden beverages, and keep any snacks out of sight. To assist with improving nutritional choices (and, it is claimed, for adopting companies to attract more repeat customers), it is becoming possible for consumers at point of service to obtain on their receipt immediate personalized information describing the nutritional value of their order and how it might be made healthier in future choices. This approach combines both information and the makings of an action plan. Such a system is possible now through a program sponsored by the U.S. Department of Veteran Services called the Veterans Canteen Service (U.S. Department of Veterans Affairs, 2014) and products for the general population are coming available (e.g., Smart-Receipt, 2014). As the American Heart Association (2013) has stated, with regard to prevention of heart disease: "Your lifestyle is not only your best defense against heart disease and stroke, it's also your responsibility."

Issues for Reflection and Discussion

1. Compare and contrast the public health and medical models in a two-page summary. Be prepared to deliver it in a 5-minute presentation.
2. Of the seven major strategies in wellness and prevention counseling, which one seems most doable for you? Which one seems most challenging?
3. The point was made that "combinations of strategies work best." Why might this be the case?
4. How could you assist a client to begin building everyday wellness and prevention actions into her life?
5. Assess your competencies in the seven broad wellness and prevention strategies discussed in this chapter. Where may you be the strongest? The weakest? What are the implications of your assessment?

References

AARP. (2014, October). Leaning in to lend support. *AARP Bulletin, 55*(8), 8.

Ackerson, B.J., & Korr, W.S. (2007). Mental health policy and social justice. In E. Aldarondo (Ed.), *Advancing social justice through clinical practice* (pp. 359–369). Mahwah, NJ: Erlbaum. doi:10.4324/9780203936689

Altmaier, E., & Hansen, J.-I.C. (2012). *The Oxford handbook of counseling psychology*. New York, NY: Oxford University Press.

American Counseling Association. (2014). *20/20: Consensus definition of counseling*. Retrieved from http://www.counseling.org/knowledge-center/20–20-a-vision-for-the-future-of-counseling/consensus-definition-of-counseling

American Heart Association. (2013, January 23). *Lifestyle changes*. Retrieved from http://www.heart.org/HEARTORG/Conditions/HeartAttack/PreventionTreatmentof-HeartAttack/Lifestyle-Changes_UCM_303934_Article.jsp

American Psychological Association. (2013). Guidelines for prevention in psychology. *American Psychologist, 69*(3), 285–296. doi:10.1037/a0034569

American School Counselor Association. (2005). *The ASCA national model* (2nd ed.). Alexandria, VA: Author.

Anchor, S. (2010). *The happiness advantage: The seven principles of positive psychology that fuel success and performance at work*. New York, NY: Crown Business.

Association for Specialists in Group Work. (2000). ASGW professional standards for the training of group workers. *Journal for Specialists in Group Work, 25*, 327–342. doi:10.1080/01933920008411677

Bardon, J. (1985). On the verge of a breakthrough. In D. Brown & D. Kurpius (Guest Editors), Consultation. *The Counseling Psychologist, 13*, 355–362. doi:10.1177/0011000085133003

Beers, C. W. (1908). *A mind that found itself: An autobiography*. New York, NY: Longman, Green. doi:10.1037/10534-000

Bell, L.A. (2007). Theoretical foundations of social justice education. In M. Adams, L.A. Bell, & P. Griffin (Eds.), *Teaching for diversity and social justice* (2nd ed., pp. 1–14). New York, NY: Routledge. doi:10.4324/9780203940822

Bergmann, J., & Sam, A. (2014). *Flipped learning: Gateway to student engagement*. Arlington, VA: International Society for Education in Technology.

Bergstrom, D. A. (1982). Collaborating with natural helpers for delivery of rural mental health services. *Journal of Rural Community Psychology, 3*, 5–26.

Berman, M. G., Jonides, J., & Kaplan, S. (2008). The cognitive benefits of interacting with nature. *Psychological Science, 19*, 1207–1212. doi:10.1111/j.1467-9280.2008.02225.x

Bloom, B. L., Hodges, W. F., & Caldwell, R. A. (1982). A preventive program for the newly separated: Initial evaluation. *American Journal of Community Psychology, 10*, 251–264. doi:10.1007/bf00896493

Borders, D. (2012). Dyadic, triadic, and group models of peer supervision/consultation: What are their components and is there evidence of their effectiveness. *Clinical Psychology, 16*, 59–71. doi:10.1111/j.1742-9552.2012.00046.x

Briggs, A. (2013). The school psychologist as social justice advocate. In D. Shriberg, S. Song, A. H. Miranda, & K. Radliff (Eds.), *School psychology and social justice: Conceptual foundations and tools for practice* (pp. 294–310). New York, NY: Routledge. doi:10.4324/9780203121245

Brodsky, A. E. (1999). "Making it": The components and process of resilience among urban, African-American single mothers. *American Journal of Orthopsychiatry, 69*, 148–160. doi:10.1037/h0080417

Bronfenbrenner, U. (1979). *The ecology of human development: Experiments by nature and design*. Cambridge, MA: Harvard University Press.

Buzzell, L., & Chalquist, C. (2009). *Ecotherapy: Healing with nature in mind*. San Francisco, CA: Sierra Club Books.

Caplan, G. (1964). *Principles of preventive psychiatry*. New York, NY: Basic Books.

Carkhuff, R. R., & Berenson, B. G. (1976). *Teaching as treatment*. Amherst, MA: HRD Press.

Castro, M. (2012). Revolutionalizing gender. *MEDICC Review, 14*, 6–9. doi:10.1590/s1555-79602012000200003

Centers for Disease Control and Prevention. (2013). *Effective behavioral interventions*. Retrieved from http://www.cdc.gov/hiv/prevention/programs/ebis/

Chestnut, J. (2011). *The wellness and prevention paradigm*. Victoria, Canada: TWP Press.

Choi, J., Price, R. H., & Vinokur, A. D. (2003). Self-efficacy changes in groups: Effects of diversity, leadership, and group climate. *Journal of Organizational Behavior, 24*, 357–372. doi:10.1002/job.195

Clanton Harpine, E. (2013). *Prevention groups*. Thousand Oaks, CA: Sage.

Community Development Society. (2014). *About CDS*. Retrieved from http://www.comm-org/about-us

Conyne, R. (1987). *Primary preventive counseling: Empowering people and systems*. Muncie, IN: Accelerated Development.

Conyne, R. (2004). *Preventive counseling: How to empower people in systems and settings* (2nd ed.). New York: Routledge.

Conyne, R., & Clack, R. (1981). *Environmental assessment and design: A new tool for the applied behavioral scientist.* New York, NY: Praeger.

Conyne, R., & Cook, E. (Eds.). (2004). *Ecological counseling: An innovative conceptualization for person-environment interaction.* Alexandria, VA: American Counseling Association.

Conyne, R., & O'Neil, J. (Eds.). (1992). *Organizational consultation: A casebook.* Thousand Oaks, CA: Sage.

Conyne, R., & Rapin, L. (2009, February 20). *Using group process in retirement transition workshops.* Workshop given at annual meeting of the American Group Psychotherapy Association, Chicago, IL.

Cook, E. (Ed.). (2012). *Understanding people in context: The ecological perspective in counseling.* Alexandria, VA: American Counseling Association.

Cooper, B. B. (2013, August 6). *10 simple things you can do today that will make you happier, backed by research.* Retrieved from http://blog.bufferapp.com/10-scientifically-proven-ways-to-make-yourself-happier

Council for Accreditation of Counseling and Related Educational Programs. (2009). *2009 standards for accreditation.* Alexandria, VA: Author.

Cowen, E. L. (1994). The enhancement of psychological wellness: Challenges and opportunities. *American Journal of Community Psychology, 22,* 149–179. doi:10.1007/bf02506861

Cowen, E. (2000). Community psychology and routes to psychological wellness. In J. Rappaport & E. Seidman (Eds.), *Handbook of community psychology* (pp. 79–99). New York, NY: Kluwer.

Dondero, T. (2013, November 6). Obamacare: Organizations help Washington State APIs overcome language barriers, indecision. *International Examiner.* Retrieved from http://www.iexaminer.org/

Dougherty, A. M. (2000). *Psychological consultation and collaboration in school and community settings: A casebook.* Pacific Grove, CA: Brooks/Cole.

Dougherty, A. M. (2013). Consultation and prevention. In A. M. Doughtery (Ed.), *Prevention and consultation* (pp. 13–29). Thousand Oaks, CA: Sage. doi:10.4135/9781452275611

Evans, S. D., Hanlin, C. E., & Prilleltensky, I. (2007). Blending ameliorative and transformative approaches in human service organizations: A case study. *Journal of Community Psychology, 35,* 329–246. doi:10.1002/jcop.20151

First Ladies Health Initiative. (2014). Retrieved from http://www.firstladieshealth.com/

Gallessich, J. (1982). *The profession and practice of consultation: A handbook for consultants, trainers of consultants, and consumers of consultation services.* San Francisco, CA: Jossey-Bass.

Gallessich, J. (1985). Toward a meta-theory of consultation. In D. Brown & D. Kurpius (Guest Eds.), Consultation. *The Counseling Psychologist, 13,* 336–354. doi:10.1177/0011000085133002

Geller, E. S. (2003). Achieving an ecologically sustainable future. In T. Gullotta & M. Bloom (Eds.), *Encyclopedia of primary prevention and health promotion* (pp. 85–92). New York, NY: Kluwer. doi:10.1007/978-1-4615-0195-4_9

Gerig, M. (2007). *Foundations for mental health and community counseling: An introduction to the profession.* Columbus, OH: Merrill Prentice Hall.

Gladding, S. (2006). *Counseling: A comprehensive profession* (5th ed.). Upper Saddle River, NJ: Prentice Hall.

Granello, P. F. (2013). *Wellness counseling.* Upper Saddle Ridge, NJ: Merrill-Pearson.

Gullotta, T., & Bloom, M. (Eds.). (2003). *Encyclopedia of primary prevention and health promotion*. New York, NY: Kluwer. doi:10.1007/978-1-4615-0195-4

Horne, A. M., Bartolomucci, C. L., & Newman-Carlson, D. (2003). *Bullybusters: A teacher's manual for helping bullies, victims and bystanders (Grades K–5)*. Champaign, IL: Research Press.

Ivey, A., Ivey, M. B., & Zalaquett, C. P. (2013). *Intentional interviewing and counseling: Facilitating client development in a multicultural society* (8th ed.). Belmont, CA: Brooks/Cole, Cengage Learning.

Ivey, A., Pedersen, P. B., & Ivey, M. B. (2008). *Group microskills: Culture-centered group process and strategies*. Hanover, MA: Microtraining Associates.

Kellehear, A. (2005). *Compassionate cities: Public health and end-of-life care*. London, England: Routledge. doi:10.4324/9780203019955

Kelly, J. F., & Yeterian, J. D. (2012). Empirical awakening: The new science on mutual help and implications for cost containment under health care reform. *Substance Abuse, 33*, 85–91. doi:10.1080/08897077.2011.634965

Ketterer, R. (1981). *Consultation and education in mental health*. Beverly Hills, CA: Sage.

Ketterer, R., Bader, B., & Levy, M. (1980). Strategies and skills for promoting mental health. In R. Price, R. Ketterer, B. Bader, & J. Monahan (Eds.), *Prevention in mental health: Research, policy, and practice* (pp. 109–134). Beverly Hills, CA: Sage.

Kluger, J. (2014, October 20). Fear factor. *Time*, pp. 30–35.

Kurpius, D., & Brubaker, J. (1976). *Psychoeducational consultation: Definition, functions, preparation*. Bloomington, IN: Indiana University.

Lewis, J.A., Arnold, M.S., House, R., & Toporek, R.L. (2002). *ACA advocacy competencies*. Alexandria, VA: American Counseling Association.

Lewis, J., Lewis, M., Daniels, J., & D'Andrea, M. (2010). *Community counseling: A multicultural-social justice perspective* (4th ed.). Belmont, CA: Brooks/Cole, Cengage Learning.

Lieberman, M.A., Yalom, I.D., & Miles, M.B. (1973). *Encounter groups: First facts*. New York, NY: Basic Books.

Liu, J., Modrek, S. K., Gosling, R., & Feachem, R. G.A. (2013). Malaria eradication: Is it possible? Is it worth it? Should we do it? *The Lancet Global Health, 1*, e2–e3. doi:10.1016/s2214-109x(13)70002-0

Marmarosh, C. L., Dunton, E. C., & Amendola, C. (2014). *Groups: Fostering a culture of change*. Thousand Oaks, CA: Sage.

McWhirter, E. H., & McWhirter, B.T. (2007). Grounding clinical training and supervision in an empowerment model. In E. Alderondo (Ed.), *Promoting social justice through mental health practice* (pp. 417–442). New York, NY: Erlbaum.

MOOC. (2013, June 3). Retrieved from http://mooc.org/

Morrill, W., Oetting, E., & Hurst, J. (1974). Dimensions of counselor functioning. *Personnel and Guidance Journal, 52*, 354–359. doi:10.1002/j.2164-4918.1974.tb04041.x

MPAC. (2013). *Master's in psychology and counseling*. Retrieved from http://www.mpcacaccreditation.org/

Mrazek, P.J., & Ritchie, G.F. (2012). *Becoming a preventionist: Making prevention part of your mental health practice: A continuing education course*. Alexandria, VA: National Association of State Mental Health Program Directors.

Myers, J. (2003). Coping with caregiving stress: A wellness-oriented, strengths-based approach for family counselors. *The Family Journal: Counseling and Therapy for Couples and Families, 11*, 153–161. doi:10.1177/1066480702250162

National Center for Chronic Disease Prevention and Health Promotion. (2009). *The power of prevention*. Retrieved from http://www.cdc.gov/chronicdisease/pdf/2009-power-of-prevention.pdf

Page, B. (2011). Online groups. In R. Conyne (Ed.)., *The Oxford handbook of group counseling* (pp. 520–533). New York, NY: Oxford University Press. doi:10.1093/oxfordhb/9780195394450.001.0001

Parsons, F. (1884). The philosophy of mutualism. *Arena, 9*, 815.

Parsons, F. (1909). *Choosing a vocation*. Boston, MA: Houghton Mifflin.

Pew Research Center. (2013). *Baby boomers retire*. Retrieved from http://www.pewresearch.org/daily-number/baby-boomers-retire/

Pirog, M.A., & Good, E.M. (2013). *Public policy and mental health: Avenues for prevention*. Thousand Oaks, CA: Sage. doi:10.4135/9781452275642

Prevention Institute Alert (2013, November 22). New soda tax makes Mexico a leading guardian of public health. Retrieved from HYPERLINK "http://www.preventiontraininginstitute.org/about-us/Ip/1096-%09new-soda-tax" http://www.preventiontraininginstitute.org/about-us/Ip/1096-new-soda-tax

Prilleltensky, I., Dokecki, P., Frieden, G., & Wang, V. O. (2007). Counseling for wellness and justice: Foundations and ethical dilemmas. In E. Aldarondo (Ed.), *Advancing social justice through clinical practice* (pp. 19–42). Mahwah, NJ: Erlbaum. doi:10.4324/9780203936689

Rattray, T., Brunner, W., & Freestone, J. (2002). *The new spectrum of prevention: A model for public health practice*. Martinez, CA: Contra Costa Health Services.

Reese, R. (2013). *EcoWellness: Construction and validation of the Reese Eco-Wellness Inventory* (Unpublished doctoral dissertation). Retrieved from http://libres.uncg.edu/ir/uncg/listing.aspx?id=

Reinhardt, R. (2013, October 28). *Providing telehealth services—Opportunities and cautions*. Retrieved from http://www.tameyourpractice.com/blog/providing-telehealth-

Ritterman, T. (2014, October 8). The soda tax wars: Let's help San Francisco and Berkeley crush big soda. *Huffpost Healthy Living*. Retrieved from http://www.huffingtonpost.com/jeffrey-ritterman/the-soda-tax-wars-sf-and-_b_5922012.html

Roszak, T. (1992). *The voice of the earth: An exploration of ecopsychology*. New York, NY: Simon & Schuster.

Saker, A. (2014, October 18). Dena Cranley steps into public role: Mayor's wife unveils health initiative. *The Cincinnati Enquirer*, pp. A1, A6–A7.

Sandberg, S. (2013). *Lean in: Women, work, and the will to lead*. New York, NY: Knopf.

Sander, J. (2013). Consultation and collaboration. In D. Shriberg, S. Song, A. H. Miranda, & K. Radliff (Eds.), *School psychology and social justice: Conceptual foundations and tools for practice* (pp. 225–243). New York, NY: Routledge. doi:10.4324/9780203121245

Savery, J. (2009). Problem-based approach to instruction. In C.M. Carr-Chellman (Ed.), *Instructional-design theories and models* (pp. 143–165). New York: Routledge.

Seattle Parks & Recreation (2014, February 28). 12th Avenue project ready to dig in. Retrieved from HYPERLINK "http://www.capitolhillseattle.com/2014/02/12th-avenue-square-park-project-%09ready-to-dig-in-" http://www.capitolhillseattle.om/2014/02/12th-avenue-square-park-project-ready-to-dig-in-

Schlossberg, N. (2004). *Retire smart, retire happy: Finding your true path in life*. Washington, DC: American Psychological Association.

Seidman, E., Aber, J. L., & French, S. E. (2004). The organization of schooling and adolescent development. In K. Maton, C. Shellenbach, B. Leadbeater, & A. Solarz (Eds.), *Investing in children, youth, families and communities* (pp. 233–250). Washington, DC: American Psychological Association. doi:10.1037/10660-013

Silverman, P. R. (2004). *Widow to widow: How the bereaved help one another* (2nd ed.). New York, NY: Bruner Routledge. doi:10.4324/9780203020975

Silverman, P. (2011). Mutual help groups: What are they and what makes them work? In R. Conyne (Ed.)., *The Oxford handbook of group counseling* (pp. 511–519). New York, NY: Oxford University Press. doi:10.1093/oxfordhb/9780195394450.001.0001

Small, S., & Huser, M. (2012). Family-based prevention programs. In R. Levesque (Ed.), *Encyclopedia of adolescence* (pp. 967–976). New York, NY: Springer. doi:10.1007/978-1-4419-1695-2_161

SmartReceipt. (2014). *SmartReceipt media just got smarter.* Retrieved from http://www.receipt.com/

Social Development Research Group. (2012). Seattle, WA: University of Washington. Retrieved from http://www.sdrg.org/

Sommers, R. (2008). *Personal space: Updated: The behavioral basis of design.* Bristol, UK: Bosko Books.

Steele, F. (1973). *Physical settings and organization development.* Reading, MA: Addison-Wesley.

Substance Abuse and Mental Health Services Organization. (2013). *Community conversations about mental health.* Retrieved from http://www.samhsa.gov/communityconversations/

Taylor, S. E., Lam, D. J., Roppel, C. E., & Barter, J. T. (1984). Friends can be good medicine: An excursion into mental health promotion. *Community Mental Health Journal, 20,* 294–304. doi:10.1007/bf00757078

Toseland, R., Haigler, D., & Monahan, D. (2011). *Education and support programs for caregivers.* New York, NY: Springer.

Tsutsui, Y. (2013). Weather and individual happiness. *Weather, Climate & Society, 5,* 70–82. doi:10.1175/WCAS-D-11-00052.1

U.S. Department of Veterans Affairs. (2014). *Welcome to the VCS.* Retrieved from http://www.vacanteen.va.gov/

Vera, E., & Kenny, M. E. (2013). *Social justice and culturally relevant prevention.* Thousand Oaks, CA: Sage.

Vera, E.M., & Speight, S.L. (2007). Advocacy, outreach, and prevention: Integrating social action roles into professional training. In E. Aldarondo (Ed.), *Advancing social justice through clinical practice* (pp. 373–389). Mahwah, NJ: Erlbaum. doi:10.4324/9780203936689

Walsh, R. (2011). Lifestyle and mental health. *American Psychologist, 66,* 579–592.

Weir, K. (2013, November). Design in mind: Psychologists can help to design smart, sustainable spaces for the 21st century. *Monitor on Psychology, 44*(10). Retrieved from http://www.apa.org/monitor/

Weissberg, R.P., & Greenberg, M.T. (1998). Prevention science and collaborative community action research: Combining the best from both perspectives. *Journal of Mental Health, 7,* 479–492. doi:10.1080/09638239817360

White, B., & Madera, E. (Eds.). (2002). *American self-help clearinghouse self-help group sourcebook* (7th ed.). New York, NY: American Self Help Clearinghouse.

Williams, J.M., & Greenleaf, A.T. (2012). Ecological psychology: Potential contributions to social justice and advocacy in school settings. *The Journal of Educational and Psychological Consultation, 22,* 141–157. doi:10.1080/10474412.2011.649653

Zittoun, T., Duveen, G., Gillespie, A., Ivinson, G., & Psaltis, C. (2003). The use of symbolic resources in developmental transitions. *Culture Psychology, 9,* 415–448. doi:10.1177/1354067x0394006

Zytowski, D. (2008, February 21). 100 years of career guidance—Honoring Frank Parsons. *Kuder User News, 6*(3), 1–2.

4

COUNSELING FOR WELLNESS AND PREVENTION

Introduction

This chapter asks a BIG question:

How can counselors and other mental health professionals use wellness and prevention strategies discussed previously to promote healthiness in people, settings, and systems? That is, how is counseling for wellness and prevention done? After all, knowing what to do is important, but power really results from being able to do those things.

You have been introduced to the broad field of wellness and prevention. You considered its underlying foundations (chapter 1), the importance of "everyday wellness and prevention" practices in life (chapter 2), and how wellness and prevention fits into our healthcare system and is guided by general strategies, such as education and community organization and system intervention (COSI; chapter 3).

In seeking to consider the translation of knowledge to strategic directions, this chapter is organized by giving attention initially to general behavior change frameworks, each of which holds value for wellness and prevention, followed by examining change models that are especially sensitive to wellness and prevention in counseling. The chapter concludes by considering ways to educate and train about wellness and prevention.

General Behavioral Change Frameworks Supporting Wellness and Prevention

Several frameworks that fuel wellness and prevention are presented in the next section. We will begin by organizing them in the following box. Note at the outset how theories are organized by individual, interpersonal, and community levels, while the perspectives included are those of ecology, positive psychology, and social justice. Together, these frameworks provide a strong foundation for wellness and prevention.

General Behavior Change Frameworks Supporting Wellness and Prevention

General Theories

Individual and Intrapersonal Level Focus

–*Transtheoretical model for stages of change (TTM)* (Prochaska, Norcross, & DiClemente, 2013)
–*Health belief model (HBM)* (Rosenstock, Strecher, & Becker, 1988)
–*Theory of reasoned action and planned behavior (TRA/TPB)* (e.g., Ajzen, 1991; Fishbein, 1967b; Fishbein & Ajzen, 2010)

Interpersonal Level Focus

–Social learning theory (Bandura, 1977b)

Community Level Focus

–Diffusion of innovations (Rogers, 2003)
–*Behavior change wheel* (Michie, 2012; Michie, van Stralen, & West, 2011)

Perspectives

–*Ecological perspective* (Bronfenbrenner, 1979)
–*Positive psychology* (e.g., Snyder & Lopez, 2007)
–*Social justice* (e.g., Albee, 1986; Nelson & Prilleltensky, 2010; Kenny, Horne, Orpinas, & Reese, 2009; Ratts, 2009)

Individual- and Intrapersonal-Level Focus

The individual and intrapersonal level focus is centered on persons, whether they be taken intrapersonally ("within the skin") or as part of larger levels—separate members of groups, organizations, settings, and systems. An intrapersonal examination centers on considering one person's internal thoughts, feelings, attitudes, beliefs, assumptions, values, developmental history, behavior, and so forth. An individual examination restricts the study of larger entities to the level of collections of separate people. An example is found when the social climate of a work setting is determined by assessing and summing the perceptions of each individual. Three behavior change theoretical models are considered: (a) transtheoretical stages of change, (b) health belief, and (c) reasoned action and planned behavior (Romano, 2015).

Transtheoretical model for stages of change. The transtheoretical model for stages of change (TTM) accentuates the importance of client readiness in relation to a change project. This model suggests that the change goal depends on doing the right things (processes) at the right time (stages).

An all-too-common mistake made in programs aimed at education and behavior change, exemplified by wellness and prevention projects—is to assume that all participants for whom the program is offered are ready—right now—to receive the information and then to act on it. You read in chapter 3 that the educational strategy for producing gains in knowledge, or attitude formation, or behavioral change often proves to be unsuccessful due to many factors. A central explanation is that many recipients may lack readiness for taking in the information, appraising it, and then deciding to move ahead to apply it.

This is one reason why collaborative processes for program creation and implementation that include representatives of the targeted population are recommended for best practice in program development and evaluation (Conyne, 2010, 2013; Raczynski, Waldo, Schwartz, & Horne, 2013). Questions such as how to address participation readiness can then be introduced for discussion among the planning team. Collaborative, representative planning such as this improves the possibilities for creating program delivery strategies that respect varying levels of openness to change. Other strategies to address readiness include conducting focus groups with people who might later participate in the program, or administering needs assessment surveys to the population to be targeted allowing for identifying indices associated with readiness (Hage & Romano, 2013).

The work of Prochaska and DiClemente (1992), Prochaska, Johnson, and Lee (2009) and Prochaska et al. (2013) on a transtheoretical therapy model based on processes and stages of change is important for assessing readiness in wellness and prevention counseling. *Transtheoretical* means that this theory cuts across other ones.

The TTM includes six progressive changes of stage which, in practice, rarely occur with linearity, but more likely reflect some degree of recycling:

Stage 1: Pre-contemplation, where people either are unaware that any change in their behavior is needed to improve their health or, if there is awareness, that they have no immediate plans to take action.

Stage 2: Contemplation, where a need for change within the next six months is acknowledged, along with positive and negative factors involved.

Stage 3: Preparation, where people have developed a plan for taking some sort of action during the next month and are likely to have put some of it into play; they may have identified an exercise plan, for instance, and visited their medical doctor for advice and clearance to begin the program.

Stage 4: Action, the plan is in effect and performance is observed and charted; in the case of physical exercise, a pedometer may be worn to measure energy expended during daily 30-minute walks and weight totals may be registered daily.

Stage 5: Maintenance, a natural tendency to regress during behavior change is countered in this stage by monitoring progress and slippage in order to make necessary adjustments, and by incorporating rewards and support along the way. Maintenance of change is a challenge and it often takes years to produce routinely positive effects.

Stage 6: Termination, where people can be said to have accomplished the targeted behavior change, with no "backsliding"; in reality, this threshold is difficult if not impossible to attain as behavior change typically is a continuing process subject to both predictable (e.g., exercising regularly may become more difficult with increasing age) and unpredictable challenges (e.g., moving to a new neighborhood without sidewalks and paths and removed from convenient access to recreational facilities).

Health belief model. The health belief model (HBM) was one of the first to adapt behavioral science change theory to explain health behavior. The model is used to assist in designing wellness and prevention change program, also. Public health messages contained in mass universal education approaches, such as print educational materials or through electronic mass media frequently are based on the HBM. The model also can be useful at the level of individual and group counseling.

It was developed by psychologists working in the U.S. Public Health Service and discussed in many classic sources (e.g., Rosenstock et al., 1988). Its point of concern was how to encourage people to act on preventive information and services. For instance, a wealth of evidence-based information is available on the clear benefits of exercise for a variety of health issues (such as joint pain) and for wellness (e.g., improved cardiac function, improved mood). Yet, the vast majority of Americans do not include exercise in their daily routine. How can this gap be reduced?

The HBM is premised on the following steps:

1. Raising awareness of the seriousness of a health problem (think heart disease)
2. Raising sensitivity to one's own susceptibility of encountering it (think high cholesterol)
3. Increasing the perceived benefits of taking action (think quality of life), such as a 30-minute moderate intensity daily walking program, in relation to
4. Reducing the perceived barriers against implementing the action (think time involved in walking)

Rosenstock (1988) added a fifth concept, self-efficacy. This concept is derived from social cognitive theory, addressing one's belief in the capacity to successfully perform any action being contemplated—in this case, the ability to walk for 30 minutes a day.

The HBM has guided wellness and prevention programs in a wide range of interventions, including smoking cessation, exercise, nutrition, and high blood pressure. Its limitations trace to being a psychologically based theory that does not readily include other influencing health care factors, such as environmental, cultural, and economic ones. As well, the model does not take into account peer influences and social norms as they may affect decision making about health concerns (Granello, 2012).

Theory of reasoned action and theory of planned behavior. These related theories from social psychology hold much potential for wellness and prevention research and for program development and intervention. The theory of reasoned action (TRA) is concerned directly with the connections among a person's attitudes and beliefs about an "object," such as obesity, and the related behaviors that are controllable (Fishbein, 1967a). The intentions and attitudes about an object are understood in this theory to be powerful predictors of behavior change. Ajzen (1991) further stressed the importance of planned behavior in the theory of planned behavior (TPB) and perceived behavioral control to the theory. Here, what is under the control of a person, similar to Bandura's (1977a) concept of self-efficacy, is central.

Taken together, TRA/TPB theory conceives of behavior as tied to a person's intention to move forward, say with a weight loss program, the success of which is dependent on that person's attitudes about weight loss, attention to social norms and expectations of important others about it, and what actions are under the control of that person. Wellness and prevention program development from the TRA/TPB viewpoint would need to elicit information about an object to be prevented (say, again, obesity) from a targeted population that would specify these important dimensions: (a) attitudes, (b) social norms, and (c) what behaviors are doable and controllable (Hage & Romano, 2013). This information, then, guides any subsequent steps.

Interpersonal-Level Focus

The interpersonal-level focus situates an individual in relation to others, where mutual influence exists. The thoughts, attitudes, and behavior of these others—family, friends, colleagues, social groups—can strongly affect individuals. The existence and quality of ongoing interpersonal relationships and dynamics are assigned significance in affecting individual functioning, although other factors also can be considered at this level, including assessing perceptions with and experience with the environment. One main interpersonal model, social learning theory, will be considered.

Social learning theory. A fundamental assumption in social learning theory (SLT) is that people mutually influence one another and that learning results from one's own experience but, also, from observing and appraising the experiences and related outcomes of others. Here, personal factors, environmental conditions and influences, and behavior dynamically interact. Bandura's (1977a, 1977b) social cognitive theory was articulated from this basic assumption and it's a dominant framework underlying a range of behavior change approaches, such as cognitive-behavioral psychotherapy (see the summary by Craske, 2009). Learning accrues from observing and appraising the experiences of others and it includes a number of processes. When observing what others are modeling, the learner needs to attend, to retain, to reproduce, and to develop the motivation to apply what is being learned. Important is the sense that one possesses the capabilities to actually do what is being learned, which is the concept of self-efficacy.

Community-Level Focus

Prevention and health promotion directions took root in public health and have spread to mental health. In this expansion, practice emphases diversified to include public health's focus on populations and large groupings at the community level to mental health's concentration on individuals, small groups and families at the clinical level. In fact, both of these emphases are important and necessary.

Counselors and other mental health professionals, as I have pointed out, are steeped in the remedial-clinical level and typically are less familiar with wellness and prevention approaches conducted at the community level. These latter approaches are concerned with collective wellness and with creating, modifying, and supporting settings and systems that support healthy lifestyles and reduce or eradicate existing hazards and risk. The diffusions of innovations theory, to be summarized next, exemplifies a community-level approach to change.

Diffusion of innovations theory. This theory focuses on how innovation can be disseminated publicly. It is a major challenge in wellness and prevention to spread information to a population and throughout a community, nation, or even internationally. Consider depression, which is a major mental health challenge across the world. In fact, depression is the second largest cause of disability in the world, following back pain. Therefore, the World Health Organization (WHO), which has been discussed before, recommends that depression needs to be addressed as a global public health priority. The WHO discovered in its study of 2010 data comparing depression against more than 200 other diseases and injuries that only a small proportion of people suffering it receive treatment. The WHO (2013) is launching a global mental health action plan aimed at policy makers around the world to address this daunting problem. This initiative clearly illustrates how diffusion of an innovation, in this case the global mental health action plan, can help address wellness and prevention.

Behavior change wheel. The behavior change wheel (Michie, 2012; Michie et al., 2011) includes a three-dimensional behavioral system at its hub, captured by the acronym, "COM-B": (a) Capability to enact change; (b) Opportunity for engaging in change; and (c) Motivation to accomplish Behavior change. Think of this system alongside the stages of change model you read about earlier. This hub is surrounded immediately by a ring of nine intervention functions (e.g., education and enablement; think of these functions alongside the seven strategies for wellness and prevention discussed in chapter 3), and then by a final ring of seven policy

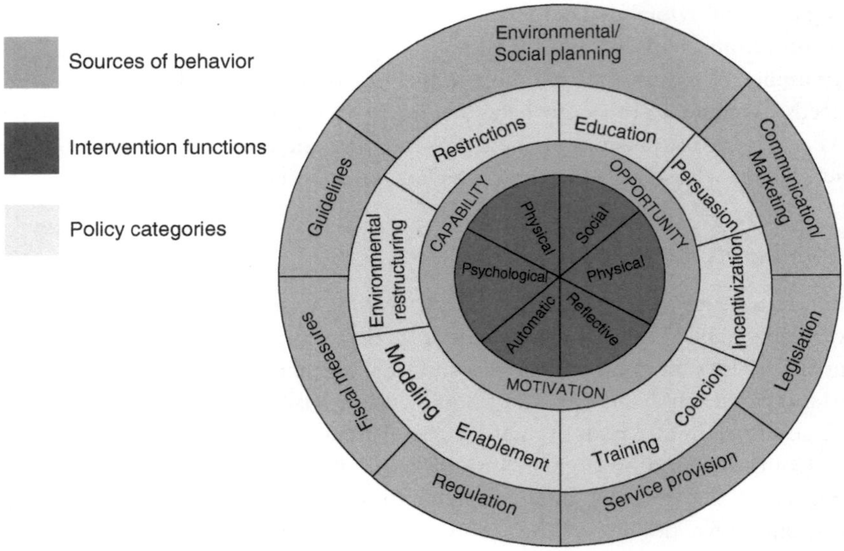

FIGURE 4.1 Behavior change wheel. The "wheel" emphasizes how capacity, opportunity, and motivation all influence change.

Source: Michie, S., Van Stralen, M. M., & West, R. (2011). The behaviour change wheel: A new method for characterizing and designing behaviour change interventions. *Implementation Science, 6*(1), 1–11. doi:10.1186/1748-5908-6-42

categories (e.g., legislation and environmental/social planning). See Figure 4.1, which depicts the "behaviour change wheel" (Michie, 2012; Michie et al., 2011).

The developers report that this new model has been used reliably with tobacco control strategies and in reducing obesity. Ongoing research continues. The behaviour change wheel would seem to hold considerable promise for guiding the creation and implementation of wellness and prevention programs due to its satisfaction of the important criteria mentioned above.

Perspectives Supporting Wellness and Prevention

Three important perspectives that contribute to wellness and prevention are addressed: (a) ecological, (b) positive psychology, and (c) social justice. These are not theories, per se, but more correctly might be understood as viewpoints, vantage points, or even "worldviews." A practical way to think of them is as lenses through which life experiences can be viewed and understood.

Ecological Perspective

That human behavior is complex is an understatement. It results from many factors, as the TRA/PB discussion suggests. Certainly, human behavior cannot be totally understood from an either an intrapersonal or an interpersonal perspective alone, or even in combination, although these are the levels around which much of traditional counseling theory, practice, and research has been centered.

An ecological perspective provides a broader scope for conceptualizing human behavior, as we discussed earlier. This perspective, first elucidated by Lewin (1936), Bertalanffy (1950), and Bronfenbrenner (1979), treats human behavior as emerging from a dynamic interplay of persons with levels of their environment. Lewin captured this relationship as $B = f(P \times E)$, where a person's behavior is a function of his or her ongoing interactions with the environment. Bronfenbrenner theorized an individual as being subject to the influences of ever increasing levels of systems, ranging from proximal (e.g., family) to distal (e.g., global); his particular terms are microsystem, mesosystem, exosystem, and macrosystem. Bertalanffy brought attention to the general systems framework, where organisms (e.g., a human) are open to, influenced by, and influence all other levels of systems.

The reciprocal interrelationship of persons with settings and systems has been portrayed in numerous, but similar, ways. As I mentioned, Bronfenbrenner's (1979) classic approach envisioned successive levels of person, microsystem (e.g., family, school), mesosystem (linkages between micro- and exosystems), exosystem (e.g., social services, neighbors), and macrosystem (political, economic, and cultural blueprint). Kasambira and Edwards (2000) picture an ecological system comprised of four levels: (a) individual or dyad, (b) primary group, (c) associated groups, such as organizations, and (d) institutional. Conyne and Cook (2004) applied this basic model to ecological counseling, which is enlisted to facilitate meaning and concordance in the lives of clients.

Other examples of the ecological perspective are notable. The WHO conception of an ecological perspective includes levels ranging from the individual, through relationships, community, and society. Orpinas and Horne (2006) adapted the WHO ecological model to apply to bullying prevention in the schools; the child is located in the center of the model, bounded successively by family, school and peers, and community and society and it also depicts associated protective factors (e.g., positive school climate) and risk factors (e.g., lack of supervision). Prilleltensky, Dokecki, Frieden, and Wang (2007), as you read about earlier, suggested an ecological model for approaching social justice in wellness and counseling, where wellness is dependent on a balance among three nodes: (a) individual (e.g., self-esteem, mastery, and control), (b) relational (e.g., caring, compassion, and social support), and (c) collective (e.g., equity, access, and justice). Thus, in this ecological viewpoint, wellness is not considered to be a property of the individual only, but it results from and is maintained by the harmonious intersection of strengths occurring at individual-relational-collective nodes. I will draw specifically this understanding of the ecological viewpoint (Prilleltensky et al., 2007) in my new model of counseling for wellness and prevention which you will read about later in this chapter.

It may be helpful at this point to explore two ecological models in a bit more detail. They both show how an individual is embedded in context, surrounded by circles of influence. In addition, the second model is geared specifically to health conditions.

Person in context. Consistent with many others, Ekpe (2010) pictures persons set within increasingly larger levels of systems, all of which are mutually influencing. These levels locate the person surrounded by these levels: (a) interpersonal, (b) institutional/organizational, (c) community, and (d) social structure, policies, and systems. See Figure 4.2.

Brief definitions of each level follow.

Individual level: Characteristics that affect individual behavior directly, including knowledge, attitudes, skills, values, beliefs, and personality traits. Wellness programs aim centrally at this level

Interpersonal level: Primary groups, interpersonal relationships, and interpersonal processes (e.g., family, peers, friends, social networks) that provide support, social identity, and role definition

Institutional/organizational level: Worksites and other formal and informal associations, with the rules, regulations, and policies that characterize them

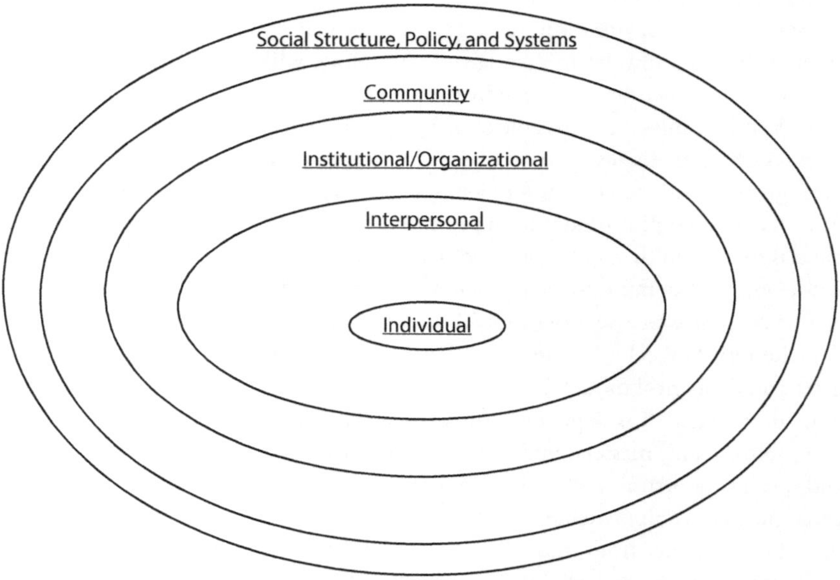

FIGURE 4.2 Person in context. An ecological perspective places people and environments in reciprocal transaction.

Source: Ekpe, S. (2010, July 2). *Person in context.* Retrieved from http://developmentcommunity.csd- i.org/profiles/generating-genuine-demand-with

Community level: Standards, norms, expectations, social climate, social networks, policies, procedures, and resources that characterize the neighborhood and community in which one lives
Social structure, policy, and systems: Local, regional, state, national, and global policies, legislation, and laws that regulate or support accountability (Ekpe, 2010)

Broad perspective of health determinants. The second ecological model (Dahlgren & Whitehead, 1991, 1992, 1993, 2006) addresses a broad socioecological approach individual health. This model maps relationships between an individual and successive environmental levels.

At the center it locates *individuals*, who are bounded by immutable fixed genes and demographic characteristics (e.g., age, gender, constitutional factors) on one side and potentially mutable lifestyle factors on the other. The *lifestyle factors* comprise personal behaviors and choices that affect health and are modifiable, such as eating and exercise patterns. The next level of influence, *social and community networks*, such as family, friends, and availability of human services, makes support and resources available for individuals, or may fail to do so. The outer ring, *general socioeconomic, cultural, and environmental conditions*, includes systemic and structural influences such as working conditions, political processes, economic policies and procedures, housing, access to services, and the provision of essential facilities. The model emphasizes the importance of counselors or other helpers intentionally intervening at all levels simultaneously, whenever possible. See Figure 4.3.

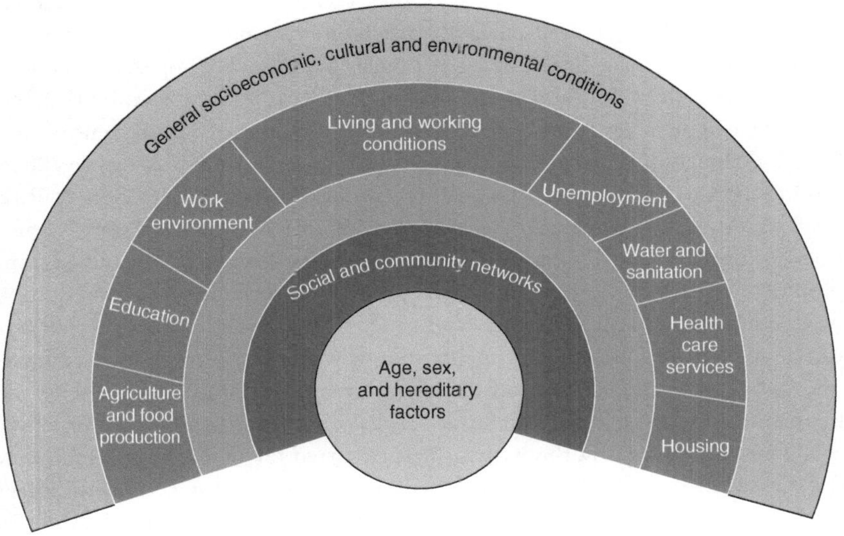

FIGURE 4.3 A broad perspective of health determinants. Health is internally and externally determined.

Source: Dahlgren, G., & Whitehead, M. (1993). *Tackling inequalities in health: What can we learn from what has been tried.* Retrieved from http://www.kingsfund.org.uk/

The formation and execution of wellness and prevention programs in counseling are well served by being oriented around an understanding of people in context and of the multiple influences of behavior. Programs and interventions developed from the vantage points of people alone, or of environments alone, are based on portions of the whole. Any gains produced are subject to fairly quick erosion. Assessing and attending to the interaction of people with their environment is a multilevel and dynamic approach that captures a wider and deeper slice of reality and, thus, holds a greater possibility for stabilizing change.

Positive Psychology Perspective

The positive psychology perspective, referred to in chapter 2 as an important part of everyday wellness and prevention, is based on a particular assumption of what is the best way to promote mental health. This approach is 180 degrees different from the medical model, which has been in effect within psychology and psychiatry (Maddux, 2000; Maddux, Snyder, & Feldman, 2003), and which has its own advantages. As you read in chapter 1, the medical model has been effectively used to correct dysfunction and to address the hundreds of clinical syndromes contained in the DSM. Instead, positive psychology alters the focus from the reduction of human psychological disabilities and disturbances to the enhancement of human strengths and abilities. This focus centers on several factors, including (a) authentic happiness (Seligman, 2002) from the eudaimonic approach, that is, happiness that is centered on meaning and self-realization (Ryan & Deci, 2001); (b) the choices people make about their lives and how they construe what occurs and matters (Maddux et al., 2003); (c) self-efficacy, hope, resilience, and optimism (Reivich & Shatte, 2002; Seligman, 2006; Snyder & Lopez, 2007; Snyder, Lopez, & Teramoto, 2010); (d) pursuit of flow and an optimal lifestyle (Csikszentmihalyi, 1990, 2009); (e) positive approaches to work and environment (Seligman & Csikszentmihalyi, 2000); (f) flourishing, meditation, and spiritual concerns (Lopez & Snyder, 2008, 2011; Seligman, 2011); and (g) signature character strengths (Peterson & Park, 2009; Peterson & Seligman, 2004), including the PERMA model: Positive Emotion (P), Engagement (E), Positive Relationships (R), Meaning (M), and Accomplishment (A). All these areas also are the province of wellness and prevention.

Positive psychology approaches can be used daily (see chapter 2), and they also can be included within the armamentarium of wellness and prevention counselors. As one example, building off the character strength of gratitude, clients can be instructed to keep a daily gratitude journal or diary in which they jot down at the end of the day, say, three things that occurred for them about which they feel pleased or grateful. Completing this exercise every day for a couple of weeks can begin to help clients refocus their attention on what is positive, and to learn how to appreciate those things, rather than to continue being fastened on negative events and situations. Emphasizing and enhancing a strengths-based approach to life and for working with client systems is consonant with positive psychology and is a hallmark of wellness and prevention counseling.

Social Justice Perspective

Social justice is another important perspective that contributes to wellness and prevention. It is open to various applications by those who hold it. As with other perspectives, social justice is at the very minimum a "worldview," providing a window through which one views and responds to life.

Social justice is increasingly being recognized as an important topic and goal in education (Bell, 2007) and it is central to certain counseling models. Community counseling, for instance (Lewis, Toporek, & Ratts, 2010), is defined in part as "a comprehensive framework that is grounded in multicultural competence and oriented toward social justice" (p. xiii). Group work provides another example of how social justice principles can be used (Conyne & Diederich, 2014; Ratts, Anthony, & Santos, 2010). The Association for Specialists in Group Work (ASGW) has developed Multicultural and Social Justice Competence Principles for Group Workers (Singh, Merchant, Skudruzk, & Ingene, 2012), which those who work with groups are encouraged to use as a guide for introducing multicultural and social justice principles and processes into their practice.

Early in its development prevention in mental health included the roots of social justice, as the twin routes to prevention were identified as competency enhancement and system change (Cowen, 1982). Especially the system change method overlaps strongly with social justice. Community counseling (Lewis et al., 2010), preventive counseling (Conyne, 1987, 2004), and ecological counseling (Conyne & Cook, 2004; Cook, 2012; Greenleaf & Williams, 2009; Williams & Greenleaf, 2012) include it as a central delivery mode. Conceptions of a "just society" and of social justice as a primary goal and method (depending on one's approach) for prevention were ushered in most clearly by Albee (e.g., Albee, 1986), and since then, they have occupied a position of prominence within the prevention literature (e.g., Kenny et al., 2009; Kenny & Medvide, 2013; Lewis et al., 2010; Pieterse, Hanus, & Gale, 2012; Prilleltensky, 2000, 2012; Ratts, Anthony, & Santos, 2010; Ratts, Toporek, & Lewis, 2010; Singh et al., 2012; Vera & Kenny, 2013; Vera & Speight, 2003).

The goals of social justice revolve around the full and equal participation of all groups in society, where the distribution of resources is equitable, all members are physically and psychological secure, and people become empowered in settings and systems to seek opportunities and grow and develop without infringing on the rights and welfare of others (Bell, 2007; McWhirter & McWhirter, 2007). Counselors work collaboratively with community members to evolve culturally relevant processes and changes that seek these goals (Vera & Kenny, 2013) across personal, relational, and collective levels of an ecosystem (Prilleltensky & Prilleltensky, 2006).

Often what is targeted for change are social pathologies, those aspects of an environment that serve to deny people a just life. For instance, the 10-year-old Center for Closing the Health Gap in Cincinnati (Curnutte, 2014) seeks to improve health in poor communities by employing two interconnected prevention strategies that are connected with social justice: (a) targeting socioeconomic factors, such as poverty, food deserts, and unemployment, and (b) reducing negative lifestyle behaviors, such as smoking, excessive alcohol consumption, and poor diet. Pieterse et al. (2012) label such actions as advocacy and prevention, where systems of oppression are to be dismantled. Watts, Abdul-Adil, and Pratt (2002) argue that educators and human service professionals are obligated to help liberate people from oppressive conditions to which they are subjected. Prilleltensky (2000) outlined a paradigm shift for promoting well-being, one that is consistent with social justice and rooted in strengths, prevention, empowerment, and community. See the next box, which summarizes some of the key concepts of social justice.

Some Concepts Central to Social Justice

Liberation
Equity
Privilege
Opportunity
Full participation
Advocacy and outreach
Empowerment
Collaboration
Diversity
Fairness
Free of exploitation and oppression
Cultural validity
Empowerment
Personal, relational, and collective wellness
Political and social collective action

Connections between holding and practicing a social justice perspective with wellness and prevention are inescapable, if not yet fully realized. As I've emphasized in various ways throughout this book, wellness is a desired state for people and for settings and systems. Humans exist and function within an ecosystem. All of it needs to be well. Especially for those who may be marginalized in society, by virtue of any number of reasons, including but not limited to—economic status, sexual and gender identity and expression, race, and ethnicity—social justice action may be mandated. The conditions these nonprivileged persons experience are radically more challenging than those faced by those in the "mainstream." Discrimination, lack of opportunity, harassment, and inequities all require change because the system that sponsors these conditions is itself sick. People can better pursue their own wellness when noxious environmental conditions such as these and others are reduced, eliminated or, better yet, prevented in the first place.

Social justice and wellness are not independent. In fact, it is the case that "wellness and justice are intertwined. Wellness requires justice, and justice without wellness has no meaning. Actions to improve wellness should reflect this state of interdependence" (Prilleltensky et al., 2007, p. 35). From this perspective, counselors work with clients and in systems to support personal needs, relational needs, and collective needs—working in all those domains—it is through the integration of these three domains that wellness can emerge. I state it once again: It is necessary that wellness not be understood as an individual level variable only. Rather, it is individual, interpersonal, organization, *and* community all wrapped together.

Models Emphasizing Counseling and Aspects of Wellness and Prevention in Counseling

Let's examine a number of counseling models that give particular attention to wellness and prevention. See the summary box, next, which organizes these models into: (a) general change approaches, (b) wellness-oriented models, (c) prevention-oriented models, and (d) wellness- and prevention-oriented models.

Change Models Emphasizing Counseling in General

–Dimensions of counselor functioning cube (Morrill, Oetting, & Hurst, 1974)
–Comprehensive mental health counseling model (Gerig, 2007)
–Ecological counseling (Conyne & Cook, 2004; Cook, 2012)

Change Models Emphasizing Wellness in Counseling

–Counseling for wellness model (Myers & Sweeney, 2005a)
–Clinical and educational wellness model (Granello, 2000)
–Counseling model for positive behavior change (CM-PBC) (Granello, 2012)

Change Models Emphasizing Prevention in Counseling

–Community counseling model (Lewis, Lewis, Daniels, & D'Andrea, 2011)
–Preventive counseling model (Conyne, 1987, 2004)

Change Models Emphasizing Wellness and Prevention

–Counseling for wellness and justice (Prilleltensky et al., 2007)
–Counseling for wellness and prevention (Conyne, 2015)

Change Models Emphasizing Counseling in General

Dimensions of counselor functioning cube. This cube model served to alter how counseling interventions were to be understood (Morrill et al., 1974). Multiple counseling interventions were possible, not simply individual or group counseling. Rather, counseling could be viewed as a kind of "multisplendored thing," capable of being employed in a variety of ways (methods), for different reasons (purposes), and with a range of recipients (targets). As Lewis et al. (2010) described, in this and similar approaches to come (e.g., community counseling, preventive counseling, ecological counseling, feminist counseling, relational-cultural counseling, empowerment-focused counseling, social justice counseling), counselors "use the wide-angle lens rather than the microscope" (p. 73).

Certainly, counseling included one-to-one remedial activity, but, according to the cube, it also legitimately embraced such other activities as community consultation, training and supervising paraprofessional helpers, and using a variety of media and social media to reach a targeted audience with a preventive message. In all, some 36 different kinds of interventions were included under the cube's umbrella.

Defining the cube's dimensions. Morrill et al. (1974) pictured counseling interventions to consist of three main dimensions: their targets, purposes, and methods. These dimensions are considered next.

The target of the intervention. Interventions may be aimed at (a) the individual; (b) the individual's primary groups, those close by and face-to-face, such as family, friendship networks, or in small groups; (c) the individual's associational groups, those that are informally or formally organized, settings such as clubs, work settings, and other organizations; or (d) the institutions or communities that influence the individual's behavior, systems such as neighborhoods, city government, community policy-making bodies, religious institutions, and so on.

The purpose of the intervention. The purpose was described as (a) remediation, (b) prevention, or (c) development. This dimension refers to why a counseling intervention is conducted and what it might expect to accomplish.

The method of intervention. The method of reaching the target population may be through (a) direct service, which involves direct professional involvement with the target, such as counseling, education, group work, and training, or (b) indirect service, such as consultation with other helping professionals or with leaders of organizations, supervision of professionals and paraprofessionals, and use of mediated interventions, such as brochures and fliers, electronic media and e-learning systems, television, and social media.

Comprehensive mental health counseling model. This mental health counseling model (Gerig, 2007) is comprehensive because it helps providers to frame their work with clients broadly. Pathology and wellness both are considered, as they are expressed throughout ecological levels. The model, then, is framed by three dimensions: (a) the level of mental health/wellness present, ranging from low to high; (b) the level of pathology present, ranging from minimal to severe; and (c) the ecological level being targeted, from the individual through the macrosystem.

How these dimensions interact in a counseling situation supports the important concept that levels of wellness and prevention, as well as mental illness, evolve through the interactions of people with levels of their environment. This P × E interaction points to the importance of understanding people in context and developing counseling interventions that emerge from that perspective and are approached contextually. It also holds out the possibility that wellness and prevention can be approached through targeting individuals, as well as families, settings, and larger systemic influences. Placing mental health and mental illness within an ecological framework is an asset.

Ecological counseling model. To counsel ecologically is to provide contextual help-giving by attending to person × environment interactions across all levels of an ecosystem. Thus, ecological counseling (Conyne & Cook, 2004; Cook, 2012) seeks to correct two large limitations of more traditional counseling: (a) it is concerned with all levels of intervention, not emphasizing one over the other, and (b) it places people within their settings, where P × E interactions are the subject of interest, not the person or the environment taken separately.

The intent of ecological counseling is to facilitate ecological concordance and harmony through applying a person-environment perspective. Eastern concepts that capture aspects of this intention are *kizuna* in Japanese, which loosely means "positive bonds," the Confucian concept *héxié shèhuì*, abbreviated as "HE," which means "harmonious society," and *yoga*, in Hindu, referring to "union."

Ecological counseling is based on a number of principles. See the following box.

Principles Underlying Ecological Counseling

Interdisciplinary	Meaning making
Metatheoretical	Concordance
Integrated view of people	Full range of targets
Individuals in Ecosystem	Parsimonious
Interactional	Collaborative
Considers multiple contexts	Empowering
Time is important	Interdependence

Change Models Emphasizing Wellness in Counseling

Counseling for wellness model. Witmer and Sweeney (1992) developed a holistic, life-span model for wellness that is based on Adlerian counseling theory and is grounded in research. They identified five life tasks that represent the characteristics of healthy individuals. (a) spirituality, (b) self-direction, (c) work and leisure, (d) friendship, and (e) love. These life tasks are further subdivided into 15 subscales. These life tasks may take on different aspects for people at different phases of human development. A retiree has different issues surrounding these life tasks than an elementary school student, for example.

Myers (1992, 2003) outlined several ways that counselors can assist others in wellness pursuits. Because in its classic sense wellness is generally understood as a process that is based on daily lifestyle choices made by individuals, counselors can further wellness by through education and helping with making choices.

Myers and Sweeney (2005b) continued their development of wellness models and approaches, supported by research. The five factor wellness model, or indivisible self model, contains these dimensions: (a) Creative Self (e.g., problem solving), (b) Coping Self (e.g., stress management), (c) Social Self (e.g., friendship), (d) Essential Self (e.g., cultural identity), and (e) Physical Self (e.g., exercise). These factors led to the development of the Five Factor Wellness Inventory (5-F WEL), an assessment measure that is grounded in research, measuring the single order factor of total wellness and five second order factors corresponding to the subscales mentioned. According to Myers and Sweeney (2008), this model and its assessment are among the most comprehensive of all wellness approaches available to counselors and mental health workers (Granello, 2012).

Clinical and educational wellness model. Granello (2000) developed this model for practical use with his clients. It is based on the life-span model (Witmer & Sweeney, 1992) and his own adaptations over time.

The overlapping domains in the clinical and educational wellness model are given in the following box.

Clinical and Educational Wellness Model Domains

–Cognition (thought processes)
–Emotional Regulation (awareness and monitoring)
–Physical Activity and Nutrition (regularity and balance)
–Preventive Self-Care (everyday wellness and prevention practice)
–Spirituality and Meaning (meaning and purpose)
–Cultural and Environmental Context*
–Social Relationships (connections with others)
–Creativity (flexibility, novelty, and resilience_

*The Cultural and Environmental Context domain is too frequently omitted or ignored in wellness programs, but it typically is a central part of prevention programs. It needs to be weighted much more heavily in wellness and prevention programs so that attention to personal, relational, and collective domains is integrated.

Counseling model for positive behavior change. According to Granello (2012), the counseling model for positive behavior change (CM-PBC) is intended for use by mental health counselors who understand how to use behavioral change approaches. It incorporates the work of Creer (1996) and by Young's (2008) REPLAN model, which contains common curative factors (relationship, efficacy, practice, lower and raise emotional arousal, activate expectations, and new learning), the REPLAN common curative factors. The CM-PBC includes stages, with each containing a series of steps (see Granello, 2012, for elaboration):

1. Determine client readiness
2. Develop goals
3. Monitor initial performance
4. Refine goals and commit
5. Perform
6. Persist

Wellness initiatives that are directed at individuals or through programs to groups and populations can address any of the dimensions that have been touched on previously. The CM-PBC applies a series of behavior change steps to promote adoption of wellness.

Change Models Emphasizing Prevention in Counseling

Community counseling model. This model of counseling first introduced in 1977 to the counseling profession in an organized framework that took a vastly different direction: emphasizing the community as a context for counseling while using a broad range of methods to produce empowerment and prevention. Its definition is as follows: "a comprehensive framework that is grounded in multicultural competence and oriented toward social justice. Because human behavior is powerfully affected by context, community counselors use strategies that facilitate the healthy development both of their clients and of the communities that nourish them" (Lewis et al., 2011, p. xiii).

Therefore, the community counseling model is employed to facilitate growth in both humans and in the communities with which they interact. It uses strategies that are focused, such as counseling, outreach, client advocacy, and community collaboration, and those that are broad-based, such as preventive interventions and macro-level change attempts involving sociopolitical advocacy. Whichever community counseling strategy is used to facilitate change in the human–context interface it is guided by attention to strengths.

Advocacy is an important community counseling—and social justice—function. Consider how counselors can advocate as change agents to assist client development. They can work on behalf of clients or with them, they can advocate to modify negative elements or processes of an environment (e.g., a school's negative social climate), or they can advocate to influence larger socio-political change (such as bullying prevention legislation). The American Counseling Association advocacy model (Lewis, Arnold, House, & Toporek, 2003) provides an inclusive framework for conceptualizing and guiding advocacy approaches.

Preventive counseling model. Preventive counseling (Conyne, 1987, 2004) is a model that emphasizes the critical importance of before-the-fact intervention including attention to competencies and to social change. The counseling for wellness and prevention model I present in this book retains much of the preventive counseling approach by drawing from contemporary literature (e.g., Aldarondo, 2007; Granello, 2012; Myers & Sweeney, 2005a; Prilletensky & Prillentensky, 2006) to expand attention to wellness dimensions, how social justice and other social system approaches need to be incorporated, and to specify more ways that wellness and prevention can be applied within individual counseling.

Preventive counseling (Belkin, 1984; Conyne, 1987, 2004) is a proactive approach that is applied across any of several levels of system and in a range of settings. It is focused more with building and broadening health (Fredrickson, 2000) than on alleviating dysfunction.

Purposes in preventive counseling. The main purpose of preventive counseling is that of prevention itself: to build and broaden strengths and capacities in people and in systems, and to reduce the incidence of dysfunction in a designated collection of people. Said very simply, preventive counseling is used to lower the probability of human suffering and to increase the opportunities for optimal human productivity, health, and satisfaction. A second purpose is to reverse the trajectory of early-stage problems so that these do not proceed toward entrenchment.

Strategies in preventive counseling. These purposes are approached through three main strategies: (a) system-centered change, (b) person-centered change, and (c) encouraging everyday prevention efforts. System-centered change is based on the assumption that people can thrive when oppressive systems are altered to become supportive. Collaborative consultation, advocacy, outreach and other methods aimed at environmental targets comprise system-centered change. Person-centered change is based on the assumption that people can become more empowered to cope with life demands. Preventive counseling can assist in enhancing coping and resilience competencies, permitting fuller and more satisfying interactions within settings and systems and promoting wellness. Everyday prevention is accomplished by people directly themselves, building routinely into their lives (as they can within the supports and constraints of their lives) healthy, wellness-oriented daily practices such as good nutrition, exercise, and social relationships. Preventive counselors can assist people to become more self-directed through providing to them a range of educational services.

Change Models Emphasizing Wellness and Prevention

Counseling for wellness and justice. This model (Evans & Prilleltensky, 2007; Prilleltensky et al., 2007) is based on the assumption that wellness and justice are yoked, resulting from personal, relational, and collective needs existing in synergistic balance. The wellness–justice nexus, then, orients counseling practice to the simultaneous promotion of wellness and justice where each dimension fuels and nurtures the other, such that counselors need to think of the following.

Domains of Wellness Yoked With Social Justice

Individual wellness
Relational wellness
Collective wellness
Optimum wellness (synthesizing the preceding domains)

How can these Wellness-Social Justice domains be incorporated practically? Consider this description of a health equity program in Seattle, the Be Active Together (BAT):

BAT Program

BAT combines health and fitness programming with public policy advocacy and community engagement to support healthy living opportunities to underserved, typically low-income communities. (Rousch, 2013, p. 1)

Activities emerging from this program include providing free and low-cost exercises to target communities, rallying community members to engage in public safety campaigns, and organizing advocacy visits to the state capitol to advance refugee, immigrant, and health and housing issues. As project director, Denise Sharify, states, "Our hope with BAT is that all our families become active in their daily lives and in their communities" (p. 2).

Through these program descriptions we can see linkages between wellness and social justice. Also evident is attention to strengths, prevention, empowerment, and community (Prilleltensky & Nelson, 2002).

Counseling for wellness and prevention model. This new model emerges from the previously discussed work in behavior change, perspectives contributing to wellness and to prevention, and existing counseling models that speak to community, wellness, and prevention. It serves as a general, umbrella framework for conducting a range of counseling interventions that seek to produce optimal, integrated wellness through empowering people, settings, and systems. More specifically, the model expands and adapts the preventive counseling model, discussed earlier, to heighten attention to wellness, while continuing a focus on prevention.

Figure 4.4 is organized to coordinate and indicate the interrelationships existing among the six central elements of the counseling for wellness and prevention model.

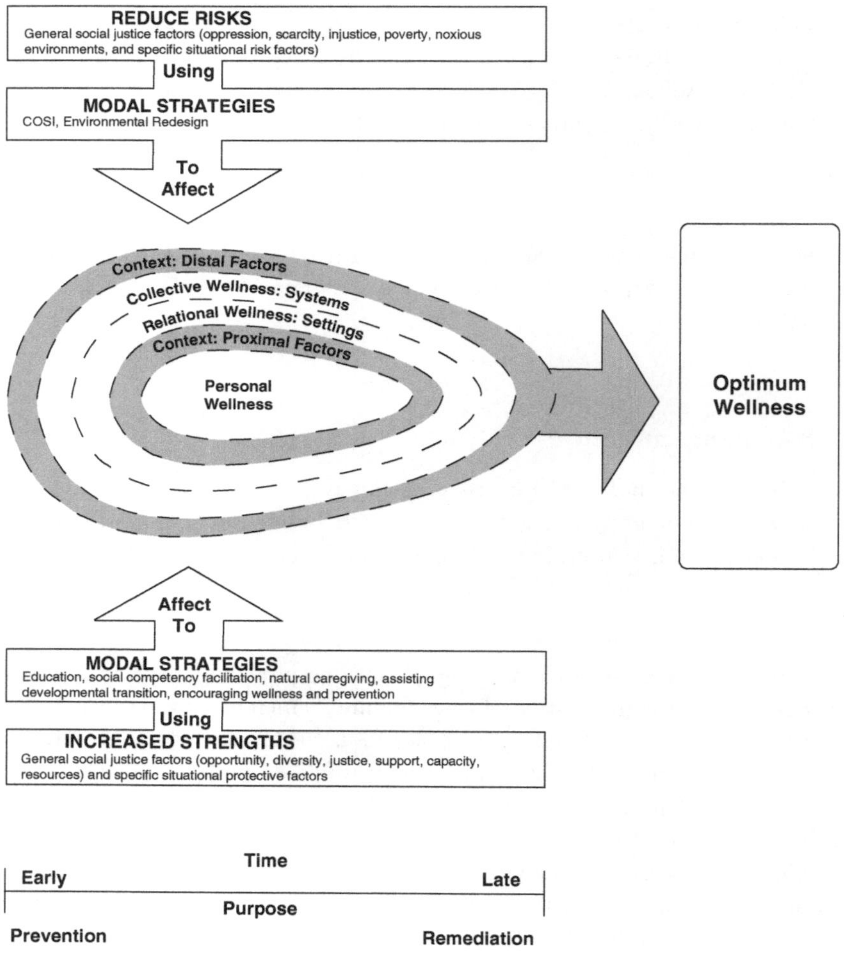

FIGURE 4.4 Counseling for wellness and prevention model. Counseling for wellness and prevention empowers people in settings and systems to progress toward optimum wellness.

(a) *Wellness and prevention contexts*:

–Proximal inputs, such as genetic predispositions and demographics, and immediate setting characteristics, such as the number and kind of resources available

–Distal inputs, including macro global influences such as economic, weather, and political conditions.

(b) *Three interrelated* wellness levels:

–Individual level, the personal focus of most traditional wellness programs

–Relational level, settings such as family, friends, work, and communities

–Collective level, systems such as governmental, political, economic, and legislative.

(c) *Incidence reduction*, the classic goal of prevention efforts, aimed at reducing or eliminating general social injustices and specific risk factors while promoting general social justice and specific protective factors:

Risk Factors

Social Justice Risk Factors: Oppression, Injustice, Poverty, Powerlessness, Noxious Environments

Specific Stressors: To fit the situation (e.g., bullying stressors)

Protective Factors

Social Justice Protective Factors: Opportunity, Diversity, Justice, Support, Capacity

Specific Protective Factors: To fit the situation (e.g., resilience protective factors)

(d) *Intervention timeline ranging from early to late*:

Early: Before-the-fact, primary prevention

Late: After-the-fact, remediation

(e) *Major strategies for wellness and prevention*:

Modal strategies aimed at reducing risk factors: Community Organization and System Intervention (COSI), Environmental Redesign.

Modal strategies aimed at promoting protective factors: Education, Competency Enhancement Facilitation, Natural Caregiver connection, Assisting Developmental Transitions, and Encouraging Everyday Wellness and Prevention.

(f) *Overall goal*:

Enhancing a state of optimum, integrated wellness through empowering people, settings, and systems.

Let's now take a look at how the counseling for wellness and prevention model connects with a contemporary issue, school shootings.

The Counseling for Wellness and Prevention Model in Relation to School Shootings

By Perry Firth

Since the Newtown shooting in which 27 were killed, there have been not only more examples of targeted school violence (sometimes called mass shootings or school shooting rampages) but raised concern over the safety of students. Even prior to this highly publicized event, the number of non-gang related mass school shootings can be traced back to the early 1900s (Cable News Network, 2014). While school shooting rampages are understood to be one of the least common forms of school violence (Borum, Cornell, Modzeleski, & Jimerson, 2010), the fear and damage they cause make them a pressing public health concern.

School shooters are created from a complex interaction among personality, temperament and behavioral characteristics, adolescent experiences, school structure and climate, family structure and cohesion, parental modeling, and community influences (CITE-FBI). It is this very complexity and intersectionality that may feel overwhelming to school professionals interested in preventing this type of violence. After all, how does one prevent something whose causes can be so multifaceted?

Counseling for Wellness and Prevention Model

The model's strengths for this type of application can be found in the framework it provides school professionals for analyzing the strengths and weaknesses present in a school's ecosystem, its emphasis on the role of distal and proximal factors in influencing the individual and environment, and in the different strategies that can be used to implement change. Further, the model is inherently ecological, acknowledging the complex roots of human behavior and development in general, and in this case, a targeted school violence threat.

Used as part of a comprehensive approach to creating a safe school, the Counseling for Wellness and Prevention Model explicitly asks school professionals to: a) assess and increase school strengths while assessing and decreasing risks; b) consider the degree to which dysfunction in the school system is the result of specific situational stressors or absent social justice factors (listed in the model); c) consider how proximal and distal factors contribute to the functioning of the school, specific individuals, and groups; and d) target interventions across multiple levels and, if needed, across contexts (for example, school and community).

These considerations create a model that is comprehensive and flexible, essential components in creating school change, while also providing opportunities to tailor interventions toward groups, systems, and individuals. Its framework also highlights the fluid and porous relationship among personal, relational, and collective wellness. Changes in functioning at one level may cause changes at others.

This model can be used preventively by school professionals prior to a student threatening violence (e.g., maybe the school psychologist had noticed that the school culture allowed bullying to go unchecked and that certain student groups seemed disenfranchised). It also can be used as an adjunct to the behavioral threat assessment process to organize individual and school-wide interventions, and as a way to prevent violence threat from re-occurring.

A Promising Strategy for School Professionals: Behavioral Threat Assessment

One answer (and arguably the best answer) to the threat of targeted school violence is the Behavioral Threat Assessment process, originally developed by the Secret Service (http://curry.virginia.edu/uploads/resourceLibrary/Virginia_Model_for_Student_Threat_Assessment_overview_paper_7–16–10.pdf) as a way to identify those individuals who pose a risk of violence. Something about how it is a broad term which may encompass variations in method, however all will have the following similarities?

When adapted for use in schools, this method enables personnel to think and plan systematically about threats, structure information gathering, use a protocol for assessing the intensity level of threats, indicate when to notify police, and connect the student in question to appropriate mental health care as needed (http://www.fbi.gov/stats-services/publications/school-shooter). Ultimately this in-depth analysis should reveal the likelihood that a threat will be carried out (http://www.fbi.gov/stats-services/publications/school-shooter). See chapter 8 for more information about the Behavioral Threat Assessment process.

It is important to connect the Behavioral Threat Assessment process with a larger, more comprehensive assessment of the overall school climate, culture and structure (http://www.fbi.gov/stats-services/publications/school-shooter). This analysis could reveal, for instance, that some student groups are given more prestige than others by both students and administrators; that class and race divides may be allowed to persist unchecked; and that some students may gain more explicit attention and approval than others. Bullying may be prevalent and a culture of silence may exist where students do not feel comfortable reaching out to administrators (http://www.fbi.gov/stats-services/publications/school-shooter). These situations have been linked to unhealthy school ecosystems that can give rise to violence.

A student threatening targeted school violence may reveal more than a personal cry for help; he (for it most often is a male) may symbolize a school climate and structural deficiencies that most likely make the lives of all students more difficult, diminishing the likelihood that individual students and the student body as a whole can achieve optimum levels of wellness and psychological well-being. It is for this reason that experts recommend incorporating threat assessment into a comprehensive model that attends to creating a safe and healthy school environment.

Counseling for Wellness and Prevention Model

The model's strengths for this type of application can be found in the framework it provides school professionals for analyzing the strengths and weaknesses present in a school's ecosystem, its emphasis on the role of distal and proximal factors in influencing the individual and environment, and in the different strategies that can be used to implement change. Further, the model is inherently ecological, acknowledging the complex roots of human behavior and development in general, and in this case, a targeted school violence threat.

Used as part of a comprehensive approach to creating a safe school, the Counseling for Wellness and Prevention Model explicitly asks school professionals to: a) assess and increase school strengths while assessing and decreasing risks; b) consider the degree to which dysfunction in the school system is the result of specific situational stressors or absent social justice factors (listed in the model); c) consider how proximal and distal factors contribute to the functioning of the school, specific individuals, and groups; and d) target interventions across multiple levels and, if needed, across contexts (for example, school and community).

These considerations create a model that is comprehensive and flexible, essential components in creating school change, while also providing opportunities to tailor interventions toward groups, systems, and individuals. Its framework also highlights the fluid and porous relationship among personal, relational, and collective wellness. Changes in functioning at one level may cause changes at others.

This model can be used preventively by school professionals prior to a student threatening violence (e.g., maybe the school psychologist had noticed that the school culture allowed bullying to go unchecked and that certain student groups seemed disenfranchised). It also can be used as an adjunct to the behavioral threat assessment process to organize individual and school-wide interventions, and as a way to prevent violence threat from re-occurring.

Competencies in Wellness and Prevention Counseling

Training of students and continuing education of practitioners is of critical importance in the helping professions and in wellness and prevention. Preparing practitioners to deliver essential competencies has become a training priority. The helping professions have addressed competencies from their own unique perspectives.

Benchmark competencies for training in professional psychology have been generated (Fouad et al., 2009), which are based on the "competency cube" (Rodolfa et al., 2005). These competencies emerge from the three domains of functions (e.g., assessment, intervention, and consultation), foundations (e.g., relationships, reflection, and individual and cultural development), and stages of professional development (from the doctoral level through continuing education). A taxonomy for training at distinct levels of professional development within psychological specialties has been created (American Psychological Association [APA], 2012) by the Commission for the Recognition of Specialties in Professional Psychology (CRSPPP). Important is the determination within counseling psychology that prevention has been identified as a foundation competency within the specialty, along with vocational and multicultural psychology.

Within the Counseling profession, a series of separate competency statements have been produced, dealing with advocacy, multicultural counseling, ALGBTIC, career, and cross-cultural counseling (American Counseling Association, 2014). Within social work, the Council on Social Work Education (2008) has stipulated 10 core competencies and practice behaviors.

Certainly, the question of competencies is of high interest within wellness and prevention counseling (APA, 2013; Conyne, Newmeyer, Kenny, Romano, & Matthews, 2008; Haggerty & Shapiro, 2013; Hawkins, Shapiro, & Fagan, 2010; Matthews, 2013; Reeser, 2007; Romano & Hage, 2000; Vera & Speight, 2003). I expand material from a recent contribution by Conyne, Horne, and Raczynski (2013), who themselves summarized a large body of work in this area, to identify key competencies in prevention. Important, too, is work underway aimed at translating the Guidelines for Prevention in Psychology (see chapter 1) into competencies.

Seven Competencies: The "Big Ones"

Seven general wellness and prevention competencies are highlighted in bold letters: three from the knowledge domain and two skills and one from each of the other domains of attitudes, and values. Similar to the "big five" traits in personality assessment (e.g., Goldberg, 1993), although without the empirical support at present, I nominate the following seven factors as essential to all wellness and prevention training efforts.

You will recognize these competencies from previous discussions. Training programs in counseling, psychology, and social work—as well as continuing education for practitioners—need to intentionally coordinate attention to knowledge, skills, attitudes, and values to support the preparation and real world functioning of wellness and prevention professionals.

Wellness and Prevention Training: Essential Knowledge, Skills, Attitudes, and Values

Knowledge
- Wellness and health promotion
- History and science of prevention
- Ecological–systemic vantage point
- Multidisciplinary sources of influence
- Incidence reduction, protective, and risk factors
- Social justice

Skills
- Basic helping
- Wellness and prevention strategies
- Group work, collaboration, consultation

Attitudes
- Personal attributes sensitive to wellness and prevention (e.g., optimism, persistence, tolerance, long-range view)

Values
- Primary prevention perspective

Primary prevention perspective (value). This is perhaps the most important competency area, and it is a value, a kind of overarching perspective, that serves to guide and to harness energies aimed at wellness and prevention ends. A primary prevention perspective is fundamentally important because its contents (before-the-fact vantage point, incidence reduction approach, strengths-oriented emphasis, systemic-ecological foundation) function as a lens through which interactions within human systems can be viewed. That lens, in fact, not only clarifies what is viewed but also redefines and refocuses mental health methods on goals of wellness and prevention. Most wellness and prevention competencies are generic, usable just as well to serve remedial purposes, too. The primary prevention perspective, however, shifts the application of helper competencies from later to earlier, from correction to promotion, from deficits to strengths, and from individual- to community-level applications. Unless trainees come to be able to value this paradigm shift then the rest of wellness and prevention training will fall short of the mark.

Wellness and health promotion (knowledge). Counseling for wellness and prevention rests upon a strengths-based knowledge base and perspective. Wellness and health promotion are emphasized but are complemented by the deficit-reduction, medical model. Both are important and necessary, but the wellness and health promotion base is critically important.

Ecological–systemic vantage point (knowledge). Wellness and prevention goals are reached through mobilizing resources existing within webs of interconnection. Human settings, relationships, support systems, networks, and person × environment interactions represent key webs of interconnection. Wellness and prevention programs strengthen individuals and their interactions with others and with the major environments of their lives—work, school, family, community. The fulcrum for change is found in dynamic systems and the connections (or lack of connections) occurring among members. Trainees need to understand the importance of ecological-systemic change and gain skills in effecting it. They need to be able to assess community needs, form collaborative relationships with key community members, and gain competencies in applying the range of COSI interventions.

Social justice (knowledge). Albee (1986) introduced discussion of the powerful contribution of social pathogens to mental health dysfunction, pointing to the value of prevention strategies targeting the reduction of those pathogens while increasing personal and social system strengths and supports. Examples of social pathogens include poverty, limited access to health care, oppression, racism, sexual harassment, and exploitation. Instances involving the cyber bullying of gay youth, sometimes even contributing to their suicide, provide one appalling example of social injustice in practice. Wellness and prevention as social justice (e.g., Kenny et al., 2009) needs to be an important element of any prevention project and, therefore, should become a central focus of training.

Wellness and prevention strategies (skills). Counseling for wellness and prevention draws from seven basic strategies, which were covered in the preceding chapter. These include: education, social competency facilitation, natural caregiving, community organization, and system intervention (COSI), assisting developmental transitions, environmental redesign, and encouraging everyday wellness and prevention practices. These strategies often are used in combination and they can be applied in individual, group, and family counseling and in broader program delivery.

Group work, collaboration, and consultation (skills). These three methods comprise the engine that drives many successful programs because, by definition, they are geared to catalyze the dynamics surrounding interconnections and relationships. These approaches also can be used responsively with effectiveness, as in therapy situations. However, in wellness and prevention, they are well situated to proactively connect people and resources. They can be used to facilitate existing networks and can be applied to create such networks when none presently exists.

Training programs, then, need to develop these competencies in trainees. As with the other important areas discussed, curricular experiences are required, coupled with supervised practice of skills.

Group skills are based on interdependence, interconnection, and interaction. Drawing from those skills that are aimed at joining interactions among people, both *collaboration* and *consultation* add direction and purpose: People are joined together to accomplish personal or task goals that they create together. These jointly determined goals, such as a school task force charged with creating a policy on obesity prevention, serve to motivate cooperative energies and the pooling of resources, intermixed to accomplish together what no one entity could hope to do independently (Clanton Harpine 2013).

Personal attributes sensitive to prevention (attitudes). Attitudes needed to become an effective counselor and therapist are well documented. Consider the necessary and sufficient conditions identified by Carl Rogers (e.g., empathy, positive regard) as a key beginning point. Wellness and prevention attributes build on those conditions and add other essential ones that center on maintaining a long-range perspective and a commitment to tolerance and social justice. Optimism, patience, persistence, and a blend of a strong process and equally strong task orientation also are necessary attributes. Training needs to infuse careful attention to development of these attributes throughout the entire program. Wellness and prevention programs and initiatives take time to develop, to deliver, and to take effect and future practitioners must be prepared for that reality.

Issues for Reflection and Discussion

1. What about the counseling for wellness and prevention model attracts you? What might you be able to do well? What would you need more education and training to do?
2. How do you think this model fits with the world of education and mental health? What seems a particularly good fit? What seems a particularly poor fit? What would need to change, if anything, to make this model work best?
3. This chapter attempted to answer an important question: "How can counselors and other helpers use wellness and prevention strategies to promote healthiness in people, settings, and systems?" What is your take-away from this discussion of theories, models, and practices?
4. Imagine you are a school counselor in a small elementary school located in an impoverished county of the state. Pick one of the approaches discussed in this chapter and think through how you might begin to apply it to address an overall problem of low morale throughout the school.

Approach chosen: ______________________________

First three steps you might take:

a. ______________________________
b. ______________________________
c. ______________________________

References

Ajzen, I. (1991). The theory of planned behavior. *Organizational Behavior and Human Decision Processes*, 50, 179–211. doi:10.1016/0749-5978(91)90020-t

Albee, G. (1986). Toward a just society: Lessons from observations on the primary prevention of psychopathology. *American Psychologist, 41*, 891–898. doi:10.1037//0003- 066x.41.8.891

Aldarondo, E. (Ed.). (2007). *Advancing social justice through clinical practice*. Mahwah, NJ: Erlbaum. doi:10.1080/08975350801905087

American Counseling Association. (2014). *Your passion. Your profession. Our purpose.* Retrieved from http://www.counseling.org/knowlec

American Psychological Association. (2012). *Education and training guidelines: A taxonomy for education and training in professional psychology health service specialties*. Retrieved from http://www.apa.org/ed/graduate/specialize/taxonomy.pdf

American Psychological Association. (2013). *Guidelines for prevention in psychology*. Retrieved from http://www.div17.org/preventionsection/PreventionGuidelines.pdf

Bandura, A. (1977a). Self-efficacy: Toward a unifying theory of behavioral change. *Psychological Review*, 84(2), 191–215. doi:10.1037//0033–295x.84.2.191

Bandura, A. (1977b). *Social learning theory*. Englewood Cliffs, NJ: Prentice Hall.

Belkin, G. S. (1984). *Introduction to counseling* (2nd ed.). Dubuque, IA: Brown.

Bell, L. A. (2007). Theoretical foundations for social justice education. In M. Adams, L. A. Bell, & P. Griffin (Eds.), *Teaching for diversity and social justice* (2nd ed., pp. 1–14). New York, NY: Routledge.

Bertalanffy, L.V. (1950). An outline of general system theory. *The British Journal for the Philosophy of Science, 1*, 134–165 doi:10.1093/bjps/i.2.134

Borum, R., Cornell, D., Modzeleski, W., & Jimerson, S. (2010). What can be done about school shootings? A review of the evidence. *Educational Researcher, 39*, 27–37. doi:10.3102/0013189X09357762

Bronfenbrenner, U. (1979). *The ecology of human development: Experiments by nature and design*. Cambridge, MA: Harvard University Press.

Cable News Network. (2014). *U.S. school violence fast facts*. Retrieved from http://www.cnn.com/2013/09/19/us/u-s-school-violence-fast-facts/

Clanton Harpine, E. (2013). Prevention groups. In R. Conyne & A. Horne (Eds.), *Prevention practice kit: Action guides for mental health professionals* (pp. 1–47). Thousand Oaks, CA: Sage.

Conyne, R. (1987). *Primary preventive counseling: Empowering people and systems*. Muncie, IN: Accelerated Development.

Conyne, R. (2004). *Preventive counseling: Helping people to become empowered in systems and settings* (2nd ed.). New York: Routledge.

Conyne, R. K. (2010). *Prevention program development and evaluation: An incidence reduction, culturally relevant approach*. Thousand Oaks, CA: Sage. doi:10.4135/9781483349176

Conyne, R. (2013). Incorporating prevention in Turkish counselor education curriculum: Considerations for competencies and strategies [Invited article]. *Turkish Psychological Counseling and Guidance Journal, 4*, 1–12. Retrieved from http://pdrdergisi.org/edergi/index.php/pdredergi/index

Conyne, R. (2015). *Counseling for wellness and prevention: Helping people to become empowered in systems and settings* (3rd ed.). New York: Routledge

Conyne, R. K., & Cook, E. (Eds.). (2004). *Ecological counseling: An innovative approach to conceptualizing person-environment interactions*. Alexandria, VA: American Counseling Association.

Conyne, R. K., & Diederich, L. T. (2014). What is group work? Thousand Oaks, CA: Sage.

Conyne, R.K., Horne, A. M., & Raczynski, K. (2013). *Prevention in psychology: An introduction to the prevention practice kit*. Thousand Oaks, CA: Sage. doi:10.4135/9781452275574

Conyne, R., Newmeyer, M., Kenny, M., Romano, J., & Matthews, C. (2008). Two key strategies for teaching prevention: Specialized course and infusion. *Journal of Primary Prevention*, 29, 375–401. doi:10.1007/s10935–008–0146–8

Cook, E. P. (Ed.). (2012). *Understanding people in context: The ecological perspective in counseling*. Alexandria, VA: American Counseling Association.

Council on Social Work Education. (2008). *Educational policy and accreditation standards*. Retrieved from http://www.cswe.org/File.aspx?id=41861

Cowen, E. (1982). Person-centered approaches to primary prevention in mental health: Situation-focused and competence-enhancement. *American Journal of Community Psychology*, 13, 31–49. doi:10.1007/bf00923258

Craske, M. (2009). Cognitive behavioral therapy. In J. Carlson & M. Englar-Carlson (Eds.), *Theories of psychotherapy series* [Video]. Washington, DC: American Psychological Association.

Creer, T. (1996). *Psychology of adjustment: An applied approach*. Upper Saddle River, NJ: Prentice Hall.

Csikszentmihalyi, M. (1990). *Flow: The psychology of optimal experience*. New York, NY: Harper & Row.

Csikszentmihalyi, M. (2009). *Creativity: Flow and the psychology of discovery and invention*. New York, NY: HarperCollins.

Curnutte, M. (2014, September 24). Improving minorities' health for 10 years. *The Cincinnati Enquirer*, pp. A-1, A-9.

Dahlgren, G., & Whitehead, M. (1991). *Policies and strategies to promote social equity in health*. Stockholm: Institute for Future Studies.

Dahlgren, G., & Whitehead, M. (1992). *Policies and strategies to promote equity in health* (Document No. EUR/ICP/RPD 414 (2)). Copenhagen: WHO Regional Office for Europe. Retrieved from http://whqlibdoc.who.int/euro/-1993/EUR_ICP_RPD414(2)

Dahlgren, G., & Whitehead, M. (1993). *Tackling inequalities in health: What can we learn from what has been tried?* Working paper prepared for the King's Fund International Seminar on Tackling Inequalities in Health, Oxfordshire, UK. Retrieved from http://www.kingsfund.org.uk/

Dahlgren, G., & Whitehead, M. (2006). *Levelling up (part 2): A discussion paper on European strategies for tackling social inequities in health*. Copenhagen: WHO.

Ekpe, S. (2010, July 2). *Generating genuine demand with social accountability mechanisms*. Retrieved from http://developmentcommunity.csd-i.org/profiles/generating-genuine-demand-with

Evans, S. D., & Prilleltensky, I. (2007). Literacy for wellness, oppression and liberation. In R. Horn & J. Kincheloe (Eds.), *The Praeger handbook of education and psychology* (Vol. 2). Portsmouth, NH: Greenwood.

Fishbein, M. (1967a). A behavior theory approach to the relation between beliefs about an object and the attitude toward the object. In M. Fishbein (Ed.), *Readings in attitude theory and measurement* (pp. 389–400). New York, NY: John Wiley.

Fishbein, M.A. (1967b). Attitude and the prediction of behavior. In M. Fishbein (Ed.), *Readings in attitude theory and measurement* (pp. 477–492). New York, NY: John Wiley.

Fishbein, M., & Ajzen, I. (2010). *Predicting and changing behavior: The reasoned action approach.* New York, NY: Taylor & Francis.

Fouad, N. A., Grus, C. L., Hatcher, R. L., Kaslow, N. J., Hutchings, P. S., Madson, M.,. . . Crossman, R. E. (2009). Competency benchmarks: A developmental model for understanding and measuring competence in professional psychology. *Training and Education in Professional Psychology*, 3, S5–S26. doi:10.1037/a0015832

Fredrickson, B.L. (2000). Cultivating positive emotions to optimize health and well-being. *Prevention and Treatment, 3*, Article 1. Retrieved from http://journals.apa.org/prevention

Gerig, M. S. (2007). *Foundations in mental health and community counseling: An introduction to the profession*. Upper Saddle River, NJ: Pearson Prentice Hall.

Goldberg, L.R. (1993). The structure of phenotypic personality traits. *American Psychologist, 48*, 26–34. doi:10.1037/0003–066x.48.1.26

Granello, P. (2000). Integrating wellness work into mental health private practice. *Journal of Psychotherapy in Independent Practice, 1*, 3–16. doi:10.1300/j288v01n01_02

Granello, P. (2012). *Wellness counseling*. Boston, MA: Pearson.

Greenleaf, A.T., & Williams, J.M. (2009). Supporting social justice advocacy: A paradigm shift towards an ecological perspective. *Journal for Social Action in Counseling and Psychology, 2*, 1–14. Retrieved from http://jsacp.tumblr.com/

Hage, S., & Romano, J. (2013). *Best practices in prevention*. Thousand Oaks, CA: Sage.

Haggerty, K., & Shapiro, V. (2013). Science-based prevention through communities that care: A model of social work practice for public health. *Social Work in Public Health, 28*(3–4), 349–365.

Hawkins, J., Shapiro, V., & Fagan, A. (2010). Disseminating effective community prevention practices: Opportunities for social work practice. *Research on Social Work Practice, 20*, 518–527. doi:10.1177/1049731509359919

Kasambira, K. P., & Edwards, L. (2000, June). *Counseling and human ecology: A conceptual framework for counselor educators*. Paper presented at the 8th International Counseling Conference, San Jose, Costa Rica.

Kenny, M., Horne, A., Orpinas, P., & Reese, L. (Eds.). (2009). *Realizing social justice: The challenge of preventive interventions*. Washington, DC: American Psychological Association. doi:10.1037/11870–000

Kenny, M. E., & Medvide, M. B. (2013). Relational influences. In S. D. Brown & R. W. Lent (Eds.), *Career development and counseling: Putting theory and research to work* (2nd ed., pp. 329–356). Hoboken, NJ: John Wiley.

Lewin, K. (1936). *Principles of topological psychology*. New York, NY: McGraw-Hill.

Lewis, J., Arnold, M., House, R., & Toporek, R. (2003). Advocacy competencies. Retrieved from http://www.counseling.org/Resources

Lewis, J., Lewis, M., Daniels, J., & D'Andrea, M. (2011). *A multicultural–social justice perspective* (4th ed.). Belmont, CA: Brooks/Cole.

Lewis, J., Toporek, R., & Ratts, M. (2010). Advocacy and social justice: Entering the mainstream of the counseling profession. In M.J. Ratts, R.L. Toporek, & J.A. Lewis (Eds.),

ACA advocacy competencies: A social justice framework for counselors (pp. 239–244). Alexandria, VA: American Counseling Association.

Lopez, S., & Snyder, C. (2011). *The Oxford handbook of positive psychology*. New York, NY: Oxford University Press. doi:10.1093/oxfordhb/9780195187243.001.0001

Maddux, J. (2000). Stopping the "madness": Positive psychology and the deconstruction of the illness ideology and the DSM. In C. Snyder & S. Lopez (Eds.), *Handbook of positive psychology* (pp. 13–25). New York, NY: Oxford University Press. doi:10.1093/oxfordhb/9780195187243.013.0007

Maddux, J., Snyder, C. R., & Feldman, D. (2003). Mental health, adulthood. In T. Gullotta & M. Bloom (Eds.), *Encyclopedia of primary prevention and health promotion* (pp. 696–704). New York, NY: Kluwer. doi:10.1007/978–1–4615–0195–4_103

Matthews, C. (2013). Teaching prevention: Preparing the next generation of psychologists. In E. Vera (Ed.), *The Oxford handbook of prevention in counseling psychology* (pp. 76–90). New York, NY: Oxford University Press. doi:10.1093/oxfordhb/9780195396423.001.0001

McWhirter, B., & McWhirter, E. H. (2007). Toward an emancipator communitarian approach to the practice of psychology training. In E. Aldarondo (Ed.), *Advancing social justice through clinical practice* (pp. 391–416). New York, NY: Erlbaum. doi:10.4324/9780203936689

Michie, S. (2012). *The behaviour change wheel: A method for designing effective interventions*. Dublin, Ireland: Implementation Science Summer School.

Michie, S., Van Stralen, M. M., & West, R. (2011). The behaviour change wheel: A new method for characterizing and designing behaviour change interventions. *Implementation Science, 6*(1), 1–11. doi:10.1186/1748–5908–6–42

Morrill, W., Oetting, E., & Hurst, J. (1974). Dimensions of counselor functioning. *Personnel and Guidance Journal*, 52, 354–359. doi:10.1002/j.2164–4918.1974.tb04041.x

Myers, J.E. (1992). Wellness, prevention, development: The cornerstone of the profession. *Journal of Counseling and Development*, 71, 136–139. doi:10.1002/j.1556- 6676.1992.tb02188.x

Myers, J.E. (2003). Coping with caregiving stress: A wellness-oriented, strengths-based approach for family counselors. *The Family Journal, 11*(2), 153–161. doi:10.1177/1066480702250162

Myers, J.E., & Sweeney, T.J. (2005a). *Counseling for wellness: Theory, research, and practice*. Alexandria, VA: American Counseling Association.

Myers, J.E., & Sweeney, T.J. (2005b). The indivisible self: An evidence-based model of wellness. *Journal of Individual Psychology*, 61, 234–245.

Myers, J.E., & Sweeney, T.J. (2008). Wellness counseling: The evidence base for practice. *Journal of Counseling & Development*, 86, 482–493. doi:10.1002/j.1556- 6678.2008.tb00536.x

Nelson, G., & Prilleltensky, I. (2010). *Community psychology: In pursuit of liberation and well-being*. New York, NY: Macmillan.

Orpinas, P., & Horne, A. M. (2006). *Bullying prevention: Creating a positive school climate and developing social competence*. Washington, DC: American Psychological Association.

Peterson, C., & Park, N. (2009). Classifying and measuring strengths of character. In S. J. Lopez & C.R. Snyder (Eds.), *Oxford handbook of positive psychology* (2nd ed., pp. 25–33). New York, NY: Oxford University Press, doi:10.1093/oxfordhb/9780195187243.001.0001

Peterson, C., & Seligman, M. E. (2004). *Character strengths and virtues: A handbook and classification*. Washington, DC: American Psychological Association.

Pieterse, A.L., Hanus, A., & Gale, M. (2012). Advocacy and prevention: Dismantling systems of oppression. In E. Vera (Ed.), *The Oxford handbook of prevention in counseling psychology* (pp. 109–124). New York, NY: Oxford Press. doi:10.1093/oxfordhb/9780195396423.001.0001

Prilleltensky, I. (2000). Bridging agency, theory and action: Critical links in critical psychology. In T. Sloan (Ed.), *Critical psychology: Voices for change* (pp. 67–81). London, England: Macmillan.

Prilleltensky, I. (2012). Wellness as fairness. *American Journal of Community Psychology, 49*, 1–21. doi:10.1007/s10464–011–9448–8

Prilleltensky, I., Dokecki, P., Frieden, G., & Wang, V.O. (2007). Counseling for wellness and justice: Foundations, practice, and ethical dilemmas. In E. Aldarondo (Ed.), *Advancing social justice through clinical practice* (pp. 19–42). Mahwah, NJ: Erlbaum. doi:10.4324/9780203936689

Prilleltensky, I., & Nelson, G. (2002). *Doing psychology critically: Making a difference in diverse settings*. London, England: Palgrave Macmillan.

Prilleltensky, I., & Prilleltensky, O. (2006). *Promoting well-being: Linking personal, organizational, and community change*. New York, NY: John Wiley.

Prochaska, J., & DiClemente, C. (1992). Stages of change in the modification of problem behaviors. *Program Behavior Modification*, 28, 183–218.

Prochaska, J. O., Johnson, S. S., & Lee, P. (2009) The transtheoretical model of behavior change. In S. Schumaker, E. Schorn, J. Ockenes, & K. Richert (Eds.), *The handbook of health behavior change* (3rd ed., pp. 59–83). New York, NY: Springer.

Prochaska, J., Norcoross, J., & DiClemente, C. (2013). Applying the stages of change. *Psychotherapy in Australia*, 19, 10–15. Retrieved from http://www.psychotherapy.com.au/journal/

Raczynski, K., Waldo, M., Schwartz, J. P., & Horne, A. (Eds.). (2013). *Evidence-based prevention*. Thousand Oaks, CA: Sage.

Ratts, M.J. (2009). Social justice counseling: Toward the development of a "fifth force" among counseling paradigms. *Journal of Humanistic Counseling, Education, and Development*, 48, 160–172. doi:10.1002/j.2161–1939.2009.tb00076.x

Ratts, M. J., Anthony, L., & Santos, K. N. (2010). The dimensions of social justice model: Transforming traditional group work into a socially just framework. *The Journal for Specialists in Group Work, 35*(2), 160–168. doi:10.1080101933921003705974

Ratts, V., Toporek, R., & Lewis, J. (2010). *ACA advocacy competencies: A social justice framework for counselors*. Alexandria, VA: American Counseling Association. Retrieved from http://www.counseling.org/

Reeser, L.C. (2007). Educating for social change in the human service profession. In E. Aldrondo (Ed.), *Advancing social justice through clinical practice*. Mahwah, NJ: Erlbaum. doi:10.1080/08975350801905087

Reivich, K., & Shatte, A. (2002). *The resilience factor: Seven essential skills for overcoming life's inevitable obstacles*. New York, NY: Broadway Books.

Rodolfa, E., Bent, R., Eisman, E., Nelson, P., Rehm, L., & Ritchie, P. (2005). A cube model for competency development: Implications for psychology educators and regulators. *Professional Psychology: Research and Practice, 36*(4), 347–354. doi:10.1037/0735–7028.36.4.347

Rogers, E. M. (2003). *Diffusion of innovations* (5th ed.). New York, NY: Free Press.

Romano, J. (2015). *Prevention psychology: Enhancing personal and social well-being*. Washington, DC: American Psychological Association.

Romano, J., & Hage, S. (2000). Prevention and counseling psychology: Revitalizing commitments for the 21st century. *Counseling Psychologist, 28*, 733–763.

Rosenstock, I. M. (1988). Adoption and maintenance of lifestyle modifications. *American Journal of Preventive Medicine*, 4(6), 349–352.

Rosenstock, I., Strecher, V., & Becker, M. (1988). Social learning theory and the health belief model. *Health Education Quarterly*, 15, 175–183. doi:10.1177/109019818801500203

Rousch, T. (2013, October 30). Supporting health equity in Seattle. *The Voice*. Retrieved from http://voice.seattlehousing.net/

Ryan, R., & Deci, E. (2001). On happiness and human potential: A review of research on hedonic and eudaimonic well-being. *Annual Review of Psychology, 52*, 141–166. doi:10.1146/annurev.psych.52.1.141

Seligman, M. (2002). *Authentic happiness: Using the new positive psychology to realize our potential for lasting fulfillment*. New York, NY: Free Press.

Seligman, L. (2006). *Theories of counseling and psychotherapy: Systems, strategies, and skills* (2nd ed.). Upper Saddle River, NJ: Pearson.

Seligman, M. E. (2011). Flourish. New York, NY: Simon & Schuster.

Seligman, M., & Csikszentmihalyi, M. (Eds.). (2000). Positive psychology [Special issue]. *American Psychologist, 55*(1), 5–14. doi:10.1037/0003–066x.55.1.5

Singh, A. A., Merchant, N., Skudrzyk, B., & Ingene, D. (2012). Association for specialists in group work: Multicultural and social justice competence principles for group workers. *Journal for Specialists in Group Work, 37*(4), 312–325. doi:10.1080/01933922.2012.721482

Snyder, C. R., & Lopez, S. J. (2007). *Positive psychology: The scientific and practical explorations of human strengths*. Thousand Oaks, CA: Sage.

Snyder, C.R., Lopez, S.J., & Teramoto, J. (2010). *Positive psychology: The scientific and practical explorations of human strengths* (2nd ed.). Thousand Oaks, CA: Sage.

Vera, E., & Kenny, M. E. (2013). *Social justice and culturally relevant prevention*. Thousand Oaks, CA: Sage. doi:10.4135/9781452275598

Vera, E. M., & Speight, S. L. (2003). Multicultural competencies, social justice, and counseling psychology: Expanding our roles. *Counseling Psychologist, 31*, 253–272.

Watts, R., Abdul-Adil, J., & Pratt, T. (2002). Enhancing critical consciousness in young African- American men: A psychoeducational approach. *Psychology of Men and Masculinity, 3*(1), 41–50. doi:10.1037/1524–9220.3.1.41

Williams, J.M., & Greenleaf, A.T. (2012). Ecological psychology: Potential contributions to social justice and advocacy in school settings. *Journal of Educational and Psychological Consultation, 22*, 141–157. doi:10.1080/10474412.2011.649653

Witmer, J.M., & Sweeney, T.J. (1992). A holistic model for wellness and prevention over the lifespan. *Journal of Counseling and Development*, 71, 140–148. doi:10.1002/j.1556-6676.1992.tb02189.x

World Health Organization. (2013). *Mental health action plan*. Geneva, Switzerland: Author. Retrieved from http://www.who.int/en/

Young, M. (2008). *Learning the art of helping: Building blocks and techniques* (4th ed.). Upper Saddle River, NJ: Prentice Hall.

SECTION II

Wellness and Prevention Applications

You read in section I about the foundations of wellness and prevention in counseling. Theory, methods, strategies, and models all were considered, as well as building wellness and prevention into daily living. Now we move to wellness and prevention *applications* that counselors and other professional helpers can apply in their work with clients and client systems.

Wellness and Prevention Approaches, Programs, and Initiatives

These approaches, programs, and initiatives are framed by the ecological perspective that we discussed in earlier chapters. Chapters 5–8 describe applications connected to each ecological level, as follows:

Individual and Group: Approaches to be taken (chapter 5)

Relational I: Settings of Families and Schools: Programs (chapter 6)

Relational II: Settings of Communities and Workplaces: Programs (chapter 7)

Collective: Systems: Societal initiatives, such as political, legislative, and health care (chapter 8)

To assist readers in comparing programs contained in chapters 6 (families and schools) and 7 (communities and the workplace), a common descriptive framework is applied to each program. We answer, What is it? How is it done? What works? Why does it work?, and provide implications for counselors and other helpers.

Note to Faculty Instructors: When assigning readings, you may find it useful to split chapters 6 (families, schools) and 7 (communities, the workplace).

It is helpful conceptually to set wellness and prevention programs and initiatives within ecological levels. However, it's also important to realize the important maxim that *in practice* effective wellness and prevention interventions typically are not constrained within any one ecological level. Rather, wellness and prevention approaches, programs, and initiatives that work cut across levels, combining and coordinating multiple strategies. A good example can be found with the FAST (Families and Schools Together) program described in chapter 7, which I identified as a community program. Well, it is. But it also could just as well be classified as a school program or as a family program. It cuts across these levels, which is one of the reasons that it can produce positive results in children and adolescents.

Note that wellness and prevention applications at the individual and group counseling levels typically do not involve structured programs. Rather, wellness and prevention approaches are embedded within ongoing work and take advantage of emerging dynamics. A counselor may assist her client to carefully implement a new exercise routine or to strengthen her social connection by volunteering at the Girls Club. Or, a group leader may help members plan how they will apply constructive feedback skills learned in the group to situations they could very well face in the future.

Program Selection Criteria Used in This Book

Programs are salient for settings, including families, schools, communities, and workplaces. Remarkable progress has been realized over the last 20 years in the number of effective programs that are now available (Romano, 2015). The difficulty in identifying examples for inclusion in this section was not due to a shortage of such interventions; the challenge was to cull just 12 of them from all the other worthy contenders. Establishing program selection criteria helped with this task. These criteria are presented next, which are similar to those contained in the National Registry of Effective Programs and Practices (NREPP, n.d.) document "Questions to Ask as You Explore the Possible Use of an Intervention." Keep in mind that these criteria also could serve as a checklist for others to use themselves when they need to identify good wellness and prevention programs.

Program Selection Criteria Checklist Use in This Book

- Clear prevention wellness and prevention goals and orientations
- Easy to find
- Actively in use
- Evidence base demonstrating effectiveness
- Acceptable study designs used
- Intervention well described
  –What settings? What populations?
  –What are its core dimensions?

- Intervention materials available
- Staffing requirements
- Training and support available
- Widespread implementation
- Dissemination results available
- Program costs reported
- Positive external evaluations, drawn online accessible registries
- Were included in previous book edition and kept and updated if met most criteria, above, were met

Systems initiatives also can strongly influence wellness and prevention. This is especially the case in the area of public policy and legislation (Pirog & Good, 2013). Counselors and other professional helpers and researchers have contributed to the development of important initiatives in the areas of health care and education. In turn, policies and legislation in these areas, such as the National Prevention Strategy and the Healthy People directives, can serve as touchstone resources for guiding practitioner actions.

Online Resource Directories Containing Effective Wellness and Prevention Programs

Certainly, counselor researchers, practitioners, faculty members, and students all can benefit by being informed about effective wellness and prevention programs that already exist. A number of searchable online resource directories have emerged over the last few years that identify effective wellness and prevention programs. Programs and initiatives contained in these directories have been designated as excellent, promising, and/or as model programs. I will discuss two examples of directories, involving the Substance Abuse and Mental Health Administration's (SAMHSA) NREPP and the Center for the Study and Prevention of Violence Blueprints for Healthy Youth Development.

The SAMHSA produces a list of prevention programs, with brief descriptions and follow-up information. SAMHSA uses the NREPP to identify programs that first rest upon a science base, meaning that they are deemed to be conceptually sound and internally consistent, with program activities that are related to program conceptualization and that are reasonably well implemented and evaluated. Upon that platform, then, prevention programs are judged as being "promising" programs if they produce some positive outcomes, as being "excellent" programs if they consistently produce positive outcomes and are strongly implemented and evaluated, and as being "model" programs if they also are available for dissemination and if technical assistance is available from the program developers.

The Center for the Study and Prevention of Violence Blueprints for Healthy Youth Development Web site at the University of Colorado (2012–2014) also contains extensive information related to the evaluation of prevention programs. Evaluation criteria used in the Blueprints project include (a) evidence of deterrent effect within a strong research design; (b) evidence of sustained effects that endure beyond the length of the prevention program of at least 1 year; (c) multiple site replication, demonstrating that the prevention program can be replicated effectively; and (d) evidence of attention to important mediating effects (e.g., risk and protective factors) and if the program is cost effective in relation to benefits. These are stringent criteria.

A set of useful online search registries that can point the way to effective wellness and prevention programs and initiatives is contained in the next box.

Some Useful Online Search Registries

- NREPP-SAMHSA's National Registry of Evidence-based Programs and Practices (http://www.nrepp.samhsa.gov/)
- Blueprints for Healthy Youth Development (http://www.blueprintsprograms.com/about.php)
- What Works Clearinghouse (http://www.ies.ed.gov/ncee/wwc/)
- Child Trends (http://childtrends.org/)
- Social Programs That Work (sponsored by the Coalition for Evidence-Based Policy) (http://evidencebasedprograms.org/about-this-site)
- Promising Practices Network (http://www.promisingpractices.net/)
- National Institute of Justice, Crime Solutions (http://www.crimesolutions.gov/about.aspx)
- EpisCenter (through Penn State; http://www.episcenter.psu.edu/ebp)

Fit of Online Registries Within Planning of Wellness and Prevention Projects

Uncovering excellent wellness and prevention program examples can be very helpful in the planning stage of the wellness and prevention program development process, which also includes stages of implementation and evaluation (Conyne, 2010, 2013; Raczynski, Waldo, Schwartz, & Horne, 2013). While space does not allow for discussion of program development and evaluation, the planning steps excerpted in the following indicate where using the online search directories can fit. Please refer to the references cited for more detail on the entire program development and evaluation process.

Plan the Program (from Conyne, 2013)

1. Lay the groundwork for community, collaboration, and cultural relevance
2. Analyze local context and conduct professional literature review
3. Create problem statement
4. Develop preventive goals, objectives, strategies, and evaluation
5. Obtain inputs and resources (Note: Online registries fit here)

Now, let's move on to the chapters of section II, beginning with wellness and prevention within both individual counseling and group work.

References

Conyne, R. (2010). *Prevention program development and evaluation: An incidence reduction, culturally-relevant approach.* Thousand Oaks, CA: Sage.

Conyne, R. (2013). *Program development and evaluation in prevention.* Thousand Oaks, CA: Sage.

National Registry of Effective Programs and Practices. (n.d.). *Questions to ask as you explore the possible use of an intervention.* Retrieved from http://www.nrepp.samsha.gov/pdfs/questions_to_ask_developers.pdf

Pirog, M., & Good, E. (2013). *Public policy and mental health: Avenues for prevention.* Thousand Oaks, CA: Sage.

Raczynski, K., Waldo, M., Schwartz, J., & Horne, A. (2013). *Evidence-based prevention.* Thousand Oaks, CA: Sage.

Romano, J. (2015). *Prevention psychology: Enhancing personal and social well-being.* Washington, DC: American Psychological Association.

University of Colorado. (2012–2014). *Blueprints for healthy youth development.* Retrieved from http://www.blueprintsprograms.com/

5

PERSONAL WELLNESS

Individual Counseling and Group Work

You must be the change you want to see in the world.
—Mahatma Gandhi, Indian political and spiritual leader (1869–1948)

Introduction

This chapter begins the second book section that examines wellness and prevention applications. It is framed around the pragmatic question: How is counseling for wellness and prevention done?

We will start with individual counseling and group work because most wellness and prevention work conducted by counselors and other mental health professionals revolves around these methods. These approaches reside within the personal wellness level of the counseling for wellness and prevention model discussed at the end of the preceding chapter.

Individual counseling and group work are the essential, "bread-and-butter" methods of the helping professions, although involvement with settings and systems certainly is waxing. Gandhi's quotation, above, is salient. Wellness and prevention counseling efforts, as any others oriented toward change or progress, can be delivered best by "change agents" who are whole and healthy themselves. Helping others starts first with helping ourselves.

Wellness and Prevention Through Individual Counseling

How can individual counseling and group work be structured to support wellness and prevention? We will consider this question in this chapter segment (see Figure 5.1).

FIGURE 5.1. Individual counseling session. Counseling for wellness and prevention occurs within individual counseling.

Source: iStock photo

Prevention in mental health has followed the public health tradition. It emphasizes a before-the-fact community and system change approach, while also embracing competency enhancement. *Wellness* in mental health emphasizes a personal responsibility approach, where individuals are encouraged within the supports and constraints of their life context to seek optimal health through establishing and maintaining positive health practices. Most attention in prevention has been given to communities and systems, while wellness has focused most on individual persons. Wellness and Prevention together, the focus of this book, combine the strengths of each approach to seek optimal health in people, and in settings, and in systems through personal and environmental changes. The aim is to enhance both personal and environmental competence (Conyne & Rogers, 1977; Steele, 1973)

Wellness and prevention counseling with individual clients and with group members, therefore, utilizes personal and environmental strengths to help clients resolve existing problems that they bring to sessions *and* learn how to apply learning that is gained to prevent future flare-ups. The fulcrum for change pivots explicitly around helping clients move toward optimal health to enhance current functioning and to avert impending onslaughts, not only with the reparation of problems and dysfunction (Conyne, 2014a).

During counseling and group work clients can learn to identify and develop assets that work for them, such as possessing a sense of fairness or an interest in others. They also can learn how to take positive advantage of aspects of their environment that support their healthy functioning, or to alter what constrains or reduces it.

Outside of counseling, individuals can and should take actions to protect and promote their own bio-psycho-social health. You will recall that the focus of chapter 2 was devoted to this matter, showing how evidence-based everyday wellness and prevention practices—exercising or eating nutritiously, for example—can be adopted by people to move themselves forward. Individuals also can learn how to mobilize their focus, when appropriate, to seek change in their environment to benefit themselves and others. As an example, they can learn stress management techniques, such as relaxation, to combat a corrosive stressor, such as an over-demanding work situation. However, they might also learn how to take actions to change stressors in the work situation itself, such as negotiating with one's supervisor and colleagues a way to re-distribute some work assignments. Importantly, these same approaches can be used by counselors with clients inside the counseling relationship, too.

A General Process for Wellness and Prevention Approaches in Individual Counseling

Individual counseling with a wellness and prevention focus follows the same general template as typical mental health counseling. It also can be embedded easily within regular mental health counseling practice.

The general process can be conceptualized as occurring in five major steps:

Step 1: Form beginnings of a sustainable helping relationship.
Step 2: Conduct a wellness and prevention assessment.
Step 3: Develop a personalized wellness and prevention counseling plan, including pertinent strategies.
Step 4: Apply the plan.
Step 5: Evaluate process and outcomes.

These five steps are considered next.

Step 1: Form Beginnings of a Sustainable Helping Relationship

Foundations of an open and trusting working relationship between counselor and client need to be initiated. This process includes orienting the client about expectations for counseling, modeling therapeutic qualities of empathy, caring, instillation of hope and optimism, and creating an overall climate of collaboration and authenticity.

Step 2: Conduct a Wellness and Prevention Assessment

You read about screening in chapter 4. Because wellness and prevention counseling is concerned principally with broadening and building strengths to enhance optimal wellness, screening and assessment pivots around identification of assets. Attention is given to the following areas, adapted from Granello (2000, 2012) and Wilson (2004, 2012).

Lifestyle history. How has the client been leading her or his life over time? What is the level of healthiness present? To what does the client attribute healthy behavior?

Social support and involvement with others. What is the breadth and depth of the client's social support network? What is the level of client engagement with others? To what degree is the client connected or disconnected with others?

TLC practices. What is the client's involvement with major TLCs (Walsh, 2011)? As discussed earlier in this text, TLCs offer a range of evidence-based possibilities that can be potent in promoting wellness and prevention within individuals. The TLC areas can form the basis for a wellness and prevention screening and assessment and for subsequent action steps. Examination of these areas can supplement the areas addressed in a more traditional psychological screening and assessment. Of particular interest is how the client is performing in terms of key wellness and prevention practices: (a) exercise, (b) nutrition and diet, (c) relationships, (d) relaxation and recreation, (e) stress management, (f) involvement with nature, (g) religion/spirituality, (h) sense of purpose, and (i) service to others.

Medical and CAM involvement. What is the client's involvement with health care providers, and for what conditions and/or goals? Consideration is given to traditional medical care through licensed health care providers, any involvement with complementary or alternative providers, and use of supplements that may have been prescribed or are taken on one's own initiative.

Stressors. What external factors impinge negatively on the client? Consider factors related to the physical, work, and social environment, including social pathogens such as oppression, finances, and lack of control, among others.

Stress management and coping skills. What are the ways the client uses to mitigate, manage, and cope with stressors? Some of these ways may be considered as being positive (e.g., yoga and friendships) while others might be more negative (e.g., ignoring stress or self-medicating through drugs).

Environmental change skills. To what degree does the client possess environmental competency which, you'll recall, is the capacity to adapt appropriately to situational characteristics (such as functioning effectively within a team at work) and also to be able to change aspects of an environment that are stressful (such as positively confronting a caustic team member). Two examples of environmental competency include: Can the client assess situational supports and constraints? Does the client possess a mindset supporting taking action to benefit herself/himself and others?

General personal and environmental skills and strengths. What is the full spectrum of skills and strengths possessed by the client? What are sources of strength and support existing in the environment? How are these strengths used to negotiate and to enjoy life? What strengths might be drawn from during wellness and prevention counseling?

Instruments exist for this purpose, which I earlier described, including the Lifestyle Assessment Questionnaire (LAQ) of the National Wellness Institute (1989), Testwell (National Wellness Institute, 2000), and the Wellness Evaluation of Lifestyle (WEL Inventory; Witmer & Sweeney, 1992). A structured wellness and prevention assessment interview also can be conducted. The purpose is to identify what may be working and not working in terms of wellness and to collaborate with the client to construct a wellness and prevention plan.

Step 3: Develop a Personalized Wellness and Prevention Counseling Plan, Including Pertinent Strategies

Explain the strengths-based orientation in the service of wellness and prevention. Because clients typically understand that counseling is concerned with problem identification and reduction or elimination, it's appropriate to validate that viewpoint while emphasizing that strengths and what works well provide the leverage for change and for moving toward optimal wellness. This "strengths" thesis (Smith, 2014) needs to be reinforced continually as wellness and prevention counseling proceeds, even with clients who may be burdened by highly demanding challenges. Current deficits, such as anxiety, often can be reduced by identifying and then broadening existing strengths.

Collaboratively set strengths-based goals to enhance wellness and prevention. A key to wellness and prevention counseling is to set positive goals with clients that are to be attained through using and maximizing existing strengths and by developing and using new strengths that may be needed. Deficits are acknowledged and not discounted but care is given that they do not dominate the course of counseling. While a client may feel like a failure, the counselor would lead the client to see where successes and strengths exist now or in the past (there always are some) and together to create goals for counseling that take full advantage of those assets. These goals are then particularized, making them specific, performance-based, attainable, measurable, and observable (SPAMO).

Select wellness and prevention strategies that fit the situation. In chapter 3 you read about the major strategies associated with wellness and prevention counseling at the individual, relational (settings), and collective (systems) levels. All strategies except COSI are relevant for use in individual counseling: (a) education, (b) social competency facilitation, (c) connect with natural caregivers; (d) environmental redesign, (e) assist developmental transitions, and (f) encourage everyday wellness and prevention. Which strategies are selected emerge from an application of four criteria: the fit with client goals, the probability of success, the potential yield, and concordance with the cultural context surrounding the client (Conyne & Rogers, 1977; Dewey, 1933; Vera & Kenny, 2013). These strategies are listed in the following box, followed by a discussion of each.

Strategies in Wellness and Prevention for Individual Counseling

A. Educate
Psychoeducation
Ecological techniques (person–environment interaction focus)
- Reconstrue
- Transcend
- Encapsulate
- Redesign
- Exit existing situation
- Select a new situation
- Advocate
- Deliver remedial counseling with wellness and prevention focus

B. Facilitate Social Competency
C. Connect With Natural Caregivers
D. Assist Developmental Transitions
E. Encourage Everyday Wellness and Prevention

Strategy A: Educate.

Psychoeducation. A primary educational strategy in wellness and prevention is psychoeducation. Here, the counselor presents to the client relevant and timely evidence-based information about health practices and they collaborate about how to possibly implement the information into daily practice. Areas to be addressed in this way can be drawn from TLCs and everyday wellness and prevention using psychoeducation.

Example of Edie drawing from exercise. Here is an example of how an everyday wellness and prevention practice can become part of an individual counseling session with a client, Edie, a 50-year-old woman who works as a data processor. Accomplishment of work tasks requires her to enter and process data. Edie sits at her office computer for 8 hours each work day entering data. Adding to the sedentary nature of her work life, Edie reports spending most leisure time reading or watching television—again, engaging in sedentary activities. She reported spending little to no time doing things actively, even choosing to drive to the grocery store located four blocks from her apartment rather than walking there. Now, Edie did not come for counseling to discuss her work and how she spends her free time. Rather, she reported being concerned with feeling increasingly "tired and sad."

Of course, many factors contribute to Edie's condition. The counselor decided early in her work with Edie to provide her with education about one of these factors, the effects of a primarily sedentary life. She drew from results of several confirming studies of postmenopausal American women (e.g., Seguin et al., 2012, 2014), including finding that those women who spent the greatest amount of time sitting and resting (excluding sleeping) died earlier than peers who were active, even while controlling for variables including physical mobility and function, overall fitness, and demographics. Women who spent 11 or more hours each day in a sedentary position were 12% more likely to experience premature death than were those in the most energetic group, that is, those spending 4 or fewer hours in inactivity each day.

The counselor pointed out to Edie that even making small changes in her daily life—ones that she could do now—could begin to make a difference that would serve to improve her mood, as well as contribute to the prospects for a higher quality and longer life. The counselor suggested to her:

> Find ways to move around each day. At work, get up after entering data every 20 minutes or so to stretch and walk around for 5 minutes or so. At home, get up during TV commercials and move around. In other words, do what you can every day to break up long periods of sitting. These will be good first steps to consider trying. We can then talk some about other ones, such as how to become increasingly more active, but that will come later. Along the way, you may begin to notice yourself beginning to feel a bit better because even small amounts of exercise, such as we have been talking about, can improve how you look and feel.
>
> Now, I'm wondering how these ideas seem to you, Edie?

Carefully implemented (and with the approval of a physician, if a plan larger than light walking is designed), even relatively minimal but consistent increments of physical exercise can help edge a person toward a higher level of overall wellness (Ratey & Hagerman, 2013). You can see by this example that wellness and prevention counseling with an individual client is concerned with engaging the person quickly with doable action steps.

Ecological techniques. During 1970–1990, considerable activity centered around the application of an ecological/ecosystem model to individuals, groups, and communities (e.g., Banning, 1989; Banning & Kaiser, 1974; Bronfenbrenner, 1979; Conyne, 1975; Conyne & Clack, 1981; Conyne & Rogers, 1977; Dahr, Corazzini, & McKinnon, 1977). At the individual level, this approach was referred to as "life space design," or "ecotherapy." This ecological thrust then diminished, to be renewed in the new millennium through works on such topics as ecological counseling (Conyne & Cook, 2004; Cook, 2012), and on the connection of ecology with prevention (e.g., Centers for Disease Control and Prevention, 2013).

Drawing from Willi (1999), Wilson (2004) pegged the goal of ecological psychotherapy as "facilitating the development of a personal niche in which the individual can experience interpersonal effectiveness" (p. 163). Conyne and Rogers (1977), in their article "Psychotherapy as Ecological Problem Solving," previously had discussed five ecologically-based educational techniques to be used in individual counseling: reconstruing, transcending, encapsulating, redesigning, and exiting; selecting is an additional important technique. These first five techniques were adapted from Kaiser (1975). Moos (1975) developed the technique of selecting a new or different environment.

All these ecologically based educational techniques are appropriate for use in wellness and prevention individual counseling. They might be used independently or together. Moreover, as Conyne and Cook (2004) pointed out and which was presented in chapter 4, ecological approaches to counseling reflect a unique perspective (person × environment) that can be used in conjunction with existing theories of counseling, such as cognitive-behavioral or existential) and they also can borrow methods from those theories.

Let's take a common case situation and apply each ecological technique to it. Imagine Corbin, a 17-year-old college freshman now in his fifth week of the fall semester. His resident advisor referred him for counseling at the university counseling center for help with severe homesickness. Corbin describes himself as feeling totally alone and unhappy and is afraid his grades also are beginning to suffer.

Reconstrue. This is a technique drawn from the cognitive-behavioral approach (e.g., Ellis, 2011). Corbin can learn how to reframe aspects of his life that are upsetting, to view them from a different perspective. The wellness and prevention counselor helps Corbin to understand that it is not being away from home, for instance, that causes his unhappiness directly but his own interpretation of being away from home. After all, there are plenty of new freshman who are feeling just the opposite of Corbin, points out the counselor. A goal is to help Corbin learn to gain a sense of perspective that he can apply successfully to his current negative experience as he improves his overall wellness. He may reconstrue his distance from home as an opportunity to experience novel situations and new people. In addition, the counselor works with Corbin to help him anticipate future challenges and how reconstruing can be used to avert problems.

Transcend. This technique emerges from Eastern and humanistic philosophic theories and practices. Focusing on one's breath, for instance, is a key element of meditation and of yoga. Beginning to master breath-focusing can allow one to literally become oblivious to external onslaughts (such as a yipping dog in the next door apartment) by allowing it to pass through, by "becoming tranquil in the midst of chaos" (Conyne & Rogers, 1977, p. 301). Transcending also can be used to de-escalate the intensity of persistent and upsetting situations, such as his rumination about being away from home. Therefore, Corbin can learn to transcend the difficulty for periods of time, to give himself a needed break and some distance from its constant impingement, while also calming his nervous system. "Breathe, Corbin" can become a useful mantra for him and he can be taught and then practice its execution in counseling. Transcending can then become a life-long technique Corbin can use to advance his sense of well-being and to lessen the intensity and the grip of internal and external challenges.

Encapsulate. Willi (1999) underscores the importance of people finding their own ecological niche in a larger setting. A person-environment niche replicates the animal world where bears hibernate in a den, dogs find cozy, protected spots where they can sleep, and so on. Corbin has yet to find his niche at the university; these sometimes take time to find and adopt. They do not need to be elaborate, but they do need to comfort, support, and protect. For Corbin finding such a spot might help counterbalance the absence of "home" that he is experiencing. In effect, he would be locating or creating a "home place," a niche, at the university. And, it might just be the end seat next to the big pillar at the study table in the library. In any case, it would be a spot he might try to occupy each time he goes there to study, a niche he could think of as his own. Of course, once feeling safer, Corbin then might begin to feel more able to reach out, to become more involved, to pursue personal and academic goals with more verve and with less fear.

Redesign. (This also is one of the major wellness and prevention strategies that we have listed previously.) From the ecological perspective, environmental redesign is a technique from architecture and environmental design disciplines. The following quotation captures its essence for our purposes: "If the cold, gray walls of the student union building are beginning to depress you, try giving them a face-lift" (Conyne, 1975, p. 151). As I write in my office at Seattle University where I'm located this academic year in an invited position, employees are at work redesigning their hallways and offices. New paint ("that ugly, old pink color is going," I've heard more than once), new office furniture and arrangements, and different traffic patterns are emerging each day, it seems. Staff offices are being moved, after collaborative discussion, to better link people with functions. Environmental redesign is in full force here, and we shall see if satisfaction and productivity increase as a result.

Initially a goal is to take advantage of what already is available, such as moving into nature more often or finding a way to activate a social network that had been neglected to become dormant. Otherwise, it sometimes is necessary to find ways to change, or to redesign, aspects of an environment that themselves are hindering wellness. For instance, clients may need to be counseled not only in how to cope more effectively with a difficult boss but, also, in how to influence positive changes in the behavior of the boss.

In Corbin's case, as he longs for home, he could be led to identify what changes he might make in his physical environment to lessen the intensity of his homesickness, contribute to his satisfaction and happiness, and bolster his studying. This collaborative discussion might yield some possibilities. For instance, bringing some photos from home of family members and of his beloved dog (his room contains no personal of family mementos) might help. Reporting that his residence hall floor is incredible noisy, Corbin might begin to trek to the university library to study, perhaps even to apply for a study carrel, which still are available. Such environmental redesign steps can help sometimes to shape a more hospitable and productive environment, lifting a person's life experience.

Exit. Sometimes it's best to leave a noxious environment or situation. Some people exit too quickly, others not soon enough. Some continue on and on and on, unable to take action but full of remorse at the same time. Corbin really is only beginning his college experience, even though he could feel it's been going on too long already. Five weeks into it, though, is only about one-third of the first semester of his first year in college. The counselor can help Corbin gain perspective about this time frame (rightfully, using the technique of reconstruing). Time is needed to make a transition. However, exiting could be discussed, if only as a test of Corbin's commitment. Talking about it could lessen any fantasies or attractions he might hold in relation to exiting. Talking about exiting, in fact, might strengthen a resolve to stay and to improve that staying. This represents an existential viewpoint; we sometimes become more enlivened and present in the here and now when we become more aware of our eventual life exit/death. If, however, exiting is selected after weighing and evaluating the options realistically, then the counselor can assist Corbin to sort through and apply that decision.

Select. Moos (1975) suggested an intentional choice process to harmoniously match a person with a different environment. In this technique, exiting a situation always is paired with moving toward a potentially concordant person-environment (P × E) relationship. Are there aspects of Corbin's life at the university that might be better served if he were to select a different opportunity structure there? For instance, is there a different residence hall that might fit his needs and style better? Another major? Even another college or, perhaps, leaving college to move into another carefully selected pursuit that might be more compatible?

Advocate. Advocating for change in toxic social systems or in those that just don't work has been at the center of social justice and prevention (e.g., Lewis, Arnold, House, & Toporek, 2003). This technique looks outward and is action oriented. Its intent is to influence external change in a surrounding environment to more positively support people who inhabit or use it. This stance may involve developing the capacity to take extraordinary steps in ordinary circumstances. Think of Rosa Parks refusing to move to the back of the bus in the Jim Crow Montgomery of the 1950s. Or of Sharon Cohen (Toner, 2014), who created "Figure Skating in Harlem," a program helping 200 low-income students a year gain life skills through ice skating.

A client who feels constrained by limited local resources supporting outdoor walking, running, and biking—which is the unfortunate case in many urban and suburban neighborhoods—may be encouraged to advocate in their community for developing new paths, such as what could emerge through adopting a "rails to trails" project. This example represents the client's use of advocacy to alter an existing physical environmental situation. Clients also may be supported in counseling to use advocacy to influence positive change in sociopolitical conditions that are thwarting healthy functioning. Joining a community action group aimed at increasing opportunities for gay and lesbian persons or speaking to the school board about the needs for establishing a bullying prevention program are examples. The focus of advocacy is the opposite of person change to fit an environment; rather, its purpose is to shape the physical or the socio-cultural-political aspects of the environment to better fit the person. In the latter case, conditions such as oppression, racism, homophobia, and bullying represent some examples.

In talking more with Corbin the counselor discovers that he has been harassed by some male students on his residence hall floor for his unwillingness to join them in teasing and taunting two other residents. In selecting advocacy, Corbin would work to mobilize forces aimed at stopping the harassment, to remove it from re-occurring. The counselor might present advocacy as an option, if it seems appropriate and possible to enact. If well received, then the counselor would work with Corbin to develop an action plan.

Deliver remedial counseling with a wellness and prevention focus. All individual counseling can include a wellness and prevention focus as an important vehicle to assist problem resolution and move toward a more optimal state of wellness. This approach is consistent with a general strengths-based approach to counseling and therapy, referred to previously (Smith, 2014), where both client and contextual assets can be identified and used to assist with struggles. What is emphasized are in the following box.

Sleuthing for Strengths in Wellness and Prevention Individual Counseling

- Focusing on what works, not what is failing
- Noting the positive resources clients possess
- Accentuating contextual strengths surrounding clients
- Causing clients to identify and maximize their strengths

Corbin was referred to counseling, as you recall, due to intense feelings of homesickness. Counseling with a wellness and prevention focus would seek to help Corbin improve his mental and emotional state by detecting his assets and leveraging them. It turns out, Corbin is kind, he likes people and they generally like him (except for those engaged in harassing him), and he possesses good problem solving skills, too; he has buried these strengths, though, in his despair. Counseling can help to unearth them, to bring them to light again so that Corbin can see and re-claim them. Taking these steps may aid in lifting the black cloak of emptiness he has been shrouding in and help him to move into brighter days ahead.

Strategy B: Facilitate social competency strategy. This strategy is used to further strengthen the capacities of clients to function well with others and in groups of people. Being socially competent is critically important for attaining a satisfying and effective life in the complex society in which we live. Take work life, for example. Being able to work effectively in a team—sometimes referred to as being a "good team player"—is cited often as one of the predictors of success and is one of the core characteristics often looked for by employers in applicant job interviews. A compilation and analysis of evaluations of the top employee characteristics by the University of Kent, Careers and Employability Services (n.d.) placed teamwork at number two, just after communication skills.

Wellness and prevention counseling typically accords importance to social competency, especially when conducted through group work, which is based on social interaction. In individual counseling, clients practice in social competency enhancement can be accomplished through focusing on the interactions occurring between the counselor and client, by examining the quality of social interactions reported by the client, by referral to group counseling or a psychoeducation group, and by connecting clients with existing social competency opportunities in the community.

In Corbin's case, connecting him with a university resource might work very well in helping ameliorate his homesickness while enhancing his overall social competency. Breaking this continuous loop of rumination can be very helpful by itself and becoming involved with other people holds much potential value. The university campus and most other forms of communities naturally contain a wide variety of resources for involvement and becoming connected with other people. At the university, for instance, the counselor might examine with Corbin descriptions of the numerous student organizations that are registered; there may be well over 100 of them, spanning social fraternities, religious groups, recreational clubs, and social justice organizations, to mention just a few. The goal is to find at least one possibility that Corbin could check out and potentially join, at least for a trial run. His experience with that organization, say, it's the Film Society, can then be monitored during counseling, particularly for effects on Corbin's well-being and on his developing social skills.

Strategy C: Connect with natural caregivers. Counselors can connect clients with help-giving resources in the community that are offered by non-professionals or encourage clients to connect with people whom they've talked about as being particularly understanding and helpful. A self-help group, such as alcoholics anonymous represents the first condition, while a helpful uncle or a barber who listens well represents the second instance. The resident advisor who referred Corbin for counseling, it turns out, is someone whom Corbin said he has come to like and "can talk with." This RA, then, might be one of these "natural caregivers," a person whom the counselor might subtly encourage Corbin to talk with about his life. This amounts to "going with the flow," taking positive advantage of available resources to get support and help. It's an example of how clients can take responsible action for self-improvement by connecting intentionally with someone or a resource right in their own environment. Clients can learn from this approach and apply it as a kind of life lesson.

Strategy D: Assist developmental transitions strategy. Use of this strategy within individual wellness and prevention counseling guides the counselor to look for how developmental markers, or transition points, may affect a client's situation. As all of us move through life we automatically pass through definable and generally predictable transition points which, by themselves, introduce particular challenges that need to be met more or less successfully. Children leave their home to begin kindergarten or elementary school. High school graduates confront what comes next in their lives. At work's end, adults face retirement or other relevant alternatives that might fit. These are examples of naturally occurring transitions. In addition, unanticipated crisis transitions can pop up, demanding us to cope and adapt. Hurricanes and other natural disasters, being fired from work, the accidental death of a loved one, and tragic shootings that are taking place all too frequently in schools and the workplace.

In Corbin's case, the counselor realizes that the challenges of being away from home for the first time and the demands of academic courses accompany the college freshman year developmental transition that Corbin faces. It is entirely adaptive and to be expected that any freshman, new to the college environment and separated from family and friends and the other comforts of home, will experience at least some level of adversity. However, Corbin may not be aware of this normative developmental explanation and, even if he were, he is the one dealing with it now, after all; for him, it is not just a textbook theory.

But there is power in conceptualizing situations in terms of developmental transitions, when that connection fits. The counselor can identify the set of developmental tasks that arise in the freshman year, such as forming new friends and remaining connected with home but not being traumatized by its physical absence, and use this kind of information to help the client to more fully understand what is being experienced. There can be a great sense of relief found when a client realizes that all freshmen must deal with similar issues he or she is facing and that having some difficulties in doing so is much more common than not. "You mean, it's not all me?" can be a reassuring awareness. Moreover, teaching clients about the concept of developmental transitions can provide them with a valuable life tool that can assist their preservation of wellness and facilitate how they more positively can understand and cope with life challenges to come.

Strategy E: Encourage everyday wellness and prevention strategy. As with TLCs, everyday wellness and prevention practices provide a blueprint toward a healthier life. Associating with positive people, getting outside to walk, sleeping well, living without physical or psychological threat, and eating whole foods are representative (see chapter 2 once again). Evidence-based research has provided counselors with a curriculum of positive wellness and prevention attitudes and behaviors that they can present selectively to clients, or refer to in their ongoing counseling with clients.

Hearing Corbin complain about feeling tired and alone at the university provides an avenue for the counselor to draw from everyday best practices to suggest that he might check out the university recreation center's free services for exercising and also for increasing possibilities for meeting other like-minded students.

These occasions in counseling provide counselors with "teachable moments" that they can use to help clients learn valuable wellness and prevention information they can apply in their lives immediately and over time.

Step 4: Apply the Plan

The client implements the counseling plan that he or she creates with the counselor to work on goal accomplishment and move toward a higher state of wellness. Counselor and client work together throughout the process to envision how strategies and goals are to be linked, with action steps articulated.

Step 5: Evaluate Process and Outcomes

Create formative and summative evaluation. Criteria for formative and summative evaluation are set (Conyne, 2010, 2013; Raczynski, Waldo, Schwartz, & Horne, 2013). Formative evaluation is used to guide the counseling implementation plan and feedback obtained along the way allows for keeping progress on course or for correcting wayward energies. In addition to examining if actions taken (or not) are in line with the plan's design, satisfaction, effort, and efficiency also are addressed during counseling discussions. If Corbin had planned to begin volunteering at a homeless shelter in the next week, for instance, a formative evaluation check at the upcoming counseling session can examine if this step occurred and how it is going. If it did not happen, then adjustments can occur.

Summative evaluation is conducted at the end of counseling to determine how effective counseling has been. Goal accomplishment, overall satisfaction, state of wellness, and transferring and application of learning can be examined. This end-stage evaluation can be conducted through structured discussion in counseling and may include relevant assessment measures. For instance, if a wellness and prevention instrument was administered at the beginning of counseling, it might be re-administered at the end to provide on source of information about change.

How satisfied is Corbin with his overall counseling experience, and with his goal accomplishment? What did he learn? What can be transferred and applied into the future? How has Corbin's level of wellness changed? Of particular importance is to help Corbin gauge if and how much the intensity of his homesickness has diminished and, alternately, what his overall level of well-being is now in relation to his college experience.

Wellness and Prevention Through Group Work

Group Work Foundations

A *group* is a living, dynamic open system set within a context. It is comprised of more than two people and characterized by a shared purpose, interconnection, and interaction among its members (Bemak & Conyne, 2004; Forsyth, 2009). It is a "web of life" (Capra, 1996). See Figure 5.2.

FIGURE 5.2. Meeting of support group. Counseling for wellness and prevention occurs within group work.

Source: iStock photo

Group work is an umbrella term, spanning a range of group-level applications (Association for Specialists in Group Work [ASGW], 2000): (a) task groups, aimed at the accomplishment of work-related goals; (b) psychoeducation groups, which transmit information and use processes aimed at helping members enhance or develop wellness and prevention life skills, such as stress management; (c) counseling groups, which activate interpersonal problem solving aimed at correcting various problems in living that do not typically carry a diagnosis; and (d) psychotherapy groups, used to help members resolve deeper and broader psychological and emotional issues that might often carry a diagnosis (Conyne, 2013).

Group work involves help-giving or task accomplishment occurring within a group setting. Capable professionals apply relevant group theory and processes to promote interdependent functioning among group members in order to accomplish personal, interpersonal, or task goals (ASGW, 2000; Conyne, Wilson, & Ward, 1997).

Supporting Research

As we saw earlier in chapter 4 with the counselor functioning cube (Morrill, Oetting, & Hurst, 1974), group work is a major counseling intervention that can be used for remedial, developmental, and preventive purposes. Clearly, this is where wellness and prevention with groups comes into play.

A fairly large body of work has emerged over the last several years addressing "prevention groups" (e.g., Clanton Harpine, 2013; Conyne, 2014b; Waldo, Schwartz, Horne, & Cote, 2011). Conyne and Horne (2001) co-edited a *JSGW* special issue, "The Use of Groups for Prevention," that summarized an examination of a large data set attesting to the effectiveness of prevention groups. Empirical studies reported in that journal's special issue demonstrated how prevention groups that were successful in developing skills and lowering risk for specific sub-groups of children and adolescents (e.g., angry and aggressive children; Shechtman, 2001), for late adolescents (e.g., college students with eating disorders; Sapia, 2001), and with adults (parents of children diagnosed with AD/HD; McDonnell & Mathews, 2001) tended to emphasize interactive, participative processes, focused group discussion, and cooperative exercises.

In another case, Conyne and Clanton Harpine (2010) co-edited a *Group Dynamics* special issue, "Prevention Groups: Evidence-Based Approaches to Advance the Field." Among other articles, it contained four lengthy evidence-based studies of prevention programs that relied on the use of group methods. These studies integrated the best available research on their topic, combined with clinical experience, professional judgment, cultural adaptation where needed, and collaboration in program design and delivery. The group-based prevention programs included the Strengthening Families Program (SFP; Kumpfer, Whiteside, Greene, & Allen, 2010), which demonstrated significant improvements in family functioning; the Incredible Years Parent Training Program of Webster-Stratton (Borden, Schultz, Herman, & Brooks, 2010), which demonstrated how IY can strengthen parent and child competencies as a means for promoting resilience; two projects by McWhirter and McWhirter (2010), showing how a prevention group aimed at families of domestic violence can reduce violence and the threat of violence and how a prevention group program aimed at improving school-based mental health can increase positive aspects of mental health; and on A. Horne's bully busting program (Bell, Raczynski, & Horne, 2010), which was able to increase teacher reports of self-efficacy, knowledge, and skills in promoting a healthier school environment as an antidote to bullying by students.

Note elements drawn from a definition of prevention groups, below, and their connection with wellness and prevention. Pay attention to the emphasis on competency enhancement and health promotion:

> Prevention groups enhance members' strengths and competencies, while providing members with knowledge and skills to avoid harmful situations and mental health problems. . . . Two key ingredients for prevention groups are that they be directed toward preventing problems and promoting health and wellbeing and that they highlight and harness group processes. (Conyne & Clanton Harpine, 2010, p. 194)

It is apparent, then, that wellness occupies a central position in prevention groups.

Let's take a closer look at these kinds of groups, which I will refer to as wellness and prevention groups. Note that they are offered in *stand-alone* form and also are *embedded* as a component within a more complex program, such as a multistage, several year community-wide substance abuse prevention program, or in a wellness workshop. Note that most of the programs that will be reported on in the next chapters on wellness and prevention in settings and in systems contain group formats as important features. Regardless of being stand-alone or embedded, however, the same general principles and processes apply.

Wellness and Prevention Groups: Psychoeducation Format

Psychoeducation is a particularly common, and useful, facet of wellness and prevention groups (Brown, 2004; Kalodner, Coughlin, & Seide, 2014; Raczynski & Horne, 2014). It can be tailored for use in stand-alone groups or in embedded ones.

In this approach important wellness and prevention life skills (such as problem solving, or active listening) are described and modeled by the group leader, then members practice the skills in the group, receive feedback, and consider how to apply them. This cycle can be repeated. Importantly, all these events occur within a group, which naturally contains the advantages associated with social facilitation, direct experience, vicarious observation, interpersonal processes, peer feedback, leader modeling, and application—if, of course, the group leader promotes and manages the group processes effectively.

To assist with promoting effective leadership of wellness and prevention groups, group leaders can be guided by best practice suggestions (ASGW, 2007), giving attention to the major steps of planning, performing, and processing. Let's briefly examine each of these steps.

Planning. The intent in this step is to create a detailed wellness and prevention group plan in collaboration with representative members of the targeted population. An example of such a plan is presented later in this chapter. Plan contents need to emerge from a local assessment and from review of a relevant research base, and incorporate input from the representative members. Thus, the plan should be based on a strong evidence base that is fitted to local conditions. Its overall intent is provide guidance for the group leader in helping members satisfy group and individual member wellness and prevention goals through maximizing strengths and harnessing positive group conditions. Drawing from TLC's and Everyday Wellness and Prevention supports these directions.

Performing/delivering. The wellness and prevention group pivots around the concepts of interdependence, interaction, cohesion, maximizing strengths, and seeking to reach overall wellness and prevention goals. The power of the group resides in the ability of the group leader to create with members a positive working climate. Such a climate allows for the emergence of interdependent bonds while retaining autonomy, the development of positive and therapeutic conditions, and it facilitates member interaction. These are essential conditions to promote as group leaders.

Processing/meaning derivation. Processing is necessary to convert experience into meaning. We do not learn much from experience itself, even though it's necessary and important in group work. We learn from reflecting on experience and identifying principles that matter for future application (Conyne, 2013; Ward & Ward, 2014).

Two forms of processing are important: (a) leader assisting members to process events and experiences within group sessions; and (b) leader or member processing between group sessions. *Within*-session processing can occur around a critical event and/or at the end of sessions. The goal of it is to help members learn about themselves, each other, and the group from their joint experience, and to connect learning with wellness and prevention goals. One model for *between*-session processing that has been found useful is called "deep processing" (Conyne, 1999). It moves through successive stages of examining and discussing objective observations, subjective assessments, relevant theory, application decisions for the immediate group, and continuing to evolve a personal approach that can work generally.

The following box summarizes these suggestions (adapted from Conyne, 2014b).

Best Practice Suggestions for Leading Wellness and Prevention Groups: Stand-Alone or Embedded

Planning Steps

- Conduct ecological assessment (people in context)
- Identify relevant research support base
- Collaborate with community representatives in planning
- Set group goals for wellness and prevention (TLCs, everyday wellness and prevention practices)
- Maximize strengths
- Create a detailed plan for conducting the wellness and prevention group

Performing/Delivering Steps

- Balance attention to information, skills, interaction, and group process
- Enhance cohesion among members as a driving force
- Systematically present skill development opportunities
- Optimize interconnection, interaction
- Develop positive, therapeutic conditions
- Attend to generating feedback

- Consider concrete application steps in and out of group
- Emphasize aspects of both wellness and prevention

Processing/Meaning Derivation Steps

- Process within and between each session
- Evaluate group process and wellness and prevention outcomes over time

A Detailed Plan for a Wellness and Prevention Group

The last item in the box under the "Planning Steps" indicates that a detailed group plan needs to be produced. This plan is used to guide wellness and prevention group sessions. General group goals can be established around therapeutic life change (TLC) areas or by drawing from everyday wellness and prevention areas. See the following illustration, which originated in a collaboration with my University of Cincinnati colleague, Dr. Robert Wilson; it is adapted specifically from Conyne (2014b):

1. *General Description of the Wellness and Prevention Group*
2. *General Outline of the Wellness and Prevention Group*
   a. Background and Rationale for the Wellness and Prevention Group
      - ★ What is the contextual situation, based on your ecological assessment?
      - ★ For what population is it intended?
      - ★ Is it a stand-alone or an embedded group?
      - ★ If it is to be embedded, describe its fit within the larger program

   b. General Goals for the Wellness and Prevention Group Experience
      - ★ What general goals do you intend to achieve for this group?
      - ★ Specify connections with which *TLCs* or areas drawn from Everyday Wellness and Prevention?

   c. Time Period for the Wellness and Prevention Group
      - ★ Hours/session
      - ★ Sessions/week
      - ★ Number of weeks

   d. Leader(s)
      - ★ Who will lead (solo, co-led)? If to be co-led, what characteristics of co-leader are desired?
      - ★ If to be co-led, how will co-leader selection occur?
      - ★ How will you process your work between sessions, and overall?

e. Methods
   * What general topics will be covered? Connection with *TLCs* or Everyday Wellness and Prevention?
   * What general methods or techniques will be used?

f. Recruitment—Screening (if appropriate for this type of group)
   * How will members be recruited?
   * How will they be screened for inclusion?

g. Processing
   * How will you assist members to reflect on their ongoing group experience?

h. Application
   * How will you assist members to identify learning that can be applied in their daily lives?

i. Evaluation
   * How will the Wellness and Prevention group be evaluated to determine effect of its delivery, and member outcome?

3. *Session by Session Description of Planned Events in the Wellness and Prevention Group*
   a. In each session, what wellness and prevention goals do you intend to achieve? Think in terms of the SPAMO acronym:

   Specific, **P**erformance-based, **A**ttainable, **M**easurable, **O**bservable

   b. What strategy (strategies) do you plan to use to achieve each of the goals listed?
   c. How will you monitor process your progress toward goal achievement?

The following is an example:

Session 1—Total time, two hours

Goal 1—To help members become acquainted.

Member Tasks—To learn each other's names and something about each member.

Strategy—(a) brief introduction by each member, (b) member interviews in pairs and report to the group.

Time Required—Strategy (a): 20 min; strategy (b): 10 min per interview; processing 20 min.

Physical Setting—Members seated in a circle except when dividing into pairs for interviews.

Materials Needed—None

Method—(a) for self-introductions, each member will be asked to give his or her name and a short statement of how he or she is feeling "right now;" (b) for the paired interviews, each member chooses another member and then finds a spot to interview his or her partner for ten minutes...

<<material omitted for example>>...

Processing—The group leader will invite discussion of feelings about introducing self, introducing others, being introduced by others... leading to a discussion of "self-presentation" and "stage-fright."

Session 2—Total time, two hours

Goal 1—To identify thoughts and feelings about being in this wellness and prevention group.

Member Tasks—To identify greatest benefit and greatest concern about being in this group.

Processing—Each member will be asked to disclose how it felt to talk about concerns and expected benefits.

Goal 2—To begin the process of individual identification of wellness and prevention goals.

Member Tasks—To write as concretely as possible one wellness and prevention goal they would like to accomplish by the end of this group; to be prepared to share this goal with the rest of the group and be open for feedback.

Processing—Each member will be provided with opportunities to reflect within sessions on group processes and events and on the meaning they are deriving from their experience.

Leader(s) will process between sessions the group and their work.

Example of a Stand-Alone and of an Embedded Wellness and Prevention Group

Wellness and prevention groups are frequently offered in schools and mental health centers as stand-alone vehicles for promoting emotional and behavioral health. Related, they also can serve to support and complement other forms of treatment, such as individual psychotherapy. A separate way these groups are used is to infuse or embed them within larger, more comprehensive programs. What follows are brief examples of each mode.

Stand-Alone Example 1. School counselors in middle schools are expected to assist students as they cope with the predictable developmental transitions occurring for elementary students (Villalba, 2007), and in early adolescence (Brannigan, 2007). These can be troubling periods for many students, involving a range of social, emotional, behavioral, and academic challenges. Wellness and prevention interventions organized around psychoeducation formats have proven to be effective methods (Dagley & English, 2014; Villalba, 2007; Webb, Brigman, & Campbell, 2005).

Brannigan (2007) described an example of such a group, with results showing promise. It was formed to assist seven students new to middle school (sixth graders) build their academic competence through identifying their learning styles, strengths, and learn how to seek help, when needed. A total of 16 sessions were held, occurring once a week during the 30-minute lunch period (students also ate).

The curriculum *Learning to Learn, Revised* (Fender, 2004) was used to guide discussion and group procedures for Sessions 1–4, with a focus on assessing learning style and skills. Self-advocacy and communication with teachers were the focus of Sessions 5–8. Group members were encouraged to address peer interaction and collaboration aimed identifying academic success strategies in Sessions 8–16. The author observes, "Where sessions I-VI contained some mini-lecture, information giving, and learning exercises, the remaining sessions purposefully centered on group process and deepened the focus on peer relationships and support" (Brannigan, 2007, p. 57). It is this blending of content with interactive process, provided at a propitious developmental transition point, that can make wellness and prevention groups such a valuable strategy.

Stand Alone Example 2: The group checkup. Lots of innovative work is occurring in health care provision, some of which is being spawned, or required, by the Patient Protection and Affordable Care Act. The Group Checkup (Park, 2013) offers one example. Since 2005, an increasingly large number of U.S. family medicine practices have been moving to offer 90-minute group visits for conducting routine physicals. These visits include taking vital signs, and each person being seen privately for a few minutes while a nurse answers questions and leads a group discussion with the others. In another health care example, Catholic Health Partners is offering group treatment (coupled with training group practitioners) to provide cost-effective and quality care that takes advantage of the therapeutic power of groups (Markham, 2013).

Embedded example. The Incredible Years (IY) Parent Training Program (Borden et al., 2010) is a well-researched, 30-year initiative that is based on resilience. This program is based on a collaborative group process model that is intended to strengthen parent and child competencies. As well, the program seeks to reduce specific negative child outcomes, such as conduct problems, as the resiliency of both children and their families is promoted. Evidence indicates that this program promotes positive parenting, consistency, problem solving, cohesion, the use of family support networks, and family resilience (Black & Lobo, 2008; Webster-Stratton, cited in Borden et al., 2010).

This illustration of an embedded wellness and prevention group asks facilitators to catalyze group discussions of desired skills that are presented through video vignettes that demonstrate children and parents interacting in a range of family contexts. Role-plays also are employed to help parents to practice skills, to verbally process their observations and experience, and to consider how to include the skills in their parenting styles. Group facilitators also use cognitive reframing to assist parents to reconstrue irrational thoughts and to increase positive coping strategies, and they also consistently encourage self-praise and self-care as positive parenting strategies.

Important aspects of this group program are that facilitators attend to and use what the researchers term "key group process components" (e.g., creating a group environment of trust) to enhance curricular concepts, as well as other factors such as repeated modeling of skills and their practice by group members. The researchers emphasize that these group process components enhance the effectiveness and efficiency of the IY curriculum. See Borden et al. (2010) for an in-depth discussion of how these key group processes are embedded (e.g., in the pre-group stage, collaborating with parents about how to reduce barriers and stigma) within developmental stages of the parenting groups.

As I mentioned earlier, most of the wellness and prevention programs described in the next two chapters focused on *settings* include embedded groups as important vehicles. Notice how programs accomplish this task.

Issues for Reflection and Discussion

1. What are your thoughts about building wellness and prevention into individual counseling practice? What might be the biggest challenges you could face when trying to do this?
2. Suppose you were a school counselor and were asked to provide a group aimed at career issues for middle school students. What might you do to ensure the group was based on a wellness and prevention orientation?
3. Consider your preferences for providing counseling services. Do you tend to lean more toward individual or to group formats? What factors contribute to your preferences?
4. Think how you can help clients pivot toward identifying their strengths as a key part of accelerating wellness and prevention in their lives. List three ways you might do this:
   a. ______________________________
   b. ______________________________
   c. ______________________________

5. Helping clients to advocate for needed change in their lives can be important and sometimes necessary. Think of a client who lives in poverty or in a destructive relationship. Consider how you might help such a client to examine environmental conditions and to possibly take reasonable action to seek positive change. Discuss issues surrounding advocacy with a partner.

References

ASGW (2007). *Association for Specialists in Group Work Best Practice Guidelines: 2007 revision.* Retrieved from http://asgw.org/pdf/Best_Practices.pdf

Association for Specialists in Group Work. (2000). *Professional standards for the training of group workers.* http://asgw.org/pdf/training_standards.pdf

Banning, J. H. (1989). Creating a climate for successful student development: The campus ecology manager role. In U. Delworth, G. R. Hanson et al. (Eds.), *Student services: A handbook for the profession* (2nd ed., pp. 304–322). San Francisco, CA: Jossey-Bass.

Banning, J.H., & Kaiser, L.R. (1974). An ecological perspective and model for campus design. *The Personnel and Guidance Journal, 52*, 370–375. doi:10.1002/j.2164–4918.1974.tb04043.x

Bell, C. D., Raczynski, K. A., & Horne, A. M. (2010). Bully Busters abbreviated: Evaluation of a group-based bully intervention program. *Group Dynamics: Theory, Research, and Practice*, 14, 257–267. doi:10.1037/a0020596

Bemak, F., & Conyne, R. (2004). Ecological group work. In R. Conyne & E. Cook (Eds.), *Ecological counseling: An innovative approach to conceptualizing person–environment interaction* (pp. 195–218). Alexandria, VA: American Counseling Association.

Black, K., & Lobo, W. (2008). A conceptual review of family resilience factors. *Journal of Family Nursing, 14*(1), 33–55. doi:10.1177/1074840707312237

Borden, L.A., Schultz, T.R., Herman, K.C., & Brooks, C.M. (2010). The Incredible Years parent training program: Promoting resilience through evidence-based prevention groups. *Group Dynamics: Theory, Research, and Practice, 14*, 230–241. doi:10.2037/a0020322

Brannigan, M. (2007). A psychoeducational group model to build academic competence in new middle school students. *Journal for Specialists in Group Work, 32*, 61–70. doi:10.1080/01933920600978554

Bronfenbrenner, U. (1979). *The ecology of human development: Experiments by nature and design*. Cambridge, MA: Harvard University Press.

Brown, N.W. (2004). *Psychoeducational groups* (2nd ed.). New York, NY: Routledge.

Capra, F. (1996). *The web of life*. New York, NY: Anchor Books.

Centers for Disease Control and Prevention. (2013). *The social-ecological model: A framework for prevention*. Retrieved from http://www.cdc.gov/violenceprevention/overview/social-ecologicalmodel.html

Clanton Harpine, E. (2013). *Prevention groups*. Thousand Oaks, CA: Sage.

Conyne, R. (1975), Environmental assessment: Mapping for counselor action. *Personnel and Guidance Journal*, 54, 150–154. doi:10.1002/j.2164–4918.1975.tb04206.x

Conyne, R. (1999). *Failures in group work: How we can learn from our mistakes*. Thousand Oaks, CA: Sage.

Conyne, R. (2010). *Prevention program development and evaluation: An incidence reduction, culturally-relevant approach*. Thousand Oaks, CA: Sage. doi:10.4135/9781483349176

Conyne, R. (2013). *Group work leadership: An introduction for helpers*. Thousand Oaks, CA: Sage.

Conyne, R. (Ed.). (2014a). *Group work practice kit: Improving the everyday practice of group work*. Thousand Oaks, CA: Sage.

Conyne, R. (2014b). Prevention groups. In J. DeLucia, C. Kalodner, & M. Riva (Eds.), *Handbook of group counseling and psychotherapy* (pp. 531–543). Thousand Oaks, CA: Sage. doi:10.4135/9781452229683

Conyne, R., & Clack, R. J. (1981). *Environmental assessment and design: A new tool for the applied behavioral scientist*. New York, NY: Praeger.

Conyne, R. K., & Cook, E. (Eds.). (2004). *Ecological counseling: An innovative approach to conceptualizing person-environment interactions*. Alexandria, VA: American Counseling Association.

Conyne, R., & Clanton Harpine, E. (Eds.). (2010). Prevention groups: Evidence-based approaches to advance the field. Special Issue: Group Dynamics: *Theory, Research, and Practice, 14*, 193–280.

Conyne, R., & Horne, A. (Eds.). (2001). The use of groups for prevention. *Journal for Specialists in Group Work*, 26, 205–289. doi:10.1080/01933920108414220

Conyne, R., & Rogers, R. (1977). Psychotherapy as ecological problem-solving. *Psychotherapy: Theory, Research, and Practice, 14*, 298–305. doi:10.1037/h0086541

Conyne, R., Wilson, F. R., & Ward, D. (1997). *Comprehensive group work: What it means and how to teach it*. Alexandria, VA: American Counseling Association.

Cook, E. P. (Ed.). (2012). *Understanding people in context: The ecological perspective*. Alexandria, VA: American Counseling Association.

Dagley, J. C., & English, E. (2014). *Group work in schools*. Thousand Oaks, CA: Sage.

Dahr, D., Corazzini, J., & McKinnon, R. (1977). An environmental redesign program for residence halls. *Journal of College Student Personnel, 18*, 11–15.

Dewey, J. (1933). *How we think*. Buffalo, NY: Prometheus Books. doi:10.1037/10903–000

Ellis, A. (2011). Rational-emotive behavioral therapy. In R. J. Corisini & D. Wedding (Eds.), *Counseling psychotherapies* (9th ed., pp. 196–234). Belmont, CA: Brooks/Cole.

Fender, G. (2004). *Learning to learn* (Rev. ed.). Nashville, TN: Incentive.

Forsyth, D. (2009). *Group dynamics* (5th ed.). Belmont, CA: Wadsworth.

Granello, P. (2000). Integrating wellness work into mental health private practice. *Journal of Psychotherapy in Independent Practice*, 1, 3–16. doi:10.1300/j288v01n01_02

Granello, P. (2012). *Wellness counseling. Boston*, MA: Pearson.

Kaiser, L. R. (1975). Designing campus environments. *National Association of Student Personnel Administrators Journal, 13*, 33–39.

Kalodner, C., Coughlin, J. W., & Seide, M. (2014). Psychoeducational and counseling groups to prevent and treat eating disorders and conditions. In J. DeLucia-Waack, C. Kalodner, & M. Riva (Eds.), *Handbook of group counseling and psychotherapy* (2nd ed., pp. 484–494). Thousand Oaks, CA: Sage. doi:10.4135/9781452229683.n35

Kumpfer, K. L., Whiteside, H.O., Greene, J.A., & Allen, K. C. (2010). Effectiveness outcomes of four age versions of the Strengthening Families Program in statewide field sites. *Group Dynamics: Theory, Research, and Practice, 14*, 211–229. doi:10.1037/a0020602

Lewis, J., Arnold, M., House, R., & Toporek, R. (2003). *Advocacy competencies*. Retrieved from http://www.counseling.org/Resources

Markham, D. J. (2013, August 15). *The power of group therapy for population health*. Retrieved from http://www.hhnmag.com/

McDonnell, K.A., & Mathews, L.L. (2001). Promoting enhanced parenting: A group for caregivers of children diagnosed with AD/HD. *Journal for Specialists in Group Work, 26*, 276–288. doi:10.1080/01933920108414219

McWhirter, P., & McWhirter, J. J. (2010). Community and school violence and risk reduction: Promoting resilience through evidence-based prevention groups. *Group Dynamics: Theory, Research, and Practice, 14*(3), 242–256.

Moos, R. (1975). Social ecology: Multidimensional studies of humans and human milieus. In S. Arieti (Ed.), *American handbook of psychiatry* (2nd ed., pp. 914–931). New York, NY: Basic Books.

Morrill, W., Oetting, E., & Hurst, J. (1974). Dimensions of counselor functioning. *Personnel and Guidance Journal, 52*, 354–359.

National Wellness Institute. (1989). *Lifestyle Assessment Questionnaire*. Stevens Point, WI: Author.

National Wellness Institute. (2000). *Testwell*. Stevens Point, WI: Author.

Park, A. (2013, September 2). The group checkup. *Monitor*. Retrieved from http://time.com/

Raczynski, K., & Horne, A. (2014). Psychoeducational and counseling groups for bullying. In J. DeLucia-Waack, C. Kalodner, & M. Riva (Eds.), *Handbook of group counseling and psychotherapy* (2nd ed., pp. 495–505). Thousand Oaks, CA: Sage. doi:10.4135/9781452229683

Raczynski, K., Waldo, M., Schwartz, J., & Horne, A. (2013). *Evidence-based prevention*. Thousand Oaks, CA: Sage.

Ratey, J.J., & Hagerman, E. (2013). *Spark: The revolutionary new science of exercise and the brain*. New York, NY: Little, Brown.

Sapia, J.L. (2001). Using groups for prevention of eating disorders among college women. *Journal for Specialists in Group Work, 26*, 256–266. doi:10.1080/01933920108414217

Seguin, R., Buchner, D. M., Liu, J., Allison, M., Manini, T., Wang, C.Y.,. . . LaCroix, A. Z. (2014). Sedentary beahvior and mortality in older women. *American Journal of Preventive Medicine, 46*, 122–135. doi:10.1016/j.amepre.2013.10.021

Seguin, R., LaMonte, M., Tinker, L., Lui, J., Woods, N. F., Michael, Y.,. . . LaCroix, A. Z. (2012). Sedentary behavior and physical function decline in older women: Finding from the Women's Health Initiative. *Journal of Aging Research, 2012*, 1–10. doi:10.1155/2012/271589

Shechtman, Z. (2001). Prevention groups for angry and aggressive children. *Journal for Specialists in Group Work, 26*, 228–236. doi:10.1080/01933920108414214

Smith, E. J. (2014). *Strengths-based therapy: Connecting theory, practice and skills*. Thousand Oaks, CA: Sage.

Steele, F. (1973). *Physical settings and organization development*. Reading, MA: Addison-Wesley.

Toner, K. (2014, February 13). *For Harlem skaters, it's not about Olympic gold*. Retrieved from http://www.cnn.com/

University of Kent, Careers and Employability Services. (n.d.). *What are the top ten skills that employers want?* Retrieved from http://www.kent.ac.uk/careers/sk/top-ten-skills.htm

Vera, E., & Kenny, M. (2013). *Social justice and culturally relevant prevention*. Thousand Oaks, CA: Sage.

Villalba, J.A. (2007). Incorporating wellness into group work in elementary schools. *Journal for Specialists in Group Work, 32*, 31–40. doi:10.1080/01933920600977556

Waldo, M., Schwartz, J., Horne, A., & Cote, L. (2011). Prevention groups. In R. Conyne (Ed.)., *The Oxford handbook of group counseling* (pp. 452–468). New York, NY: Oxford University Press. doi:10.1093/oxfordhb/9780195394450.001.0001

Walsh, R. (2011). Lifestyle and mental health. *American Psychologist, 66*, 579–592.

Ward, D., & Ward, C. (2014). *How to help leaders and members learn from their group experience*. Thousand Oaks, CA: Sage.

Webb, L. D., Brigman, G. A., & Campbell, C. (2005). Linking school counselors and student success: A replication of the student success skills approach targeting the academic social competence of students. *Professional School Counseling, 8*, 407–413. Retrieved from http://www.schoolcounselor.org/school-counselors-members/publications/professional-school-counseling-journal

Willi, J. (1999). *Ecological psychotherapy: Developing by shaping the personal niche*. Seattle, WA: Hogrefe & Huber.

Wilson, F. R. (2004). Ecological psychotherapy. In R. Conyne & E. Cook (Eds.), *Ecological counseling: An innovative approach to conceptualizing person–environment interaction* (pp. 143–170). Alexandria, VA: American Counseling Association.

Wilson, F.R. (2012). Assessment, diagnosis, and treatment planning from the ecological perspective. In E. Cook (Ed.), *Understanding people in context: The ecological perspective in counseling* (pp. 179–206). Alexandria, VA: American Counseling Association. Retrieved from http://www.counseling.org/

Witmer, J., & Sweeney, T. (1992). Wellness and prevention as a model for counseling and human development throughout the life-span. *Journal of Counseling and Development, 71*, 140–148. doi:10.1002/j.1556–6676.1992.tb02189.x

6

RELATIONAL WELLNESS

Family and School Programs

The Family Setting

We grow up in families and schools. These relational settings are vital to development and they provide uniquely important sites in which to conduct wellness and prevention counseling. See Figure 6.1.

When a family functions well, it can positively guide and shape children's development. A positive family can provide a continuing source of purpose, support, challenge, and enjoyment in all family members' lives.

When the family is not functioning well its members can suffer a number of difficulties, ranging from disaffection to dysfunction and illegal behavior. It is no surprise that strategies to lower risk factors, such as poverty and absence of support, frequently assume considerable importance in wellness and prevention counseling programs.

As well, strategies to enhance protective factors are indispensable in family wellness and prevention programs. For instance, the Strengthening Families initiative of the Center for the Study of Social Policy (2012) follows a five-factor framework to bolster protective factors: (a) enhance parental resilience, (b) access and/or develop social connections, (c) obtain concrete support when needed, (d) increase knowledge of child development and of parenting itself, and (e) build the social and emotional competence of children.

Wellness and prevention programs targeting the family seek to assist at the "ground level." Regardless of the traditional or nontraditional nature of a family, these programs address what is the most basic unit of importance in human development in our society.

Effective wellness and prevention programs typically cross settings, and this point is especially valid for the family setting. Reviews of wellness and prevention programs that are restricted to the family setting indicate that few such efforts

FIGURE 6.1. Enjoying family time outdoors. Counseling for wellness and prevention occurs with families.

Source: iStock photo

exist. Rather, attention to the family setting is often incorporated within broader setting applications, such as the school or the community.

Counseling for wellness and prevention programs focused on family settings frequently emphasize parent training. These programs typically educate parents or other adult caretakers of children in parenting skills and strategies. Once trained, the caregivers are assisted in practicing these skills and strategies with their children. Parent involvement prevention programs frequently involve families in the process of implementing the program through participating in events, activities, or strategies that are embedded naturally with learning principles—such as working with others, listening, sharing ideas, and talking about what works. These family programs take place either in the home of the family or they involve family members off-site in some intentional form of family involvement (Catalano, Berglund, Ryan, Lonczak, & Hawkins, 2002).

This chapter segment will examine three family programs that have been widely evaluated as being effective:

- Functional Family Therapy (FFT) (Alexander et al., 1998; Alexander, Waldron, Robbins, & Neeb 2013): FFT is a family-based prevention and intervention program that is used to target high-risk youths and their families (treatment) or at-risk youths and their families (prevention). In doing so, FFT employs a strength-based model that focuses on risk and protective factors.
- FAST Track (Bierman et al., 1996; Conduct Problems Prevention Group, 1992, 2007): This is implemented in family, individual, and school settings.

It seeks to reduce conduct problems while promoting development of academic, behavioral, and social skills.

- Triple P: Positive Parenting Program (Matsumoto, Sofronoff, & Sanders, 2010; Sanders, 2008; Triple P Positive Parenting Program, 2014): This is a set of programs providing graduated intensity to fit the parent-child situation, with a general goal of enhancing the knowledge, skills, and confidence of parents in order to prevent behavioral, emotional, and developmental problems in children and adolescents.

Family Program Examples

Program Primary Wellness and Prevention Counseling Strategies
Functional Family Therapy: Education, relationships, skills
FAST Track: Education, risk/protective factors, strengths, multilevel
Triple P: Education, training, skills, COSI

Functional Family Therapy

What is functional family therapy? Functional family therapy (FFT) (Alexander, Robbins, & Sexton, 2000; Alexander et al., 2013; Sexton & Alexander, 2002) is a family-based prevention and intervention program that is used to target high-risk youths and their families (treatment) or at-risk youths and their families (prevention). The program starts with the family in order to effectively intervene with an individual and extend to the wider ecosystem surrounding and influencing clinical issues.

Family-based, FFT is a strength-based model that focuses on risk and protective factors. It uses a multisystemic and multilevel approach to treat and prevent the broad range of problems encountered by juveniles in relation to delinquent and criminal behavior. It focuses on the treatment system, individual and family functioning, and the therapist as key factors. FFT combines and integrates a number of components within its model, including clinical theory, empirically supported principles, and extensive clinical experience, seeking to provide specific and individualized interventions.

Original developers of FFT (Alexander & Parsons, 1973) realized more than 40 years ago that the development and rate of juvenile delinquency, drug abuse, and violence were increasing much faster than were the successful treatment programs. FFT was created with the family at the center of treatment and prevention, and with the evolving belief that identifying and building family members' strengths was a critically important part of the process. Moreover, Alexander et al. (2000) and Alexander et al. (2013) maintain that FFT can exert a so-called dual effect involving successful treatment of youth who are presently offending through changing risk and protective factors within the family system while also exerting a primary preventive effect on siblings who are at risk but not yet offending.

How is it done? FFT targets youth 11–18 years of age across a range of ethnic and cultural groups, while also providing assistance to younger siblings. It is a short-term, multiphase, goal-directed, systematic intervention involving an average of 12 sessions over a 3- to 4-month period for milder cases and up to 30 hours of direct services for more challenging ones. FFT has evolved into an intervention model including systematic training, supervision, and process and outcome assessment.

FFT works first to identify and develop the inner strengths of family members, as well as seeking to enhance a sense that they can improve their situations. This avenue is very consistent with positive psychology tenets. Also, centering initial activity around strengths provides the family with a "platform for change and future functioning" that can lead to greater self-sufficiency, lowered treatment needs, and much reduced costs.

The clinical model includes five major components, in addition to pretreatment. These are as follows:

1. Pretreatment: Seeks to assure that relationships between family therapists and referral sources are positive and collaborative, that the referral process is responsive and timely, and that it adequately orients and prepares those referred.
2. Engagement Phase: This early phase intervention emphasizes engagement and motivation, where establishing a family focus to the work includes increasing hope and positive expectations for change. The intent is to be immediately responsive, to listen, help, respect, to "match," and to develop and maintain a positive, strength-based relational perspective, respecting and attending to cultural factors.
3. Motivation Phase: Emphasis is placed on creating a positively motivating helping context, maximizing hopefulness and promoting self-efficacy. Therapists focus on relationship dimensions, maintaining a strength-based approach.
4. Relational Assessment: Emphasis is given to promoting and understanding interactions and relations among family members, replacing an individual perspective with a relational one. Both intra- and extrafamily processes and competencies are considered as interaction patterns, functions, resources, and resistances are examined.
5. Behavior Change Phase: Forward actions include changing ineffective behavioral patterns through skill building and developing positive coping approaches. Activities incorporate modeling and promoting positive behavior, learning from psychoeducation information provided, and communication and conflict resolution training.
6. Generalization Phase: This late-phase intervention is concerned with broadening positive family functioning, developing plans for resisting relapse, and identifying strategies for connecting effectively with community systems.

Generalization is emphasized, where the primary goal is to improve the family's capacity to impact the multiple systems in which it is embedded (e.g., school, community, juvenile justice system).

For a sample, Sexton and Alexander (1999) described the early phases of engagement and motivation as typically including the following:

Goals: Develop alliances, reduce negativity and resistance, improve communication, minimize hopelessness, reduce dropout potential, develop family focus, increase motivation for change.
Risk Factors Addressed: Negativity and blaming, hopelessness
Protective Factors Addressed: Credibility, alliance, treatment availability
Assessment: Behavior (e.g., risk and protective factors presented), relational problems (e.g., needs), and context (risk and protective factors). Assessment is multilevel, multidimensional, and multimethod and focused on family functioning, not on diagnostic assessment.
Therapist/Interventionist Skills: Interpersonal skills (e.g., validation, reframing), high availability to provide services.

What works? FFT is a model Blueprint prevention programs, as judged by the Center for the Study and Prevention of Violence and it has been evaluated very positively by several other sources. These include the American Youth Policy Forum, the Office of the U.S. Surgeon General, the Centers for Disease Control and Prevention, and the Office of Juvenile Justice and Delinquency Prevention. The FFT model has spread to 220 sites and is being implemented in the Netherlands, Norway, and in several U.S. states (including Washington, Florida, Louisiana, Oregon, California, Pennsylvania, New York, and Ohio).

The program always has required a comprehensive evaluation of process and outcomes. From 1973 to the present, research data demonstrate that FFT is highly successful when compared with residential treatment, standard juvenile probation services, and alternative therapeutic approaches. Indices, such as reduced recidivism, lowered rearrests, reductions in offending by the siblings of adolescents in treatment, and lowered costs of service have clearly favored FFT. For example, in the state of Washington, it is estimated that effectively delivered FFT reduces recidivism by 30%; at a $2,500 cost on average for each program participant, the cost benefit is $7.50 for every dollar spent (Washington State Institute for Public Policy, 2002). These savings support the value of well-executed wellness and prevention programs.

Why does it work? FFT derives its effectiveness by emphasizing factors that are essential to positive change and to their generalization. Its programmatic phases are tied to specific factors associated with positive change. Strengths are recognized and valued. Risk and protective factors that are both person- and system-centered are incorporated within assessment and behavior change. The approach is oriented within the context of the family and attends systematically to connected systems. Care is given to nurturing the relationship between the family and the provider.

Implications for counselors and other helpers. FFT occupies a unique place in prevention programs, aside from its validated effectiveness. It is both a treatment and a wellness and prevention program. FFT, therefore, illustrates how a powerful approach can be used, on the one hand, to target offending adolescents and their families (treatment) or, on the other, at-risk adolescents and their families (wellness and prevention). It is a program that has been replicated across 15 states where thousands of adolescents and families are served each year. Moreover, a range of trained professionals are using this approach, both for treatment and for wellness and prevention—including licensed mental health counselors.

By spanning the treatment–wellness and prevention spectrum, FFT is highly compatible with counselors and other helpers who understandably are interested in identifying prevention approaches they can use which fit well with their ongoing work. FFT's focus on strengths and relational dynamics builds a natural bridge linking treatment and prevention. This proven program offers professional counselors and other mental health professionals who are prepared to work with families a wellness and prevention vehicle that can be used perhaps more readily than can some other equally excellent programs that we will examine next.

FAST Track Prevention Project

What is FAST Track? FAST Track is a multisite, comprehensive, and long-term prevention program that includes multiple settings: the family/home, school, and the individual. Research on the program has been continuously conducted and published since its origins in 1992, including studies by Bierman et al. (1996), Conduct Problems Prevention Research Group (2010, 2011), Foster and Jones (2007), and Lochman et al. (2010). The project has been implemented in several locations throughout the United States and in other English-speaking countries, including Great Britain, Canada, and Australia.

The FAST Track program is premised on an ecological and developmental perspective that antisocial behavior has its origins in the interaction of multiple influences. Risk levels increase when children and families reside in low-income, high-crime neighborhoods where marital conflict and other forms of instability are more likely to occur. In such situations, consistent and positive parenting practice is difficult to maintain, especially if children may be impulsive. In turn, these children's readiness and preparation for performing well in school is threatened, and their repertoire is often inadequate for coping with social, emotional, and academic demands in school. As well, parents from such situations often are unable to relate well with school staff and may find it uncomfortable within the school environment.

How is it done? The FAST Track approach hinges on the conception that improving child competencies, parenting effectiveness, school context, and school–home communications will contribute to preventing certain behaviors across the period from early childhood through adolescence. It is guided by an ecological developmental theory based on the interaction of multiple influences on the development of behavior, holding that multiple stressors and influences on children and families can increase their risk levels. In such contexts, some families that experience marital conflict and instability can cause inconsistent and ineffective parenting.

On the basis of the preceding developmental model, the wellness and prevention strategy includes providing intensive interventions during transitions located at school entry and from elementary to middle school to high school. FAST Track also is predicated on a unified model of wellness and prevention that includes both universal (teacher-led curriculum, called PATHS) and components administered only to high-risk students.

The wellness and prevention intervention includes a universal-level classroom program and social-skill training, academic tutoring, parent training, and home visiting aimed at improving competencies and reducing problems in a high-risk group of children selected in kindergarten. Its overall purpose is to prevent chronic and severe conduct problems for children at high risk for long-term antisocial behavior. The program seeks to reach its wellness and prevention goal by increasing communication bonds and interaction competencies among children and parents, by enhancing children's cognitive, social, and problem-solving skills, and by improving peer relationships. It can be implemented in urban and rural areas for girls and boys of varying social class, ethnicity, and family composition.

The universal intervention of a teacher-led curriculum (PATHS) continues from first through fifth grades and includes 57 lessons. These lessons are taught about three times a week, with each lesson lasting 20–30 minutes. The lessons address skills for understanding and communicating emotions (40%), skills for increasing positive social behavior (30%), and skills for self-control and social problem solving (30%).

The high risk program spans Grades 1–6 but is most intense during transitions occurring upon entry into first grade and from grade school to middle school. At that level, the program is multidimensional and includes the following:

- Parent and child training groups meeting biweekly in second grade and then once per month for all other years
- Home visits occurring biweekly to reinforce parenting skills, foster parents' problem-solving capacity, and to promote parents' feelings of efficacy and empowerment of children, and child case management activities occurred as needed.

During the middle and high school phase (Grades 6–10), three standard prevention activities are delivered. These address the transition from middle school to high school, adolescent developmental issues in parent and youth groups, and vocational opportunities (e.g., life skills, budgeting skills, job interview skills) in Grade 7 and 8 youth forums.

Generally, FAST Track services are delivered through classroom skills training, peer group interventions, and parent groups. All service providers receive specific training. Parent groups are facilitated by clinicians experienced with high-risk families and who hold advanced degrees in counseling or social work.

What works? The FAST Track Prevention Project has been evaluated generally positively by several sources (e.g., as a Promising Blueprint program, and as being effective by the Center for Mental Health Services). An evaluation by Greenberg, Lochman, and McMahon (1996) and by the Conduct Problems Prevention Research Group (1992, 2000) indicated that the FAST Track Prevention Project addressed 10 positive youth development constructs: social, emotional, cognitive, and behavioral competence, self-efficacy, resiliency, bonding, recognition for positive behavior, opportunities for prosocial involvement, and prosocial norms. Participants in the FAST Track experimental program were found to use health services less than other students (Jones et al., 2010), and needed emergency medical services less often. Research of the FAST Track program yielded strong evidence for successive three-year cohorts favoring first grade program participants (n = 448) over controls (n = 450). The program children consistently showed better social skills, more positive peer relations, better reading skills, and more positive emotional and social coping skills, with some indication of fewer conduct problems. Parents of the program children were shown to be more involved in their children's schools, to be more positively involved with their children, and to use more effective discipline strategies. Observers of children's aggressive, disruptive, and oppositional behavior in the classroom reported fewer related problems for program children. In terms of process evaluation, several positive results were obtained, including fidelity with which teachers delivered the curriculum.

Other research has found mixed results. For instance, the Conduct Problems Prevention Research Group (2007) found some significant effects for high risk groups but none between intervention and control groups for students in Grades 3 and 6. Another study by the Conduct Problems Research Group (2011) found no significant main differences for the intervention but a subgroup analysis found positive results for higher risk youth.

Why does it work? On balance, research supports the FAST Track intervention and prevention program. The prevention program works because it is comprehensive and long term. Its conceptual base is well developed, focused on a universal program and on a high-risk program organized around developmental transitions. Multiple set of skills are addressed across three domains (social, cognitive, problem solving), parents and peers are involved, and multiple methods are incorporated (parent training, home visitations, social skills training, academic tutoring, PATHS classroom curriculum). The prevention program is delivered within a carefully constructed research design, including program and control students. Both outcome and process evaluations are planned for and conducted. The prevention program is coordinated across family and school settings.

Implications for counselors and other helpers. Mental health professionals, school counselors, and school psychologists frequently are confronted with child and family problems that often are centered around existing poor social skills, discipline problems, and disruptive behavior at home and in the classroom. Individual, group, and family counseling and therapy typically are the reactive responses, often with positive results. The FAST Track Prevention Project, however, illustrates how counselors and associated helpers could collaborate with others to create wellness and prevention programs aimed at both reducing the occurrence of these kinds of problems and at developing competencies in children and parents. This kind of approach might engender even broader empowering consequences due to its early stage and comprehensive focus.

Triple P: Positive Parenting Program

What is Triple P? Triple P, standing for Positive Parenting Program, is featured in the *National Prevention Strategy* (U.S. Surgeon General, 2011), as an award-winning program. It is really a sequential series of programs that are geared to a wide range of parenting challenges and to intended to positively address the broad range of emotional, behavioral, and developmental issues experienced by children and teenagers. The overarching goal of these programs is to prevent childhood and adolescent problems that can occur in a family, school, and community *before* they emerge while fostering family environments that support and encourage children and adolescents to actualize their promise.

How is it done? Triple P Positive Parenting Program (2014) is deliverable through a suite of programs, each of which targets a particular population or set of problem areas to be prevented. A universal, population program is available, as are increasingly specialized programs for parents of children with disabilities, with weight or other health problems, for parents who are experiencing transitional stress (e.g., divorce), or for indigenous families.

Triple P is a multilevel system that is tailored to different kinds of developmental and population issues. The program seeks to enhance practical parenting strategies and strengthen parent–child relationships by incorporating community wide media strategies, outreach to primary care services and community agencies, and behavioral counseling into a system of parenting and family support (Prinz, Sanders, Shapiro, Whitaker, & Lutzker, 2009).

Each level of the program differs in its intensity, ranging from information dissemination as a chief component, to a "light-touch" program for those whose problems are less pronounced, to more intense programs for parents coping with high, at-risk situations in their families. Delivery of the programs is shaped to fit circumstances along a continuum of low to high risk. Combinations of large public seminars, online work, self-help interventions, personal consultations, and group courses are all available to mesh with the particular context.

Training of program deliverers is accorded high importance. Therefore, specialized training in the Triple P approach is required in order to conduct the program. Six thousand practitioners have been trained to deliver Triple P. They are drawn from a broad range of disciplines and professions, including doctors, psychologists, counselors, social workers, police officers, teacher's aides, child safety officers, and clergy.

What works? Triple P was developed at the University of Queensland, Australia by Professor Matt Sanders. It now has been fanned out to 25 different countries, including the United States, with program materials translated into 17 languages being internationally implemented to enhance practical strategies for parenting aimed at strengthening relationships between parents and children.

Research has been accumulating to support the program over a 30-year period, leading to Triple P being the most extensively researched parenting program in the world, according to its Web site. Moreover, the program is ranked by the United Nations as the number one family prevention program in the world owing to its strong evidence base.

Population-based randomized trials demonstrate reduced rates of child maltreatment, out-of-home placements, and child injuries. Comparisons favoring treatment over control conditions across counties in South Carolina, in Santa Cruz, California, and in San Francisco, California, produced lowered rates of hospital and ER admissions from child abuse injuries, reduction of significant mental health problems in children, and decrease in parents' depression levels, stress, and other emotional problems. The National Registry of Evidence-Based Programs and Practices (NREPP; 2014), an online searchable registry of mental health and substance abuse programs, rates Triple P highly as an evidence-based program. On the NREPP's 4-point scale, the five Triple P studies that were investigated produced average ratings of 3.0, which is impressive. In addition, a 3.8 rating for readiness of dissemination supports its capacity for use right now. A large meta-analysis of 55 studies (Nowak & Heinrichs, 2008) of Triple P found that it causes positive changes in parenting skills, child problem behavior, and parental well-being, with the amount varying as a function of the intensity of the intervention.

Why does it work? This program works because of many factors. Program materials are comprehensive and professionally produced. They have been clinically tested to match with differing levels of parental and childhood/adolescent needs, from low to high intensity. This helps to make the program flexible and adaptive, as opposed to being one-size-fits-all. The materials, as mentioned earlier, have been translated into 17 languages and possess a high degree of cultural responsiveness. Those implementing the program are practitioners who have received specific training in the Triple P system. The Triple P approach has been found to be widely effective due to many of the preceding features.

In addition, the program is cost effective. Pairing a program scope and intensity with family needs reduces unnecessary expenditure of resources that can be tied to over-servicing and mismatching. Parents are encouraged to set their own goals and to adopt the program strategies they think will best fit their needs. This kind of self-regulation is said to be a program hallmark and it encourages parents to problem solve and become increasingly independent in applying aspects of the program while reducing a need for relying on close, continuing support from program personnel. Cost effectiveness can be measured in saved dollars associated with prevention gains over program cost expenditures. For instance, return on investment conducted by the Washington State Institute of Public Policy showed that delivering the standard Triple P program could save a community $1,788 per participant through reduction of child mental health problems (Lee et al., 2012).

Implications for counselors and other helpers. Practitioners seeking a culturally sensitive and well-researched wellness and prevention program that aims at helping parents to enhance their family effectiveness should find Triple P to be of particular benefit. Its capacity for alteration to fit local contexts, coupled with its orientation of empowering parents, matches well with the need for evidence-based programs to be adjustable. The program's clear emphasis on before-the-fact intervention provides counselors who use it the opportunity to help parents and children create meaningful change in the trajectory of their lives together.

Conclusion: Family Programs

The three family-based wellness and prevention programs described in this chapter, Family Functioning Therapy, FAST Track, and Triple P, each demonstrates important ways to positively affect family functioning and to exert a preventive influence. Mental health, school counselors, and school psychologists all need to be aware of the role of family dynamics in the overall development of strengths and deficits found in family members they may working with—remedially, developmentally, or preventively. Prevention programs that may be located in a different setting, such as a school, neighborhood, or workplace, usually can improve their effectiveness by incorporating family influences within their design and delivery.

Common ingredients have been identified that span effective wellness and prevention programs (as we have seen in earlier chapters) and in family-based prevention programs, particularly. Most recently, Kumpfer and Alvarado (2003) have reported on two federal studies (National Institute of Justice's, Office of Juvenile Justice and Delinquency Prevention project in 1989 and the Center for Substance Abuse Prevention's Prevention Enhancement Protocol System in 1998). Through this review process, the authors identified effective family preventive interventions (behavioral parent training, family skills training, and family therapy) and what accounted for this effectiveness. Effective family-focused prevention interventions were those that:

1. Were comprehensive, multicomponent programs that could modify a broader range of risk and protective processes in children than single-faceted programs could.

2. Emphasize family strengths (e.g., resilience and protective processes), instead of deficits, are generally more effective in addressing families experiencing relationship problems than are programs centered more specifically on either parents or children alone.
3. Address family relations, communication, and monitoring provided by parents.
4. Produce enduring effectiveness results when they are able to change cognitive, affective, and behavioral dynamics within the ongoing family environment.
5. Recognize that higher risk families need an increased dosage or intensity of intervention (25–50 hours) than do lower risk families (5–24 hours), due to the involvement of more risk factors and fewer protective factors.
6. Recognize that age and developmental appropriateness are necessary for family programs.
7. Introduce developmentally appropriate interventions when a family is receptive to change and growth.
8. Introduce family interventions as early as possible in situations of greater dysfunction.
9. Tailor the wellness and preventive program within the cultural traditions of the family, which improves recruitment, retention, and sometimes effectiveness.
10. Build incentives, such as child care and transportation, into prevention programs in order to increase recruitment and retention.
11. Use trainers and staff who are competent, warm, humorous, use empathy well, and are able to structure training so it is organized and directive.
12. Use interactive skills training methods (e.g., homework practice, role playing, active modeling, CDs/videos) rather than passive, didactic learning approaches to increase client satisfaction and program effectiveness, and
13. Employ a collaborative process with participants to foster empowerment and the identification of support and participant-based solutions.

When working in the area of family-based prevention, these guidelines can be very helpful to providers.

The School Setting

Perhaps the single best organized setting available for locating and delivering wellness and prevention programs is the school. A range of physical, environmental, and behavioral factors that may negatively influence a student's personal and academic development typically are found in schools (Meyers & Swerdlik, 2003). Moreover, schools present unparalleled opportunities for developing and supporting student strengths. See Figure 6.2.

There are many reasons for schools being a valuable entry point and resource setting for wellness and prevention. The most obvious one is that children and adolescents are required to attend school and, thus, can be found in one spot. Second, children and adolescents spend large, continuing portions of their everyday

FIGURE 6.2. Classroom. Counseling for wellness and prevention occurs in schools.

Source: iStock photo

lives (at least from September through mid-June, some 5,400 hours) in school. Third, the mission of schools and the goals and purposes of wellness and prevention programs coincide around an intent to improve outcomes for students. Fourth, schools provide convenience and accessibility to parents and family members, in addition to students, allowing the capacity to include them in skill building and other activities. This is an important point, especially for families of limited resources whose children may be at elevated risk for academic and personal difficulties. Fifth, schools provide an ongoing structure through which wellness and prevention programs can operate (Branden-Muller & Elias, 1991; Brown & Bolen, 2003; McMahon, Ward, Pruett, Davidson, & Griffith, 2000; Ross, Powell, & Elias, 2002).

Therefore, the school setting affords a significant opportunity for engaging students and important others, such as teachers and parents, in prevention activities. In addition, the school is an organized setting that can be coordinated with other settings, such as family and community, for wellness and prevention programming (Kolbe, Collins, & Cortese, 1997).

Schools provide an ecology that incorporates students and adults in important ongoing processes and structures. These processes and structures include a complex organizational structure, cultural norms and values, social and peer groups, classrooms, clubs, athletics, music, cafeterias, faculty lounges, temporal patterns, and physical structures, among others (Oxley, 2000). Settings within schools and schools themselves as settings are naturally occurring, ecological units of activity that provide milieus that are rich for prevention programs. Also important are the contextual relationships of schools with other systems, such as the community and with state and national policies and legislation (Conyne & Mazza, 2007).

It may not be surprising, then, that schools are frequent sites for wellness and prevention programs and that there are a number of school-based programs that have been recognized for their quality. Greenberg et al. (2003) recently observed that school-based prevention and youth development programs are most beneficial when they simultaneously can increase students' personal and social assets while also enhancing the quality of the school environment itself.

In this chapter segment, we will examine three programs that have demonstrated impressive evidence of effectiveness:

- *Life Skills Training* (Botvin & Griffin, 2012; Botvin, Griffin, & Nichols, 2006; Botvin & Kantor, 2000; Botvin & Tortu, 1988; Botvin, Schinke, Epstein, Diaz, & Botvin, 1995): This is a research-validated substance abuse wellness and prevention program proven to reduce the risks of alcohol, tobacco, drug abuse, and violence.
- *Seattle Social Development Project* (Catalano et al., 2002; Haggerty & Kosterman, 2012; Hawkins et al., 1992; Herrenkohl, Hemphill, Mason, Toumbourou, & Catalano, 2012; O'Donnell, Hawkins, Catalano, Abbott, & Day, 1995; Hawkins, Catalano, & Kosterman, 1999; Lonczak, 2002; Seattle Social Development Research Group, 2012): This is a program which is part of the Social Development Research Group (SDRG) and aimed at understanding and promoting healthy behaviors and positive social development for a variety of populations. Look for the special focus that is presented on these SDRG programs, especially "Communities that Care," contained in the highlighted box later in this chapter.
- *Olweus Bullying Prevention Program* (Bauer, Lozano, & Rivara, 2007; Olweus, 1991, 1992, 1993): This is a multilevel, multicomponent program intended to reduce and to prevent bullying in elementary and secondary schools.

School Program Examples

Program Primary Wellness and Prevention Counseling Strategies

Life Skills Training: Education, skills, psychoeducation, group interaction

Seattle Social Development Project (A Social Development Research Group Program): Education, risk and protective factors, assisting developmental transitions, community development

Olweus Bullying Prevention Program: Education, assisting developmental transitions, COSI aimed at system change at all ecological levels

Life Skills Training

What is Life Skills Training? The Life Skills Training (LST) program is a research-validated substance abuse prevention program proven to reduce the risks of alcohol, tobacco, drug abuse, and violence. It targets the major social and psychological factors that promote the initiation of substance use and other risky behaviors and uses a coordinated set of educational and behavioral change approaches to reach goals. The program has demonstrated effectiveness not only with White students but, also, with Hispanic and African American populations, with behavioral effects on smoking, alcohol, marijuana use and on multiple substances and illicit drugs (Botvin, 2011; Botvin & Tortu, 1988; Botvin & Kantor, 2000; Botvin, Griffin, Paul, & Macauley, 2003).

LST is designed to impact substance abuse knowledge, attitudes, skills, and norms. A foundation for the program is that social skills are key vehicles that people need to function effectively, and that their mastery improves the quality of life and can prevent a host of both specific and general negative consequences. The program is a group-based approach to teach life skills (but also uses other methods) aimed at resisting social influences that may encourage drug use and to promote the development of self-management and interpersonal skills. The life skill components that are taught follow a cognitive-behavioral approach and involve episodes of instruction, demonstration, behavioral rehearsal, feedback, social reinforcement, and focused practice that includes homework assignments and booster sessions. Life skills represent a particularly strong potential for everyday prevention due to their highly teachable nature.

LST is a program intended for elementary (starting at Grade 3), middle and junior high school students (sixth to seventh grades), and for high school students. In addition, the LST program is tailored to transitions, to parents, and to the workplace. The program is available in Spanish and has been implemented in 36 countries.

At the elementary level, LST is the most frequently used evidence-based program across the nation to prevent drug and alcohol use. At the middle school level, the LST program is aligned with the Common Core Standards, a single set of clear educational initiatives for K–12. The program is supported by more than 30 scientific studies and it is recognized as a Model or an Exemplary program by several major organizations: U.S. Department of Education; U.S. Department of Justice, Office of Juvenile and Delinquency Prevention; Center for Substance Abuse Prevention; National Institute on Drug Abuse; American Medical Association; Office of National Drug Control Policy; Centers for Disease Control and Prevention, Coalition for Evidence-Based Policy; and Blueprints for Healthy Development.

Its goal is to prevent drug use among students. This substance abuse wellness and prevention program targets major psychological and social factors that reduce risky behaviors and the use of substances. It makes use of a carefully developed training regimen in life skills and social resistance aimed at enhancing confidence and developing necessary life skills. Psychoeducation groups are a main vehicle for conducting the training. Attention is given not only to specific resistance skills but, also, to the enhancement of generic personal and social skills, such as in communication or problem solving, that students can learn to use effectively when presented with challenging life situations.

The program takes as a conceptual touchstone the research of Jessor (1982), indicating that health-compromising behaviors appear to be positively correlated. This condition suggests that a number of problem behaviors may be caused by the same set of basic factors. Thus, the set of underlying factors that lead to substance abuse, for example, may also lead to other problem behaviors, too, such as academic difficulty and depression. Therefore, the LST program seeks to target factors that are linked to a range of later dysfunctions and problem behaviors through training in skill sets that are both specific to the behaviors to be prevented (in this case, substance abuse) and are aimed at increasing general personal and social competence.

Social learning theory (Bandura, 1997) and problem behavior theory (Jessor & Jessor, 1977) theoretically undergird the program components. Substance abuse is conceptualized as being socially learned and functional, resulting from an interaction of personal and social-environmental factors and where modeling and social reinforcement play important roles. Learning new skills and how to apply them—that is, gaining personal and social competence that can be acted on—is the basic fulcrum for prevention in this program.

As cited in Botvin and Tortu (1988), objectives of the LST program are to (a) provide resistance skills against direct and indirect social pressures to drink excessively, smoke, or use marijuana; (b) help students to manage anxiety, especially social anxiety; (c) increase self-esteem, autonomy, self-confidence, and self-mastery; (d) increase awareness of the negative consequences of substance abuse; and (e) enhance attitudes and behaviors that support not using substances.

How is it done? The LST program includes three major parts: (a) general self-management skills, (b) social skills, and (c) information and skills specifically related to drug use. Each part contains a number of 45-minute sessions that can be delivered as an intensive mini-course or once a week. Skills are taught in a psychoeducation group format using strategies of instruction, demonstration, feedback, reinforcement, and practice.

Areas covered within the three major components include the following:

Specific knowledge and information. Sessions address knowledge and information that are particular to substances and substance abuse.

General decision-making skills. Sessions address making decisions and independent thinking and also how the media and advertising influence decisions.

General self-directed behavior change skills. Sessions address self-image and self-improvement. An 8-week self-improvement project is started at this point.

General coping with anxiety skills. Sessions address common anxiety-arousing situations and practicing skills and techniques for coping.

General social skills. Sessions address verbal and nonverbal communication skills, social skills aimed at overcoming shyness, social skills dealing with boy-girl relationships, and assertiveness training.

LST is delivered in 15 sessions in year 1, 10 sessions in year 2, and 5 sessions in year 3. A critically important facet of the program is incorporation of booster sessions following the main program (10 sessions for eighth graders and 5 sessions for ninth graders). These booster sessions are used to help thwart tendencies to regress and to reinforce the skills and their application.

What works? As mentioned, LST is one of the prevention programs evaluated by the *Blueprints* project as being both an excellent and a model program, and by OJJDP and SAMHSA as a model program. LST also has been evaluated by NIDA as an effective program and by the Department of Education–Safe Schools as exemplary, as well as by other evaluation agencies. In terms of program outcomes, over a dozen studies consistently demonstrate that LST dramatically reduces gateway drug use. That is, the program has been shown to reduce the rate of increase in target behaviors (e.g., smoking) in program participants, or in the proportion of adolescents in the program manifesting the behaviors, compared to those in comparison groups. Cross-cultural studies show that LST is effective with a diverse range of adolescents from different cultures. Moreover, results indicate that the program results are durable, and that the program is effective whether it is delivered by teachers, peer leaders, or health professionals.

More specifically, averaging outcomes over several studies, LST has been found to cut tobacco, alcohol, and marijuana use from 50% to 75%, with long-term follow-up results (6 years post program) showing that LST cuts polydrug use up to 66%, reduces pack-a-day smoking by 25%, and decreases the use of inhalants, narcotics, and hallucinogens. Last, LST is cost effective. According to a study by Lee, Drake, Pennucci, Miller, and Anderson (2013) for the Washington State Institute for Public Policy, communities using the LST middle school program attain a $50 benefit for each $1 invested.

Why does it work? LST is a carefully constructed program that matches its objectives with its methodology. It is set within a sophisticated research design that allows for testing immediate outcome effects, as well as durability and replicability and has included both pilot studies and large-scale prevention trials. A variety of outcome measures is used, including self-report questionnaires and saliva samples. The inclusion of training and education in both drug-specific and in generic competencies acknowledges that trying to prevent one specific set of behaviors alone is but a partial approach; rather, programs need to be more comprehensive as there is no single and direct route between etiology and effect in mental health and educational prevention programs. The use of psychoeducation groups that include peer participation resonates well with adolescents. The program curriculum is clearly developed, training for group leaders is thorough, parental support for the program is intentionally sought and maintained, and ongoing support and consultation is made available for program implementers.

Implications for counselors and other helpers. The LST program relies on methods and intervener skills that are central to counselor training, role, and function. The use of psychoeducation groups connects with a dominant group work application for counselors in all settings (Conyne, Wilson, & Ward, 1997). As Albee and Gullotta (1997) observed about group methods, in general,

> Group can provide a simple, sustained kind of human friendship where the act of genuine, honest, trusting, and empathic caring has great growth promoting power. (p. 18)

Training and consulting with others, such as teachers, and training and supervising others, such as students and paraprofessionals, are critically important activities for counselors in the schools. Collaborating with parents, so important in the LST program, is a main-line counselor function within the schools. Fitting the program within the ongoing school environment is a task that school counselors are educated to do as part of any comprehensive and developmental school counseling program. In short, the LST prevention program affords a close and comfortable match with the school counseling mission.

Seattle Social Development Project

What is the Social Development Research Group? The Seattle Social Development Research Group (SDRG; 2012) is an interdisciplinary prevention research team located at the University of Washington that for over 30 years has pursued a mission to investigate and promote healthy behaviors and positive behaviors across diverse populations of school children. See the "Interview Notes," below, that highlight the SDRG.

The Social Development Research Group Interview Notes with Kevin Haggerty, PhD by Perry Firth

Context

To provide another voice on the application of a holistic model of wellness and prevention and an ecological orientation toward development, we decided to take advantage of the proximity of the Social Development Research Group (SDRG), which is a Seattle based, University of Washington, School of Social Work set of programs that is comprised of an interdisciplinary team of researchers interested in promoting healthy and positive behaviors in general and positive social development in particular. The Seattle Social Development Project is part of the SDRG. The following narrative is based on an interview with the Group's associate director, Dr. Kevin Haggerty. It will touch on developmental contexts, changes in the prevention field, changes in social media, and the projects that Dr. Haggerty is most excited about.

Interview Notes

Risk Factors and Developmental Context

The SDRG conducts research into risk and protective factors, and has identified certain factors that increase risk for negative outcomes like drug abuse, school dropout delinquency, violence, teen pregnancy, and depression. When asked if he felt that there were certain risks most likely to produce negative child outcomes, Dr. Haggerty responded that risk needs to be placed in a developmental context. A factor which provides the most risk in one developmental time period, may not pose the most risk in another. For example, the family is the most important institution during early childhood. Therefore, family conflict during this time period is a heightened risk factor. During adolescence friends become an important socializing force in a young which means that behaviors like drug use are influenced by their friends use. Another developmental factor is early use. For example, teens who begin drinking before age 15 are twice as likely to develop alcohol abuse or dependence in early adulthood than those who wait to initiate use. It's clear that the development of risk is very linked to developmental context.

Positive Factors and Developmental Context

As with risk, protective factors must be viewed within a developmental framework. What factor is most protective, according to Dr. Haggerty, depends on where children are in their development. Protective factors which increase the likelihood of positive youth development include opportunities for meaningful involvement with positive influences, skills to be involved, and recognition for involvement. These three conditions promote strong bonds to supportive people. This bond contributes to young people following positive norms and expectations. It's worth noting that gangs can provide many of these factors, too, which helps to explain their appeal to struggling youth. Therefore, wellness and prevention interventions must fill that need for connection, something the SDRG does through implementing interventions that capitalize on and increase protective factors and social bonding.

Change in Prevention Field

Thanks to their strong guiding theory, the SDRG has been practicing and researching since the 1980s, long enough for their orientation and methods to have evolved. Today some of their research operates from a "cells to neighborhood" perspective. For example, they are exploring genetic and epigenetic influences on substance abuse as well as the gene/environment interaction predicting substance abuse.

Social Media

It is clear that the field of wellness and prevention has been changing, and will continue to do so. When asked where he thought the prevention field was going, and what that might mean for young researchers and preventionists interested in this work, Dr. Haggerty discussed how changing technologies are altering how prevention is conceptualized. He pointed to an emerging area of research that is concerned with how social media can be used to combat social isolation, and another where technology can be used to recruit and implement parenting intervention programs.

Current Research That Excites: Communities That Care

While the Group has many different areas of research, we were interested in learning about which research Dr. Haggerty is currently most excited about. Acknowledging that this is a tough question, he narrowed his answer down to three projects in three different areas of ongoing work: Communities that Care, The Seattle Social Development Project (also known as Raising Healthy Children), and their family programs.

Communities that Care (CTC) targets adolescent problem behavior like alcohol and drug abuse using a "coalition-based approach" to prevention. It operates from a public health perspective, and true to the guiding theory of SDRG, emphasizes decreasing risk while strengthening protective factors. Implemented across five phases, it provides a framework for communities to implement evidence based programs to promote well-being. These interventions are picked based on community risk assessments that identify elevated risk factors, blunted protection and elevated problem behaviors (Haggerty & Shapiro, 2013).

Dr. Haggerty is enthusiastic about Communities that Care because the program embodies the entire philosophy of the working group and its data show that a prevention framework emphasizing risk and protective factors can lead to a third less initiation into drinking, drug use and delinquency. Moreover, technology can be harnessed to increase its dissemination.

Seattle Social Development Project

This project was described as being exciting because it shows that when teachers are taught to teach better, parents to parent better, and kids are helped to develop and use social-emotional skills, long-term benefits are seen in education, mental health, and later SES variables. Results demonstrate a breadth of outcomes, and are another clear example of the guiding theory of the group in action.

Family Programs

Dr. Haggerty is currently particularly interested in family programs which harness a model that allows self-directed use. An example is 'Staying Connected With Your Teen' a self administered intervention which strengthens family connection and skills to reduce violent behavior, risky sexual behavior, and substance use initiation.

Lessons Learned

Dr. Haggerty talked about the importance of including key leaders who control resources in the Communities that Care approach.. He noted that prevention is a long term proposition, it can take 5–10 years to achieve a collective impact on community outcomes. Moreover, building frameworks for communities and schools is very important, something that a risk and protective orientation is effective in providing.

The SDRG has identified protective factors that mitigate risk, which are: (a) bonding to pro-social families, school and peers, and (b) clear standards and norms to guide behavior. Programs sponsored by the SDRG, such as the Seattle Social Development Project and some 20 others, include strategies to enhance these protective factors. Program examples are Community Youth Development Study (CYDS), which is grounded in community development approaches; Evidence-2Success, which is aimed at children and families in disadvantaged urban areas;

and Raising Health Children (RHC), which uses a variety of interactive learning approaches to involve students. These and all other programs of the SDRG center on providing opportunities for involvement in positive roles, skill development to support that participation, and regularized systems to recognize and reinforce pro-social involvement.

What is the Seattle Social Development Project? The Seattle Social Development Project (SSDP) is one of the suite of SDRG programs that began in 1981 to study developmental pathways that contribute to both positive and to problem behavior. It also is a universal, comprehensive, evidence-based, and longitudinal wellness and preventive intervention that targets multiple risk and protective factors in both home and school. The SSDP was expanded in 1985 to include 808 fifth graders from 18 Seattle area schools. The Intergenerational Project (TIP) is underway to study children of the members of the SSDP, allowing for examination of child rearing practices and contributing to cross-generational knowledge.

The SSDP intends to reduce risk factors in childhood for drug abuse, school failure, and delinquency while seeking to increase protective factors, such as pro-social bonds, commitment to school, and attachment. It also is based on the conception that many of the same risk factors (e.g., poor and inconsistent family management practices, peer rejection) predict multiple poor outcomes, such as substance abuse, teen pregnancy, and school dropout. That is, as has been observed earlier in this book, that when preventing academic and socioemotive problems there is no single and direct linkage between one cause and one effect; rather, multiple casual factors may interact to yield any of a range of outcomes.

SSDP is based on the social development model (Hawkins, Catalano, & Miller, 1992), where strong bonds (attachment, commitment, and belief) are considered to be essential protective factors that serve to moderate social norms about childhood maladaptive behavior, such as delinquent acts. According to the model, the positive bonding of children is a function of opportunities provided within the family and classroom, possessing necessary skills to interact successfully in these environments, and for pro-social behavior to be recognized and reinforced. The social development model further holds that changing a developmental trajectory toward negative outcomes is dependent on early and sustained programmatic intervention.

How is it done? SSDP can be used for the general population of young children in the first through sixth grades. It also is appropriate for use with high-risk children from low socioeconomic conditions and with low school achievement.

SSDP emphasizes a combination of parent and teacher training. The program is intended to be developmentally appropriate throughout the application period and to reduce early conduct problems, academic failure, and peer rejection. These factors are all considered as antecedents for future dysfunctional behavior and other negative outcomes.

Parental training is presented in classes offered optionally in first to third grade, in collaboration with school and parent councils. During first and second grades, seven sessions of the "Catch 'Em Being Good" program is provided. This family management program assists parents to set appropriate expectations for child behavior, improve their monitoring of child behavior, and to support parents' use of consistent disciplinary practices. During the second and third grades, the four-session "How to Help Your Child Succeed in School" program is provided to encourage parents to improve their own communication practices, their involvement with their children, and their interaction with teachers. These sessions also address how parents can better support their children's learning, mastery of math and reading skills, and to create positive learning environments in the home. During the fifth and sixth grades, five sessions are made available to help develop family positions on drug use and to reinforce children's application of refusal skills they are learning.

Teachers receive training that focuses on proactive classroom management, cooperative learning, and interactive methods. They learn strategies for establishing clear expectations and rules, along with rewards for compliance. They discover how to organize small group learning activities, where heterogeneity is included, as an important method for increasing students' social skills and their participation and connection with peers. First-grade teachers also find out how to teach students better communication skills, negotiation, decision making, and conflict-resolution skills through the *Interpersonal Cognitive Problem Solving* (ICPS) curriculum developed by Shure and Spivack (1988). Sixth-grade teachers learn how to present refusal skills training as related to peer pressure and substance abuse.

What works? SSDP has been evaluated positively by several external sources. It has been accorded excellent status by the American Youth Policy Forum, Center for Mental Health Services, Communities That Care, National Institute of Drug Abuse (NIDA), among others. It has been judged as Promising by the Center for Substance Abuse Prevention (CASP) Blueprints, by the Department of Education-Safe Schools, as Highly Promising by Title V (OJJDP), and as a Model 1 program by the Surgeon General's Report of 2001.

A number of program evaluations have been conducted of the SSDP. These have tended to show that the project improves school performance, family relationships, and student involvement with drugs/alcohol at various class grades. Some sample results follow.

Evaluations conducted at the end of second grade of project students compared to controls, showed that white boy students exhibited lower levels of aggression and externalizing of antisocial behaviors and that white girl students exhibited lesser amounts of self-destructive behaviors. At the end of fifth grade project students, compared to controls, engaged in lower initiation of alcohol use and of delinquency behaviors, realized closer attachment to their family and to school, and improvements were realized in family management practices and family communication. Continuing with this longitudinal developmental study, at the end of Grade 11 project students, compared to controls, demonstrated reductions in drunk behavior and in drinking and driving, as well as reduced involvement in sexual activity and in violent behaviors. Presently, the SSDP is involved with an intergenerational study, a 5-year project aimed at understanding effects of SSDP participation on the children of those participants. This example of longitudinal study over many years is a very positive aspect of the SSDP.

Why does it work? The SSDP is based on a well-developed underpinning theory, connected with bonding and the understanding that a set of risk and protective factors may be associated with a range of potential outcomes. The project is carefully constructed to articulate the theory in practice, with an interconnected application of both school and family preventive activities. It is set within a developmental longitudinal research design allowing for tracking of long-term changes. The SSDP establishes itself solidly as a competency enhancement approach, integrated within multiple contexts and levels. The knowledge, attitudes, and skills that are focused on in the project are pertinent to situational needs and to developmental age progression. It, and other programs of the SDRG, provides an outstanding example of how sound theory can be translated into effective application.

Implications for counselors and other helpers. The importance of competency enhancement as a route to wellness and prevention of deficits is of natural attraction to counselors and many other practitioners. Serving in a training and consultative role is becoming of greater familiarity and importance. For instance, students of mine provided consultation and training to university faculty in how to establish and maintain classroom environments that support small group instruction, and they also taught faculty how to facilitate small group interaction. Seeking to improve classroom and family systems, as well as students/children as they move between both of these important settings, reinforces the importance of ecological connections. Following the progress of trainees across a developmental time period is a research approach that wellness and prevention counselors need to take increased advantage of as they seek to document the durability of growth and change.

Olweus Bullying Prevention Program

What is the Olweus Bullying Prevention Program? This program was initiated in the 1980s by Dr. Dan Olweus, a research professor of psychology affiliated with the Research Center for Health Promotion (HEMIL) at the University of Bergen in Norway. The program consists of multi-level, multi-component components designed to reduce and prevent school bullying in elementary and middle schools. Moreover, it seeks to improve peer relations, make schools safer and more positive settings for learning and development. Supporting goals include increasing awareness and knowledge about bullying, involving parents and teachers in bullying prevention, providing support and protection to victims, and creating clear rules against bullying.

A theoretical proposition underlying the OBPP is that bullying needs to be addressed through an intentional and planned restructuring of the social environment of a school. This concept is consistent with other outstanding bullying prevention programs, such as that of Orpinas and Horne (2006). Existing structures and processes that reward or support anti-social behavior, including bullying, are targeted for change in preference of pro-social ones (Blueprints for Healthy Youth Development, 2014).

How is it done? The OBPP is a system-wide approach that is implemented at four ecological levels: (a) individual, (b) classroom, (c) school, and (c) community. *Individual* components include developing individual plans for students and intervening with students with those having a history of bullying and/or victimization. *Classroom* components include defining and enforcing rules against bullying, discussions and activities to reinforce anti-bullying values and norms and active parental involvement in the program. The *school* level components consist of an assessment of the nature and prevalence of bullying in the school, the formation of a committee to coordinate the prevention program, introducing school rules against bullying, and development of a system ensuring adult supervision of students outside of the classroom. The *community* level components include involving community members on a Bullying Prevention Coordinating Committee, developing partnerships with community members to support a school's program, helping to spread antibullying messages and principles of best practice in the community.

What works? The OBPP is an evidence-based program that is evaluated as Promising in the *Blueprints for Healthy Youth Development* (2014), a Model program by the Substance Abuse and Mental Health Services Administration, and Effective by the Office of Juvenile Justice and Delinquency Prevention.

Statistics collated from the OBPP Web site (Hazelden Foundation, 2014) show how successful implementation of the OBPP can reduce school bullying. Outcomes reported include:

- Fifty percent or more reductions in student reports of being bullied and bullying others; peer and teacher ratings of bullying problems have yielded similar results
- Significant reductions in student reports of general antisocial behavior such as school bullying, vandalism, school violence, fighting, theft, and truancy
- Significant improvements in the classroom social climate as reflected in students' reports of improved order and discipline, more positive social relationships, and more positive attitudes toward schoolwork and school
- Greater support for students who are bullied, and stronger, more effective interventions for students who bully

Why does it work? Several factors contribute to the OBPP program's effectiveness, and these are implicit within the program's goals and methods. The program is designed to match and assist varying developmental levels of students, with versions aimed at elementary, middle school, and high school placements. Its ecological orientation also reaches the community. This allows for a comprehensive, system-wide implementation. The program also is administered universally across the school, with all students participating in most of its aspects. It allows for tailoring of program implementation so that higher risk students, either identified as being the object of bullying or as engaged with bullying, receive more individualized and higher program dosage. Readiness of the school for the OBPP is taken into account through use of an assessment questionnaire designed for that purpose. Carefully constructed and executed program materials, program training, program monitoring, and program evaluation all are accorded high value and are accompany program implementation. Small group discussions and interactive activities, such as role playing and the Bullying Circle Exercise (Olweus Bullying Prevention Program, 2012, 2014), are used to engage program participants.

Implications for counselors and other helpers. The OBPP clearly illustrates the importance of taking a system-wide approach to solving and preventing complex designated problems, such as bullying. Counselor training programs need to provide students with the necessary theoretical and practical knowledge and skills to be able to deliver not only individual-level interventions but, also, interventions that span other ecological levels: interpersonal, group, organizational, system-wide, and community. A comprehensive, system-wide focus is mandated, therefore, upon which the OBPP is based.

Conclusion: School Programs

Many in our society blame the schools for the problems of children. Others blame families for the problems of children that are brought to school. Neither is right and neither is totally wrong. The difficulties with each position are that blaming others is unproductive and harmful, and the problems of concern germinate from multiple sources in a variety of interconnected ways. It might be more accurate to state that the problems of many youth—manifested in such domains of academic performance, social relationships, physical health, attitudes toward self and others, management of feelings—arise from the mesosystems of life, the intersections and disconnects between main units such as the home and the school (McMahon, Mason, Daluga-Guenther, & Ruiz, 2014).

Therefore, it is a somewhat arbitrary analysis in which we are engaged in this and the other chapters of section II. Examining wellness and prevention programs aimed separately at the family and the school is artificial in the "real world," failing to appropriately acknowledge the dynamic interplay between school and family that contributes so strongly to health and disorder. The same observation holds for community and work settings, the subjects of the next chapter of this section.

Yet, we know that the school setting itself can be critically important to youth development, and wellness and prevention counselors can make a significant contribution at this level. The necessary overriding goal is to create throughout a school a healthy and safe environment.

School Counselors Are Needed for Wellness and Prevention Counseling in the Schools

Within the schools, certainly school counselors (and school psychologists, school social workers, and an increasing number of counseling psychologists) are the natural role occupants who are in position to make such a positive difference in their work with others, both in and out of the school. Recent research on adding just one school counselor intern to a staff documents clear positive effects, including reductions in disruptive behavior of students (20% for boys, 29% for girls), and a rise in their test scores (Collins, 2014). Yet, it is no secret that in many school districts school counselors do not exist, the unwitting victims of budget cuts and/or of misplaced priorities. Alarmingly, the national average number of school counselors to students is reaches nearly twice that of 1:250 ratio recommended by the American Counseling Association (Bidwell, 2013). In still other cases, school counselors are performing tasks that are inconsistent with their desired role. They should not, for instance, be yoked to clerical record keeping, supervising study halls, and performing disciplinary actions (among many other inappropriate activities).

The American School Counselor Association (ASCA) has developed a national model to provide a framework for school counseling programs (American School Counselor Association, 2014). This model is highly consistent with wellness and prevention counseling. It contains four interrelated components: (a) foundation, (b) delivery system, (c) management systems, and (d) accountability. The model is an organized, systematized, and comprehensive effort to produce student development in interconnected domains (academic, career development, personal/social development). One responsibility set forth for the school counselor in this model is to collaborate with teachers to present proactive, wellness, and prevention-based guidance curriculum lessons. Taken in total, the systematic and developmental role called for in this model should be expected to yield wellness and prevention effects.

The programs examined in this section fit very well within the school counselor role and function and are consistent with the ASCA developmental model. Providing life skills training for students, organizing a healthy and safe school environment that also promotes organization and clarity, and training teachers and parents in important family- and school-based skills offer school counselors (and other school personnel) tested designs that can be adapted to fit local circumstances.

A blueprint for action exists, waiting to be implemented more fully and consistently.

Issues for Reflection and Discussion

School

1. Imagine you and colleagues just received a Healthy School Grant. This is a dropout prevention grant to occur in three inner-city middle schools, with attention to the high school to which these middle schools "feed." We are intending to combine aspects of student life skills training, teacher–parent training, and ecological transition. All is well and good, except today is October 10, the funding is yet to be released, the public schools have been in session since August 27, and no staff can be hired until the grant contract is finalized!

Organize with a partner, or with a small group (whichever best fits your situation). Discuss this situation in general, and then more specifically develop ideas about the questions below: (30 minutes)

a. What do you think should be done during this lull in the action?
b. How could aspects of the three school programs discussed in this chapter be drawn from?
c. Finally, share your ideas with others and look for commonalities and differences. (30 minutes)

2. How can school counselors counter the forces so strongly in place in many school systems that serve to keep them from doing wellness and prevention counseling? Give an example.

3. There has been some work done that supports the idea that a whole school and its surrounding community be viewed a one unit of change, that is, where school and community are partners. Is this a feasible approach to take? What are the some pros and cons? Develop a list to capture these competing factors to share with others.

Family

4. How does family life affect functioning in other domains, such as school? Identify some ways. How can preventive counselors take advantage of that influence to develop effective family-based programs?

5. Which of the three family-based prevention programs described in this chapter do you resonate with the most? Why? Again, discuss your choice with a partner and compare notes. Pay close attention to what you may be saying about yourselves in the process.

6. Consider your own family history and dynamics (choose your family of origin, your present family, or another connection with people that feels like a "family"). How are you affected by this history and dynamics? What is the openness of your family culture to mental health service involvement? How might a

wellness and prevention program best be introduced so that members of your family might be attracted to it? Write a one-page analysis paper to share with others later.

References

Albee, G., & Gullotta, T. (Eds.). (1997). *Primary prevention works.* Thousand Oaks, CA: Sage.

Alexander, J., Barton, C., Gordon, D., Grotpeter, J., Hansson, K., Harrison, R.,. . . & Sexton, T. (1998). *Blueprints for violence prevention: Book 3. Functional Family Therapy*. Boulder, CO: Center for the Study and Prevention of Violence.

Alexander, J., & Parsons, B. (1973). Short-term behavior interventions with delinquent families: Impact on family process and recidivism. *Journal of Abnormal Psychology, 81*, 219–225. doi:10.1037/h0034537

Alexander, J., Robbins, M., & Sexton, T. (2000). Family-based interventions with older, at-risk youth: From promise to proof to practice. *The Journal of Primary Prevention, 21*(2), 185–205. doi:10.1023/a:1007031219209

Alexander, J. F., Waldron, H.B., Robbins M.S., & Neeb, A. A. (2013). Functional Family Therapy for adolescent behavior problems. *Contemporary Family Therapy, 35*(4), 806–807. doi:10.1007/s10591–013–9281–3

American School Counselor Association. (2014). *ASCA national model.* Retrieved from http://www.ascanationalmodel.org/

Bandura, A. (1997). *Self-efficacy: The exercise of control.* New York, NY: Freeman.

Bauer, N., Lozano, P., & Rivara, F.P. (2007). The effectiveness of the Olweus Bullying Prevention Program in public middle schools: A controlled trial. *Journal of Adolescent Health, 40*, 266–274. doi:10.1016/j.jadohealth.2006.10.005

Bidwell, A. (2013, September 16). Lack of funds leave school counselors struggling to find balance. *US News & World Report.* Retrieved from http://www.usnews.com/news/articles/2013/09/16/lack-of-funds-leave-school-counselors-struggling-to-find-balance

Bierman, K., Coie, J., Dodge, K., Greenberg, M., Lochman, J., & McMahon, R. (1996, May). *An initial evaluation of the FAST Track Program.* Paper presented at the 5th National Prevention Conference, Tysons Corner, VA.

Blueprints for Healthy Youth Development. (2014). Center for the Study and Prevention of Violence. Boulder, CO.

Botvin, G. (2011). *What demographic does LST work for?* Retrieved from http://lifeskilltraining.com/faq.php?id=4

Botvin, G. J., & Griffin, K.W. (2012, April 11–14). *Long-term outcomes from Blueprints model programs: Life Skills Training.* Paper presented at Blueprints for Violence Prevention Conference, San Antonio, TX.

Botvin, G.J., Griffin, K.W., & Nichols, T.R. (2006). Preventing youth violence and delinquency through a universal school-based prevention approach. *Prevention Science, 7*, 403–408. doi:10.1007/s11121–006–0057-y

Botvin, G.J., Griffin, K.W., Paul, E., & Macaulay, A.P. (2003). Preventing tobacco and alcohol use among elementary school students through Life Skills Training. *Journal of Child & Adolescent Substance Abuse, 12*, 1–17. doi:10.1300/J029v12n04_01

Botvin, G., & Kantor, L. (2000). Preventing alcohol and tobacco use through life skills Training. *Alcohol Research and Health*, 24, 250–257. Retrieved from http://pubs.niaaa.nih.gov/publications/arh341/toc34_1.htm

Botvin, G.J., Schinke, S.P., Epstein, J.A., Diaz, T., & Botvin, E. (1995). Effectiveness of culturally focused and generic skills training approaches to alcohol and drug abuse prevention among minority adolescents: Two-year follow up results. *Psychology of Addictive Behaviors, 9*(3), 183–194. doi:10.1037//0893–164x.9.3.183

Botvin, G., & Tortu, S. (1988). Preventing adolescent substance abuse through life skills training. In R. Price, E. Cowen, R. Lorion, & J. Ramos-McKay (Eds.), *14 ounces of prevention: A casebook for practitioners* (pp. 98–110). Washington, DC: American Psychological Association. doi:10.1037/10064–008

Branden-Muller, L. R., & Elias, M. J. (1991). Catalyzing the primary prevention revolution in the schools: The role of school psychologists. *Journal of Educational and Psychological Consultation, 2*(1), 73–88. doi:10.1207/s1532768xjepc0201_5

Brown, M., & Bolen, L. (2003). Introduction to the special issue: School-based health centers. *Psychology in the Schools, 40*, 245–251. doi:10.1002/pits.10087

Catalano, R. F., Berglund, L. M., Ryan, J. A., Lonczak, H. S., & Hawkins, J. D. (2002). Positive youth development in the United States: Research findings on evaluations of positive youth development programs. *Prevention and Treatment, 5*(1). doi:10.1037//1522–3736.5.1.515a

Center for the Study of Social Policy. (2012). *Strengthening families: A protective factor framework.* Retrieved from http://www.cssp.org/reform/strengthening-families/the-basics/protective-factors

Collins, N. (2014, September 25). School counselors do more than you think. *Pacific Standard: The Science of Society.* Retrieved from http://www.psmag.com/navigation/politics-and-law/school-counselors-youd-think-91339/

Conduct Problems Prevention Group. (1992). A developmental and clinical model for the prevention of conduct disorder: The FAST Track Program. *Development and Psychopathology, 4*, 509–527. doi:10.1017/s0954579400004855

Conduct Problems Prevention Research Group. (2007). Fast Track randomized controlled trial to prevent externalizing psychiatric disorders: Findings from grades 3 to 9. *Journal of the American Academy of Child & Adolescent Psychiatry, 46*(10), 1250–1262. doi:10.1097/chi.0b013e31813e5d39

Conduct Problems Prevention Research Group. (2010). The Fast Track Project: The prevention of severe conduct problems in school-age youth. In R.C. Murrihy, A.D. Kidman, & T.H. Ollendick (Eds.), *Handbook of Clinical Assessment and Treatment of Conduct Problems in Youth, 4*, 407-433. New York: Springer. doi:10.1007/978-1-4419-6297-3_16

Conduct Problems Prevention Research Group. (2011). The effects of the Fast Track preventive intervention on the development of conduct disorder across childhood. *Child Development, 82*, 331–345. doi:10.1111/j.1467–8624.2010.01558.x

Conyne, R.K., & Mazza, J. (2007). Ecological group work applied to schools. *Journal for Specialists in Group Work, 32*, 19–29.

Conyne, R., Wilson, F. R., & Ward, D. (1997). *Comprehensive group work: What it means & how to teach it.* Alexandria, VA: American Counseling Association.

Foster, E. M., & Jones, D. (2007). The economic analysis of prevention: An illustration involving children's behavior problems. *Journal of Mental Health Policy and Economics, 10*, 165–175. Retrieved from http://www.icmpe.net/fulltext.php? volume=10&page=165&year=2007&num=4&name=Foster%20EM

Greenberg, M., Lochman, J., & McMahon, R. (1996, May). *An initial evaluation of the Fast Track Program.* Paper presented at the 5th National Prevention Conference, Tysons Corner, VA.

Greenberg, M.T., Weissberg, R.P., O'Brien, M.U., Zins, J.E., Fredericks, L., Resnik, H., & Elias, M.J. (2003). Enhancing school-based prevention and youth development through coordinated social, emotional, and academic learning. *American Psychologist, 58*, 466–474. doi:10.1037/0003–066x.58.6–7.466

Haggerty, K. P., & Kosterman, R. (2012, June). Helping parents prevent problem behavior. *Better: Evidence-Based Education, 4*(3). Retrieved from http://www.betterevidence.org

Haggerty, K. P., & Shapiro, V. B. (2013). Science-based prevention through Communities That Care: A model of social work practice for public health. *Social Work in Public Health, 28*, 349–365. doi:10.1080/19371918.2013.774812

Hawkins, J. D., Catalano, R., & Kosterman, R. (1999). Preventing adolescent health-risk behaviors by strengthening protection during childhood. *Archives of Pediatric Medicine, 153*, 226–234. doi:10.1001/archpedi.153.3.226

Hawkins, J.D., Catalano, R., & Miller, J.Y. (1992). Risk and protective factors for alcohol and other drug problems in adolescence and early adulthood: Implications for substance abuse prevention. *Psychological Bulletin, 112*, 64–105. doi:10.1037/0033–2909.112.1.64

Hawkins, J. D., Catalano, R., Morrison, D., O'Donnell, J., Abbott R., & Day, L. (1992). The Seattle Social Development Project: Effects of the first four years on protective factors and problem behaviors. In J. McCord & R. Tremblay (Eds.), *The prevention of antisocial behavior in children* (pp. 139–161). New York, NY: Guilford.

Hazelden Foundation. (2014). *Violence prevention works: Safer schools, safer communities*. Retrieved from http://www.violencepreventionworks.org/public/index.page

Herrenkohl, T.I., Hemphill, S.A., Mason, W.A., Toumbourou, J.W., & Catalano, R.F. (2012). Predictors and responses to the growth in physical violence during adolescence: A comparison of students in Washington State and Victoria, Australia. *American Journal of Orthopsychiatry, 82*(1), 41–49. doi:10.1111/j.1939–0025.2011.01139.x

Jessor, R. (1982). Critical issues in research on adolescent health promotion. In T. Coates, A. Pederson, & C. Perry (Eds.), *Promoting adolescent health: A dialogue on research and practice* (pp. 447–465). New York, NY: Academic Press. doi:10.1016/b978-0–12-177380–9.50036–0

Jessor, R., & Jessor, S. (1977). *Problem-behavior and psychosocial development: A longitudinal study of youth*. New York, NY: Academic Press.

Jones, D., Godwin, J., Dodge, K.A., Bierman, K.L., Coi, J. D., Greenberg, M. T., & Pinderhughes, E.E. (2010). Impact of the Fast Track prevention program on health services use by conduct-problem youth. *Pediatrics, 125*, 130–136. doi:10.1542/peds.2009–0322

Kolbe, L., Collins, J., & Cortese, P. (1997). Building the capacity of schools to improve the health of the nation: A call for assistance from psychologists. *American Psychologist, 52*, 256–265. doi:10.1037//0003–066x.52.3.256

Kumpfer, K.L., & Alvarado, R. (2003). Family-strengthening approaches for the prevention of youth problem behaviors. *American Psychologist, 58*, 457–465. doi:10.103 7/0003-066x.58.6–7.457

Lee, S., Aos, S., Drake, E., Pennucci, A., Miller, M., & Anderson, L. (2012). *Return on investment: Evidence-based options to improve statewide outcomes* (Document No. 12–04–1201). Olympia, WA: Washington State Institute for Public Policy. Retrieved from http://www.wsipp.wa.gov/

Lochman, J.E., Bierman, K.L., Coie, J.D., Dodge, K.A., Greenberg, M.T., McMacho, R.J., & Pinderhughes, E.E. (2010). The difficulty of maintaining positive intervention effects: A look at disruptive behavior, deviant peer relations, and social skills during the middle school years. *The Journal of Early Adolescence, 30*, 593–624. doi:10.1177/0272431609340513

Lonczak, H. (2002). Effects of the Seattle Social Development Project on sexual behavior, pregnancy, and sexually transmitted disease outcomes by age 21 years. *Archives of Pediatric & Adolescent Medicine, 156*(5), 438–447. doi:10.1001/archpedi.156.5.43

Matsumoto, Y., Sofronoff, K., & Sanders, M. R. (2010). Investigation of the effectiveness and social validity of the Triple P Positive Parenting Program in Japanese society. *Journal of Family Psychology, 24*(1), 87–91. doi:10.1037/a0018181

McMahon, H. G., Mason, E., Daluga-Guenther, N., & Ruiz, A. (2014). An ecological model of professional school counseling. *Journal of Counseling & Development, 92*, 459–471.

McMahon, T., Ward, N., Pruett, M., Davidson, L., & Griffith, E. (2000). Building full-service schools: Lessons learned in the development of interagency collaboratives. *Journal of Educational and Psychological Consultation, 11*, 65–92. doi:10.1207/s1532768Xjepc1101_05

Meyers, A. B., & Swerdlik, M. E. (2003). School-based health centers: Opportunities and challenges for school psychologists. *Psychology in the Schools, 40*(3), 253–264. doi:10.1002/pits.10085

National Registry of Evidence-Based Programs and Practices. (2014). *Triple P-Positive Parenting Program*. Retrieved from http://www.nrepp.samhsa.gov/ViewIntervention.aspx?id=1

Nowak, C., & Heinrichs, N. (2008). A comprehensive meta-analysis of Triple P-Positive Parenting Program using hierarchical linear modeling: Effectiveness and moderating variables. *Clinical Child & Family Psychology Review, 11*(3), 114–144. doi:10.1007/s10567–008–0033–0

O'Donnell, J., Hawkins, J. D., Catalano, R., Abbott, R., & Day, L. (1995). Preventing school failure, drug use, and delinquency among low-income children: Long-term intervention in elementary schools. *American Journal of Orthopsychiatry, 65*, 87–100. doi:10.1037/h0079598

Olweus, D. (1991). Bully/victim problems among schoolchildren: Basic facts and effects of a school based intervention program. In D.J. Pepler & K.H. Rubin (Eds.), *The development and treatment of childhood aggression* (pp. 411–448). Hillsdale, NJ: Erlbaum.

Olweus, D. (1992). Bullying among schoolchildren: Intervention and prevention. In R. D. V. Peters, R. J. McMahon, & V. L. Quinsey (Eds.), *Aggression and violence throughout the life span* (pp. 100–125). Newbury Park, CA: Sage.

Olweus, D. (1993). *Bullying at school: What we know and what we can do*. Cambridge, MA: Blackwell.

Olweus Bullying Prevention Program. (2012). *Bullying circle exercise* [Handout]. Retrieved from http://www.pabar.org/public/education/projectpeace/materials/Bullying %20 Circle%20Exercise.pdf

Olweus Bullying Prevention Program. (2014). Retrieved from http://www.blueprintsprograms.com/factSheet.php?pid=17ba0791499db908433b80f37c5fbc89b870084b

Orpinas, P., & Horne, A. (2006). *Bullying prevention: Creating a positive school climate and developing social competence*. Retrieved from http://www.apa.org/pubs/books/4317082.aspx

Oxley, D. (2000). The school reform movement: Opportunities for community psychology. In J. Rappaport & E. Seidman (Eds.), *Handbook of community psychology* (pp. 565–590). New York, NY: Kluwer. doi:10.1007/978–1–4615–4193–6_24

Prinz, R. J., Sanders, M. R., Shapiro, C. J., Whitaker, D. J., & Lutzker, J. R. (2009). Population based prevention of child maltreatment: The U.S. Triple P System Population Trial. *Prevention Science, 10*, 1–13. doi:10.1007/s11121–009–0123–3

Ross, M., Powell, S., & Elias, M. (2002). New roles for school psychologists: Addressing the social and emotional learning needs of students. *School Psychology Review, 31*, 43–52.

Sanders, M. R. (2008). Triple P-Positive Parenting Program as a public health approach to strengthening parenting. *Journal of Family Psychology, 22*(4), 506–517. doi:10.1037/0893–3200.22.3.506

Seattle Social Development Research Group. (2012). SDRG projects. Retrieved from http://sdrg.org/projects.asp

Sexton, T. L., & Alexander, J. (1999). *Functional Family Therapy: Principles of clinical intervention, assessment, and implementation*. Henderson, NV: RCH Enterprises.

Sexton, T., & Alexander, J. (2002). Functional Family Therapy for at-risk adolescents and their families. In F. Kaslow (Ed.), *Comprehensive handbook of psycho-therapy: Vol. 2. Cognitive-behavioral approaches* (pp. 117–140). New York, NY: John Wiley.

Shure, M., & Spivack, G. (1988). Interpersonal cognitive problem solving. In R. Price, E. Cowen, R. Lorion, & J. Ramos-McKay (Eds.), *14 ounces of prevention: A casebook for practitioners* (pp. 69–82). Washington, DC: American Psychological Association. doi:10.1037/10064–000

Triple P Positive Parenting Program. (2014). *Triple P takes the guesswork out of parenting. Retrieved from* http://www.triplep.net/glo-en/home/

U.S. Surgeon General. (2011). *National Prevention Strategy*. Retrieved from http://www.surgeongeneral.gov/initiatives/prevention/strategy/

Washington State Institute for Public Policy. (2002). *Washington State's implementation of Functional Family Therapy for juvenile offenders: Preliminary findings* (Document No. 02–08–1201). Retrieved from http://www.wsipp.wa.gov/

7

RELATIONAL WELLNESS AND PREVENTION

Community and Workplace Programs

The Community Setting

This chapter focuses on effective programs in community and work settings. These are dominant settings for nearly all of us, and it is important to understand their connection with wellness and prevention counseling. Community and work settings are contained within the relational wellness level of the counseling for wellness and prevention model.

When considering wellness and prevention programs at this level, I am thinking of those more or less loosely organized levels that lie outside more tightly organized settings. Examples include neighborhoods, parks and recreation areas, religious centers, and music and art venues, and so on (see Figure 7.1). For the sake of discussion, I will refer to these as the community setting. Community settings strongly affect many aspects of everyday life. They make a difference in health, participation, and satisfaction. Everyone gets involved in developing and maintaining a healthy community.

Community-level wellness and prevention interventions combine individual and environmental change strategies (multi-component) across multiple settings to promote well-being and prevent dysfunction among population groups in a defined geographic location (Wandersman & Florin, 2003). These interventions typically include aspects of grassroots involvement, inter-organizational linkages, and improving community problem solving. The Spectrum of Prevention of the Prevention Institute (1999) indicates six comprehensive and interrelated strategies: (a) influencing policy and legislation, (b) changing organizational practices, (c) fostering coalitions and networking, (d) educating providers, (e) promoting community education, and (f) strengthening individual knowledge. Note that developing knowledge is but one of these six strategies, but it is the one that probably is most immediately considered by most professional mental health workers.

FIGURE 7.1 Urban park. Counseling for wellness and prevention occurs in communities.

Source: iStock photo

Community organization and social intervention (COSI; Gullotta & Bloom, 2003) is a major wellness and prevention we highlighted in chapter 3 that fits the community level especially well. It is targeted at "the collection of values, norms, processes, and behavior patterns within a community that organize, facilitate, and constrain the interactions among community members" (Mancini, Martin, & Bowen, 2003, p. 319). The social organization of a community directly impacts the capacity of a community to promote health and well-being of individuals and families living within it. Thus, we see in popular magazines various discussions of those communities considered to be the "best places to live," or the most attractive places to retire," or the "safest communities in America," and so forth.

Mancini et al. (2003) suggest that wellness and prevention effectiveness within communities is influenced substantially by "community capacity," a concept involving the willingness and ability of community members to connect with each other, to assume mutual responsibility, and to exert a collective competence aimed at reducing risks and promoting assets associated with health and with health promotion. Community capacity is realized through demonstrating a shared responsibility to produce obtainable health and prevention benefits.

Communities, of course, are complex settings. When considering introducing community-based wellness and prevention programs, counselors need to be mindful of the collaborative maxim, "Don't do *to* them, do *with* them." Likewise, interventions that are theory and evidence-based need to be adapted appropriately to fit within the social and culturally-relevant practices that characterize the community, with attention given to social disparities. Comprehensive programs also need to focus on risk reduction and strengths promotion (American Psychological Association, 2014a).

In this chapter portion you will read about three award-winning prevention programs that incorporate many of these strategies at the community level:

- *Big Brothers/Big Sisters of America (BBBSA)* (McGill, Mihalic, & Grotpeter, 1998; Public/Private Ventures, 2007), which uses both mentoring and case management approaches to assist primarily low-income youth from single parent homes.
- *Communities Mobilizing for Change on Alcohol (CMCA)* (Coalition for Evidence-Based Policy, 2013; Wagenaar et al., 1999; Wagenaar et al., 1998; Wagenaar, Murray, & Toomey, 2000), a community-organizing program to reduce adolescent access to alcohol through changing community policies and practices.
- *Families and Schools Together* (FAST, 2014; Crozier, Rokutani, Russet, Godwin, & Banks, 2010) is a multifamily group intervention developed by McDonald and initiated in 1990. It concentrates on relationship building among families, schools, and communities to increase the well-being of children and the self-efficacy of parents. (Note: FAST is not to be confused with the program described in chapter 6, FAST Track.)

Community Program Examples

Program Primary Wellness and Prevention Counseling Strategies

Big Brothers/Big Sisters of America: Education—mentoring, social competency facilitation, assisting development transitions

Communities Mobilizing for Change on Alcohol: COSI

Families and Schools Together (FAST): COSI, education, group, assisting developmental transitions

Big Brothers/Big Sisters of America

What is Big Brothers/Big Sisters of America? This wellness and prevention program is a national youth-service community-based organization that has been providing volunteer-based mentoring services to children and adolescents (age range from 6–18, typically) who are predominantly from low-income, single-parent households. The intervention was begun with the Big Sisters program in New York City in 1902; Big Brothers followed in 1904. Together, a network has been developed consisting of some 500 agencies located throughout the United States, and in 12 other countries throughout the world.

The overall purpose of Big Brothers/Big Sisters of America (BBBSA) is to help at-risk children, generally from single parent homes, to cope more effectively with their environment. BBBSA established basic requirements (called "standards") in 1922 to guide the one-to-one relationships of volunteers with children, as well as for how local agencies should operate. Eventually, these "standards" evolved into a set of Standards and Required Procedures for One-to-One Service. Compliance with these standards and procedures provides the foundation for how each agency throughout the country is to operate and lends consistency to the work of mentors with individual youth.

At the heart of the BBBSA approach to serving at-risk youth is what might be thought of as a non-prescription individual mentoring process. That is, this form of mentoring is not based on manually-driven steps and procedures, but on the development and maintenance of friendship and trust, a mining of the mutually shared experiences of everyday life that may later lead to learning and growth. Here, the quality of the mentoring relationship is vitally important. A caring adult who is not part of the family seeks to maintain a consistent availability and presence with a youth who is growing up in what might be thought of as adverse circumstances (e.g., one-parent family, low SES). The BBBSA belief is that the frequent and consistent involvement of a caring volunteer in a youth's life can serve a powerfully positive influence.

Since the 2004 edition of this book, BBBSA has extended its mentoring strategy to include a school-based program where mentors spend time with children in their school. School-based mentoring programs are the fastest growing form of mentoring in America today.

In this way, the conceptual framework for BBBSA is aligned with social control theory, where attachments to positive role models, commitment to socially appropriate goals, and involvement in conventional activities and experiences can serve a protective factor for youth. Such positive social bonding can buffer negative pressures and assist youth to refrain from involvement in problem behaviors and in delinquent pursuits.

How does it work? BBBSA is a community mentoring program accomplished through the careful construction of thousands of one-to-one mentoring relationships. In the program, an adult volunteer mentor (Big Brother or Big Sister) is intentionally matched with an at-risk child (Little Brother or Little Sister), with the goal of creating a warm, positive relationship that might then exert preventive effects. Two aspects of this match are important: (a) the appropriateness of the match itself and (b) the ongoing supervision of the match relationship that is provided by a professional staff member, who role is known as a case manager.

The youth's parent/guardian applies for their child to be matched with a mentor through a written application and child/parent interview. Potential mentors are screened by a BBBSA case worker through a personal interview, home visit, and criminal, background, and reference check to ensure that they are not a safety risk and are likely to form a positive relationship with the youth. Prior to a match being made, the youth and parent meet with the potential mentor; the match's completion requires the parent's approval.

The volunteer mentor generally meets with the child for 3–5 hours a week throughout the course of one year, and sometimes longer than one year. What occurs is not specified, except that activities (e.g., studying, cooking, playing sports) need to be in accord with the goals that were set when the match was created. These goals emerge from an extensive interview conducted by the case manager with the child and the parent/guardian. The overarching goal is to develop and maintain a mutually positive relationship through regular meetings between the mentor and child. Other more specific goals may be set, as well, related to such areas as general hygiene, peer relationships, learning a new skill, and academic performance. These goals and progress toward them are stipulated in an individual case plan that is maintained and updated by the case manager over time.

For the first year, BBBSA case workers maintain monthly contact with the mentor, as well as the youth and his or her parent, to insure a positive mentor-youth match, and to help resolve any problems in the relationship. Mentors are encouraged to form a supportive friendship with the youths, as opposed to modifying the youth's behavior or character.

The case manager oversees all aspects of the mentoring relationship, from forming the match through monitoring and terminating the relationship. An important part of the case manager role is to communicate about how things are going in and around the mentoring relationship with the volunteer, the child, and the parent/guardian. The *Standards and Required Procedures for One-to-One Service* establish the regularity of case manager contacts and communication. For instance, early in the match case manager contacts with volunteer and parent occur frequently, followed by monthly contacts during the year, and contact is made with the child at least quarterly. In all of aspects of their role, case managers are guided by the Standards, mentioned earlier.

What works? BBBSA has been judged by external reviewers very positively. It has been identified as a Model program by Blueprints for Violence Prevention and has been rated as Effective by the American Youth Policy Forum, the Center for Mental Health Services, Communities That Care, and Title V (OJDP), as a Promising program by the Center for Substance Abuse Prevention (CSAP), BBBSA has been endorsed by national evaluation associations. It is listed as a "social program that works" by the Coalition for Evidence-Based Policy (2012), and as a "program that works" by the Promising Practices Network (2009).

Much of the evidence supporting the program is in the form of anecdotal reports from a range of parties over decades, including parents, children, teachers, and case managers. Indirectly, support emerges from sets of resiliency studies examining the role of caring adults. For instance, Werner (1996) found in her long-term longitudinal study in Hawaii that high-risk boys and girls who interacted with caring adults outside the family provided an important protective factor contributing to successful transition to adulthood.

Historically, research on mentoring programs has not shown effectiveness. However, research conducted by Public/Private Ventures (P/PV) demonstrated that the BBBSA program provided many concrete benefits (Wootan, 2010). P/PV conducted an 18-month (1992–1993) comparative study of randomly selected BBBSA children compared to non-BBBSA children. Results showed that youth participants in the program (i.e., Little Brothers and Little Sisters) were 46% less likely to have initiated use of drugs or alcohol (26%), felt more competent about doing their schoolwork, attended school more frequently, obtained better grades, maintained better peer relationships, and were about one-third less likely to have hit others.

In another study, "Making a Difference in Schools: The Big Brothers Big Sisters School-Based Mentoring Impact Study" (Herrara et al., 2007), the mentoring provided through BBBSA was found to produce moderately positive effects. Improved were school attendance, academic performance, turning in assignments, scholastic self-efficacy, and reduced truancy.

Testimonial support has emerged for the mentoring program within BBBSA in two studies. Civic Enterprises (2010) assessed the educational beliefs of both Big and Little Brothers and Sisters and found that 97% of the "Littles" reported that it is very important to work hard in school (97%), to go to school and get good grades (95%), and to graduate from college (94%). An interactive online survey conducted by Harris Interactive (2009) of Littles alumni reported that mentoring helped them to do better in school (77%), reach a higher level of education than they had thought possible (65%), and keep them from dropping out of high school (52%).

In 2008, BBBSA served 255,000 youths at 470 agencies nationwide. The national average cost of making and supporting a match is approximately $1,300 in 2009 dollars. In relation to outcomes summarized above, this cost seems very acceptable (McGill, Mihalic, & Grotpeter, 1998).

Why does it work? Mentoring and its supervision are the hallmarks of this program. The idea of matching to create a warm relationship is a simple but elegant one. The basic simplicity of the program's underpinning (albeit, being connected to more sophisticated theory related to positive social bonding) is one important reason why this program works. It is understandable. It is feasible. It is not complex. It is not costly. All of these characteristics promote successful application, replication, and adaptation. Moreover, the very careful monitoring of the matching relationship through case managers, following clearly articulated standards and procedures, helps to insure that the central program component functions well and appropriately, and stays targeted on agreed-upon goals. The ongoing communication process that the case manager implements keeps the program moving ahead and allows key partners to be involved and to contribute.

Implications for counselors and other helpers. Often community-based prevention requires multiple layers and systems of involvement, and is necessarily complex and comprehensive in scope. The BBBSA program shows that a community prevention program can be very simple conceptually. This one has established well developed procedures to provide support and communication while allowing for the inventiveness and creativity of the mentoring process to emerge—consistent with goals and agreed-upon rules and procedures. Nothing can be more simple and direct than one-to-one relationships.

Of course, counselors are well trained in this basic delivery approach, whether expressed through direct contact, training and supervising of others, consulting about these programs, or developing and evaluating mentoring programs. For instance, we are employing a "near peer" voluntary mentoring component within our Counseling program, where returning students and first year students are matched. Results are very favorable, actually going both ways, with mentors and mentees alike gaining.

Communities Mobilizing for Change on Alcohol

What is Communities Mobilizing for Change on Alcohol? This is a community-organizing program designed to reduce teens' (13–20 years of age) access to alcohol by changing community policies and practices. Thus, it makes use of the COSI set of strategies we examined in chapter 3.

Communities Mobilizing for Change on Alcohol (CMCA) seeks both to limit youths' access to alcohol and to communicate a clear message to the community that underage drinking is inappropriate and unacceptable. It employs a range of social-organizing techniques to address legal, institutional, social, and health issues related to underage drinking. The goals of these organizing efforts are to eliminate illegal alcohol sales to minors, obstruct the provision of alcohol to youth, and ultimately reduce alcohol use by teens. The program involves community members in seeking and achieving changes in local public policies and the practices of community institutions that can affect youths' access to alcohol.

CMCA was developed, first implemented, and evaluated in a 15-community randomized trial by the Alcohol Epidemiology Program at the University of Minnesota School of Public Health. Since that initial trial in the early 1990s, numerous communities in the United States, Sweden, and other countries have implemented interventions based closely on the CMCA model. CMCA is based on theory and research that emphasizes how important the social and policy environment is in promoting or in retarding youth drinking of alcohol. This viewpoint reinforces the understanding that long-term prevention success is dependent on changing the social and policy environment in a community to support the prevention goals. Therefore, this initiative targets the whole community for change, rather than individual young people. Community factors receiving specific prevention attention are the policies and practices of major community institutions.

Most prevention interventions to reduce youth drinking and its negative consequences have focused on reducing the youth *demand* for alcohol, typically through school-based programs. Prevention programs that are based on information-delivery and on affective change strategies have demonstrated no lasting positive effects, while some programs based on life skills and resistance skills have shown beneficial effects; yet, the latter seem to require intense implementation, many sessions, and booster sessions.

Reducing the *supply* of alcohol represents another way toward prevention of youth alcohol used. Examples of supply reduction include increasing the legal age for purchase or consumption of alcohol, or reducing availability of alcohol via raised excise tax. Both of these approaches have shown success (Wagenaar et al., 1998).

CMCA falls within the supply reduction approach to youth alcohol drinking prevention, with its intent being to reduce youth access to alcohol. Effectively limiting teen accessibility to alcohol can directly reduce teen drinking and also communicate within the community a clear social norm that underage drinking in both inappropriate and unacceptable.

How is it done? Community organizing, a major part of the COSI strategy, is the major intervention method used in CMCA. It involves activating grassroots citizens in a community to pursue policy and institutional change. Those involved usually constitute a group independent from the existing power structure in a community, even if some members may hold leadership position in community organizations.

As mentioned, CMCA seeks to engage community citizens to change local public policies to effect the practices occurring within major community institutions in relation to youth alcohol drinking. Examples of these community institutions include law enforcement, schools, licensing departments, community events, the local mass media, civic groups, and churches and synagogues.

The objective of CMCA is to reduce youth drinking through limiting the accessibility of alcohol to them, such as through illegal sales by retailers and by adults who may provide teens with alcohol. The community organizing intervention within the program involves hiring a community organizer within each intervention community. During one application, the community organizer worked for a 2.5-year period (completing a total of 1,518 one-on-one meetings) with a wide variety of persons in policy or policy-influencing positions, and with retailers. These meetings accomplished several ends, by (a) assisting the organizers to better understand the community, including its history, culture, and the patterns of influence and power; (b) building personal and political relationships with people across the community; (c) gaining an understanding of the interests, views, and commitments of community members; and (d) providing recruitment leads of individuals to the core strategy group to be formed. During this phase, the community organizers also reviewed existing alcohol control policies, procedures, and enforcement practices.

During the second phase of the CMCA preventive intervention, a strategy team is formed, comprised of a local core leadership group. As well, a larger base of active and diverse citizens is created. These groups work to develop a base of community support and to design specific community organizing strategies. These strategies include identifying specific alcohol policy and enforcement targets for change and plans for mobilizing citizens in the community to advocate for these changes.

What works? CMCA is based on established research that has demonstrated the importance of the social and policy environment in facilitating or impeding drinking among youth. COSI used within CMCA methods draw on a range of traditions in organizing efforts to deal with the social and health consequences of alcohol consumption.

The CMCA project has received an Exemplary evaluation from the Center for Substance Abuse Prevention and is listed on the National Registry of Effective Prevention Programs (2014a). The Web site of the Alcohol Epidemiology Program (http://www.epi.umn.edu/alcohol) contains many resources related to the CMCA project and to strategies for reducing youth access to alcohol. These are available at no cost. The project also is included as a "program that works" by the Promising Practices Network (2013).

Many communities have adapted ideas and components of the CMCA project, following its original implementation and evaluation. As mentioned, the CMCA was first evaluated in a fully randomized trial across 15 communities in Minnesota, with 7 communities assigned to intervention and another 8 to controls. Baseline surveys were conducted in each community and repeated 3 years following. A multiple time-series design was implemented. Data collection included pre-and post-test surveys of 12th-grade students conduced in schools, telephone surveys of 18- to 20-year-olds and of alcohol retailers, use of direct tests to see to young buyers, and monitoring pertinent changes in the community practices of community institutions.

Results demonstrated that CMCA favorably and significantly affected the drinking behavior of 18- to 20-year-olds. They were less likely to try to buy alcohol, less likely to gather at bars, less likely to drink alcohol, and less likely to provide alcohol to other teens. Arrests for driving under the influence of alcohol also were significantly reduced. Younger adolescents were not significantly impacted by the program. Alcohol merchants reduced sales to minors and increased their checks of age identification.

Another study (Wagenaar et al., 2000) was conducted, using the CMCA to effect arrests and traffic crashes. Arrest and traffic crash data were collected from 1987 to 1995, providing a 6-year baseline and for 3 years of intervention data. Results showed net declines in the preventive intervention communities for all arrest and traffic crash indicators. Drawing from the two studies summarized, the researchers observed that the CMCA approach to limit youth access to alcohol may be effective, but that a longer intervention period is necessary.

Why does it work? Community organizing aimed at policy change represents an important wellness and prevention strategy, and this strategy was intentionally used to guide the design, implementation, and evaluation of this project. This relationship between guiding precepts and program development, implementation, and evaluation is an important reason for the program's success.

Moreover, CMCA effectiveness is tied to careful development of the community organizing function and matching the preventive method with a sensitive evaluation regimen. In terms of the first point, CMCA community organizers spent considerable time and effort getting to know people in the community and to learn about the community itself. They formed personal relationships and connected with both influential community members and with a diverse range of citizens. They worked intentionally to create a strategic plan for mobilizing community members themselves to seek desired change. In that sense, their efforts were infused by the goal of empowerment, where people gain increased control and power in affecting changes that are important for improving their condition and that of others.

Regarding evaluation, the preventive intervention was set within a solid community-based research design, allowing for proper evaluation to occur. Data resulting from the preventive intervention were collected and were synchronized with the intervention itself. A variety of measures was used, including surveys of relevant groups, archival data, alcohol purchase attempts, and drinking behaviors.

Last, the CMCA approach to preventing underage drinking through limiting the access of minors to alcohol has been disseminated through a variety of means, and the program is being adapted in many communities. This dissemination function is important for effective prevention programs.

Implications for counselors and other helpers. CMCA provides a crystal-clear example of a community-based prevention program that is purely environmental and systems oriented. (Compare this approach with those that have focused just as strictly on person-oriented variables.) It is important for counselors and other helpers to be aware of how prevention can be accomplished through leveraging environmental variables, in this case, the community policies affecting underage access to alcohol.

In an extensive university project I was involved with we gathered campus environmental assessment data about the effects on students of a number of campus conditions, such as policies, the physical space, and opportunities for socializing. We then consulted with campus administrators about the results. Two major environmental changes occurred from this effort: (a) because personal safety at night on campus emerged as a consistent concern, a new lighting system was installed to improve the visibility, and (b) because high levels of stress were consistently reported at about the mid-semester points, a mid-semester break was incorporated within the academic calendar (Conyne, 1975; Conyne & Clack, 1981).

Practitioners can collaborate with others in environmentally oriented prevention programs in various ways, such as helping to shape the interaction processes to be engaged in by community organizers. As well, counselors and other helpers can add unique components to such programs, helping them to expand beyond a reliance on environmental change only to also include attention to person-oriented change methods; in the case of the CMCA program, for example, might incorporation of skill-building workshops for community organizers be beneficial to assist them in doing their work more effectively?

Families and Schools Together: Protecting Hearts and Minds

What is Families and Schools Together? (Note: This program is not to be confused with *FAST Track* family program discussed in chapter 6.) Families and Schools Together (FAST) is a multifamily group intervention that is grounded in the schools and community. It is a systematic relationship-based intervention, with components targeted to every stage of a child's development. It legitimately could be classified alternately as being focused at the family, the school, or—as I have done here—the community level. In fact, FAST involves all three levels in interaction.

In building positive relationships, the program promotes the resilience and success of children. A major route it takes is to empower parents to support their children through consistent parenting and productive communication styles.

How is it done? Viewing FAST as a community-level intervention, the following tenet is important: "Communities should take leadership roles in providing positive relationship involvement systems, and support providers must collaborate to protect children and families." The creation of positive relationships that can be implemented and sustained within the family and community context is the critical component of this program. Skills developed are not parachuted into the family but they are nested within the real world of the child, family, and community.

The FAST program is based on several theoretical constructs: (a) social ecological theory of child development, (b) family systems theory, (c) parent empowerment, (d) community development, (e) brain development research, (f) social capital, and (g) risk and resilience models.

The program is deliverable at five baby/childhood/adolescent developmental points:

1. *Baby FAST*, for ages 0–3. This program is a family group intervention for young parents who meet together in small groups for eight weeks. Parents learn skills they can use, gain social support, and babies are targeted early in their development.
2. *Pre-K-FAST* for ages 3–6. This program is intended to prepare kids to enter school ready to learn. Parents meet together over 10 weeks, in schools or community centers.
3. *Kids FAST* (K-5), for parents and kids. This was the initial FAST program, developed to aid parents in becoming more involved with the lives of their children. Strategies include family relationship management, stimulating parental empowerment, and enhancing parent-child bonding. Parents meet weekly for 10 weeks in school or community sites.
4. *Middle School FAST*, for grades six-eight. This 10-week program that occurs in community centers or schools targets preteens and teens, which are critically important transition periods. Attending to and building protective factors are emphasized within the family context, to assist children in managing positively their increasing independence, choice-making, and responsibility.

5. *Teen FAST* for high school. This 8-week process is designed to increase leadership skills of teens. Interesting, teens recruit parents to participate in the program, not the much more typical other way around.

All of these programs are designed to:

- Connect parents and kids to their schools and communities
- Guide parents in building personal competencies and assets in their children
- Promote community service and voluntary involvement
- Use experiential learning to build assets and modify attitudes
- Conduct programs in community or after-school situations
- Involve parents actively
- Assure that parents who are capable assume and remain the main sources of protection for their children

What works? The FAST program enjoys endorsement by evaluation sources and widespread use. It has been evaluated as being evidence based. It has been recognized by SAMHSA/NREPP as an "exemplary model" program for prevention and early intervention, by the U.S. Justice Department as "exemplary" for preventing juvenile delinquency, the Promising Practices Network as a "program that works," and by the National Dropout Prevention Center as a "model" program. The program has been implemented in 46 states in this country and in 13 countries around the world (Australia, Austria, Canada, England, Germany, Kazakhstan, Netherlands, Northern Ireland, Russia, Tajikistan, and Wales). It has reached some 450,000 participants.

Findings associated with the various FAST programs include:

Pre-K FAST: 68% of teachers report improved child behavior, longitudinal studies report that FAST families outperform controls in family functioning and healthy childhood behaviors.

Kids FAST: 84% of teachers report that FAST kids improve their academic performance, 88% say kids improve their behavior.

Middle School FAST: 80% of families "graduate" from the program.

Teen FAST: FAST teens are more likely to be focused on school, 85% of teens rate *FAST* as beneficial or highly beneficial.

The FAST programs have been evaluated as being ready for use, obtaining the highest score possible of 4.0.

Why does it work? The program is based on solid theoretical and research bases that have been translated into realistic, school and community settings. It is a flexible program, designed to be configurable to meet the local needs of every community. It does not take up valuable classroom due to its after-school and community placement. Program developers maintain it supports all communities regardless of social setting, geography, or ethnic heritage and it works well in urban, inner city, rural, and suburban communities. FAST has been recognized as being highly able to engage parents. Its small group and experiential components help parents to connect with one another and aid in skill development. Skills taught to parents and to children are consonant with demands and opportunities present within their communities. The program respects parents and is able to empower them to engage with each other and their families in the real world; for example, they are able to run their own monthly family meetings. Connections and relationships at all levels are central themes throughout the FAST programs.

Implications for counselors and other helpers. The comprehensive use of multiple strategies makes the FAST program appealing to professional practitioners seeking to affect multiple sources of influence and settings. The availability of FAST programs at differing developmental levels permits counselors to apply the program across the childhood and adolescent life span. Its emphasis on relationship building and maintenance as a key change dimension connects centrally with the ethos of the helping professions. As pointed out, FAST is both a community and a family program, making its application flexible and its scope broad.

Conclusion: Community Programs

The three community-based prevention programs selected for presentation in this chapter demonstrate different approaches. Big Brothers and Big Sisters of America shows the power of ongoing and carefully monitored mentoring relationships that, with broad-scale application across many mentors-mentees, has the capacity to elevate the quality of life in a community. Communities Mobilizing for Change on Alcohol illustrates how environmental change (policy), arrived at through appreciable attention to collaborative relationships, can result in positive change within one focused area of concern (reducing alcohol problems). Families and Schools Together (FAST) includes five programs geared to the unique developmental transitions of children, all of which use multiple factors hinging on relationship development to enhance the well-being of children and the competencies of parents.

In these and other community-based wellness and prevention programs the need is to blend two sometimes competing approaches: (a) community-driven, infused by collaboration between community members and professional practitioners, and (b) research-driven (Wandersman & Florin, 2003). The grassroots tradition (community-driven) needs to be informed by the prevention science tradition that is now emerging (research-driven), and vice versa.

The Workplace Setting

Working is a central part of most adult's lives, and they spend much of their lives at work. Work settings vary widely, including hands-on, concrete applications (such as shown in Figure 7.2, of carpenters) to symbolic and highly abstract applications in complex organizations (such as scientific laboratories or computer modeling).

FIGURE 7.2 Two carpenters working on wood. Counseling for wellness and prevention occurs in the workplace.

Source: iStock photo

Work is not uniformly agreeable for all employees, of course. On the positive side, work provides income, offers a route to satisfaction and happiness, provides a way to contribute and be productive, develops opportunities for social interaction, and can provide a general purpose and organizing structure for life. Along with love, Freud identified work as a major feature of a healthy life (Freud's "lieben und arbeiten": to love and to work).

Work also can be a significant source of stress and an engine for generating psychological disorders and distress. Work-related stress has many causes (Quick, Quick, Nelson, & Hurrell, 1997), including excessive demands, economic instability, job ambiguity, unabated routine, rapid technological change, lack of control over work, and international economic competition.

Work-related psychological dysfunctions constitute one category in the top 10 occupational health risks in the United States (Quick et al., 1997). Job-related stress is a serious matter. More than one-third of working Americans reported in a 2013 national survey that they experienced chronic work stress, while their organizations did not provide adequate resources to assist them in managing that stress (American Psychological Association, 2014b).

In fact, work-related stress is the major health and safety issue for most employers in the Western world. For instance, in the United Kingdom, more than 6.5 million working days are lost each year at a cost to companies of almost £400 million. The cost to society in human as well as financial terms is greater still and the latter has been estimated at some £3.75 billion annually. Wellness and prevention-oriented organizations have been seeking not just to control these costs but to establish work systems that positively enhance mental health, reflecting a view that a sense of community is at the heart of a workplace. Moreover, improvements in organizational health show up on the bottom line (Miller, Lipsedge, & Litchfield, 2002).

The Institute of Medicine's definition of prevention applied to the workplace identified the following three types: (a) universal preventive interventions that focus on the entire work force and families; (b) selective preventive interventions that target members of the work setting or their families who are at high risk; and (c) indicated preventive interventions that are aimed at high-risk workers of their family members who are show signs or symptoms of problems.

Wellness and prevention programs within the workplace have been variously described. A general description of an organized program offered by an employer is that the program is created to support employees (sometimes also including their families) to assist them to adopt and sustain positive behaviors intended to improve their quality of life, reduce health risks, increase their personal effectiveness, and provide a benefit to the work setting's bottom line In terms of the latter, comprehensive, well-delivered programs can provide a return on investment (ROI; discussed previously in chapter 1) of up to 6:1 (Berry, Mirabito, & Baun, 2010).

The Centers for Disease Control and Prevention recommends that a workplace health program should be based on a coordinated, systematic, and comprehensive approach. A *coordinated* approach to workplace health promotion results in a planned, organized, and comprehensive set of programs, policies, benefits, and environmental supports designed *systematically* to meet the health and safety needs of all employees. A *comprehensive* approach seeks to enact interventions that are systemic, addressing multiple risk factors and health conditions concurrently, recognizing that the interventions and strategies chosen influence multiple levels of the organization including the individual employee and the organization as a whole.

A large study of workplace wellness programs by RAND Health (Mattke et al., 2013) confirms these points. The study results identified five key factors that supported success: (a) develop effective communication strategies; (b) provide opportunities for employees to take active part in the wellness activities; (c) be sure that senior leadership is fully and obviously engaged in the programs; (d) use and leverage existing resources, as much as possible; and (e) conduct continuous evaluation of the program.

In terms of wellness and prevention program delivery, the work setting provides many advantages. For instance, it affords a locale where large numbers of parents can be reached with messages related to prevention of children's use of alcohol and other drugs, and where substance abuse prevention can be integrated into a standard health promotion and wellness program. Workplace wellness and prevention programs addressing substance abuse can reduce costs in such areas as workers' compensation claims, injury, litigation, and health insurance, among others.

The work setting is a major locale in most adult's lives in this country. Today 51% of employers with 50 or more employees now offer some kind of wellness and prevention plan for their employees (Mattke et al., 2013). This figure seems impressive, perhaps, until realizing that another 49% of these organizations are not providing wellness and prevention programs.

How can these wellness and prevention programs be characterized? Baicker, Cutler, and Song (2010) analyzed 36 workplace wellness programs along many dimensions. In chapter 1, I discussed their findings in relation to the positive Return on Investment (ROI) that can attend well-delivered wellness and prevention programs. In addition, these researchers also were able to identify the most frequent foci of the programs studied and how they were delivered. Most of these 36 programs were found to emphasize multiple risk factors (75% of firms involved in the study), followed by targeting weight loss and fitness (66%), and smoking cessation (50%). Delivery methods included assessment of health risks (81%), self-help educational materials (42%), individual counseling (39%), classes, seminars, and group activities (36%), and building in incentives for participation (31%). These findings fit well with the training and competencies of mental health professionals.

To understand how wellness and prevention programs can function in the workplace, let's examine three effective examples:

- *The Healthy Workplace* (Cook, Back, Trudeau, & McPherson, 2002; Cook, Hersch, Back, & McPherson, 2004; Cook & Schlenger, 2002; Dietz, Cook, & Hersch, 2005), which includes five different programs all incorporating substance abuse prevention and promotion of a general wellness lifestyle in the workplace within a general health promotion format.
- *Coping with Work and Family Stress* (Kline & Snow, 1994; Snow, 2009; Snow & Kline, 1995; Snow, Swan, Raghavan, Connell, & Klein, 2003). Formerly titled the *Yale Work and Family Stress Project*, this program develops and evaluates preventive interventions that are based on relationships between risk and protective factors and aims to increase active coping strategies, reducing stressors and developing stress management, and building social support.
- *JOBS Project for the Unemployed* (Reynolds, Barry, & Gabhainn, 2010; van Ryn & Vinokur, 1992; Vinokur, Price, & Schul, 1995; Vinokur, Schul, Vuori, & Price, 2000), which seeks to prevent recently unemployed persons from further psychological distress and to promote self-efficacy in relation to the job search.

Workplace Program Examples

Program Primary Wellness and Prevention Counseling Strategies
The Healthy Workplace: Education and wellness, using small group formats
Coping With Work and Family Stress: Education: Group, risk and protective factors, social support
JOBS Project for Unemployed: Education, with an emphasis on psychoeducation groups

Note that these excellent prevention programs each tend to emphasize a competency enhancement approach.

The Healthy Workplace Program

What is the Healthy Workplace Program? Healthy Workplace (Cook et al., 2002) is a set of substance abuse prevention interventions for the workplace that are designed for workers who are not substance-dependent. The five Healthy Workplace interventions—*SAY YES!, Healthy Choices for Feeling Good, Working People: Decisions About Drinking, the Make the Connection series, Healthy Life 2000* (formerly Prime Life 2000), and *Power Tools*—target unsafe drinking, illegal drug use, prescription drug use, and the healthy lifestyle practices of workers. Cast in a health promotion framework and grounded in social-cognitive principles of behavior change, Healthy Workplace interventions integrate substance abuse prevention materials into popular health promotion programs, thereby defusing the stigma of substance abuse and reducing barriers to help-seeking behavior. Intervention materials are designed to raise awareness of the hazards of substance use and the benefits of healthy behaviors and to teach techniques to live healthier lives. The interventions are delivered in small group sessions using videos and print materials that can be used in any order and are selected based on the organization's goals and workforce composition (construction workers, office workers, technical/professional staff, and others).

Importantly, the Healthy Workplace program simultaneously seeks to improve the health practices of adult workers, as it is based within a wellness and health promotion framework. Integrated with health promotion activities, this program adapts social cognitive theory (SCT; Bandura, 1997), the health belief model (Rosenstock, Strecher, & Becker, 1988), and Cook's (1985) biopsychological model of healthful alternatives to form its conceptual base. Therefore, the program is positive, emphasizing the benefits of healthful behaviors and not stressing the dangers of substance abuse (although these are covered). Program materials are designed to appeal rather than to scare, by featuring healthful activities that are rewarding and fun and by presenting the program in interesting ways.

The Healthy Workplace program has been tested in a variety of work settings (e.g., large and medium-size companies, with construction workers, in manufacturing and printing facilities), and with ethnically diverse workforces (e.g., Latino, African American). Central components of the Healthy Workplace program include (a) reaching the mainstream of workers in a work setting through the positive vehicle of health promotion; (b) raising awareness of the benefits of healthful behaviors and practices, as well as the hazards of using tobacco, alcohol, and illegal drugs, and in misusing legal drugs; (c) teaching specific techniques to employees for improving health and reducing use of tobacco, alcohol, and illegal drugs; and (d) using carefully developed videos to raise self-efficacy and provide models for how healthful practices can be incorporated and substance abuse reduced.

The Healthy Workplace program is designed to increase protective factors and to decrease risk factors at the individual and organizational levels. Individual level protective factors to increase include stress-coping abilities, belief in the benefits of a healthful lifestyle, and skills to reduce alcohol and drug abuse. Organizational level protective factors to increase include management support for health promotion and low-to-moderate job stress. Individual-level risk factors to decrease include the levels of personal and work stress, denial of the benefits of a healthful lifestyle, and inadequate skills for alcohol and drug abuse reduction. Organizational-level risk factors to be reduced include lack of management support and high levels of workplace stress.

How is it done? The Healthy Workplace program consists of five wellness and prevention interventions that are delivered in small group sessions incorporating tailored videos and print materials. These interventions can be used in any sequence. They are chosen to best fit an organization's goals and the composition of its workforce.

The "*SAY YES!*" intervention is a classroom series with a multi-segment video and accompanying booklet. It is a general health promotion that contains substantial sections addressing alcohol and drug abuse. *SAY YES!* can be used within organizations that desire a general health promotion program that focuses on substance abuse prevention. The purpose of this preventive intervention is to improve health attitudes and practices and to reduce substance abuse.

The intervention can be delivered by a trainer in three sessions, each lasting about an hour. Session 1 (45 minutes) is the introduction, addressing central concepts including healthful lifestyle and well-being, personal choices and lifestyle, and the impact of alcohol and drug use on health and well-being. Session 2 (1.5 hours) focuses on drugs, alcohol, and healthy choices. Media messages are examined, and a variety of means are used (e.g., didactic presentation, video vignettes, group exercises) to compare drug and alcohol use with healthful choices involving relaxation, physical exercise, and recreational activities. Behavioral guidelines for appropriate use of alcohol or for refusing it are provided. In Session 3 (45 minutes) the emphasis is on healthy choices and action, including a step-wise process of behavior change and the setting of realistic health behavior goals.

The "*Working People*" program consists of four 30-minute small group sessions over a period of four weeks. It focuses on alcohol abuse prevention and is intended especially for a blue-collar workforce of 18- to 35-year-olds. Less attention is given to improving health practices. Session 1 is entitled "A Closer Look at Drinking." This introductory session overviews some health and safety risks and the potential negative social and lifestyle effects of irresponsible and/or heavy alcohol use. Session 2 presents some important facts about alcohol, centered on a lecture-style video. Session 3 is entitled "One More Pitcher?" It focuses on decision-making processes and alcohol consumption, setting personal limits, and on practical ways to reduce drinking. Session 4 emphasizes positive alternatives to alcohol abuse.

The "Make the Connection" intervention is a three-part series of video and print materials, with each part consisting of three 45-minute sessions: (a) the stress management connection; (b) the healthy eating connection; and (c) the active lifestyle connection. The program is intended to be included in workplace health promotion programs on stress management, weight management and nutrition, and fitness.

The "Healthy Life 2000" (formerly known as "Prime Life 2000") program contains layered interventions consisting of a series of small group sessions on stress management, healthy eating, and fitness. As well, print materials and videotapes are mailed to all employees. All components include preventive information on alcohol abuse, illegal drug use, and prescription drug use.

The "Power Tools" intervention consists of three 45-minute sessions that was developed specifically for young, blue-collar men. The intervention combines general health issues with sessions particularly devoted to alcohol and drug abuse.

For each of these five interventions, small group sessions of from 10–20 employees are essential for implementation. This, then, provides a useful example of how group work is embedded as a central feature within a wellness and prevention program. These small group sessions are generally held on-site, in the work setting's training or conference room.

Each intervention includes a training guide and back-up materials. A trainer who is familiar with the appropriate guide and has the necessary support resources (i.e., print and videotape materials) can implement the intervention.

What works? The Healthy Workplace program has been evaluated as a Model program by the Substance Abuse and Mental Health Services Administration (SAMHSA). The program has evolved over several years of developmental, implementation, and evaluation trials. Training guides, videos, and print materials for its preventive interventions have been implemented in many work settings throughout the United States, Australia, and Canada.

The Healthy Workplace wellness and prevention interventions have been field-tested in five different worksites, using pre-post repeated measure designs. Random assignment to program or control groups was accomplished in three of the five studies, and a quasi-experimental design was used in two studies. Sample sizes ranged from 108 workers (in "Working People") to around 1,500 workers (in "Healthy Life 2000"); sample sizes in the other studies were approximately 300 to 400. The Health Behavior Questionnaire, containing multiple measures of health and substance use practices and attitudes, was used for assessment. Analysis of covariance and hierarchical regression were the main statistical analytic methods employed.

Generally, these research studies have demonstrated reductions in alcohol and drug use among participants, accompanied by improvements in related health measures, such as coping with stress, and in dietary practices. More particularly, in the "Working People" intervention, alcohol consumption was decreased by 47% and the number of binge drinking days was decreased by 60%. In the "Make the Connection" intervention, participants showed increases in awareness of perceived risks associated with alcohol and drug use and between health and alcohol and drug abuse; they also showed reduced use of alcohol and drugs for relieving stress.

The Healthy Workplace program results suggest that substance abuse prevention and healthy lifestyle enhancement in work settings can be accomplished within wellness and prevention offerings without lessening the impact. Stress management health promotion programs seem to provide an especially useful vehicle.

Why does it work? Health promotion and disease prevention efforts are being used with increasing frequency within work settings. Employers and managed care organizations are interested in improving employee health and productivity while health care costs are contained. Wellness and prevention programs that address health promotion in the work setting are an attractive choice, finding a fast-growing niche.

The Healthy Workplace program fits within this evolution of care in the work setting. Moreover, combining attention to substance abuse prevention with general health promotion offers a delivery system that is acceptable to workers without diminishing program effects. The capacity of the program to grow strengths and assets, as well as to reduce negative behaviors, contributes to overall effectiveness.

Making use of group methods for delivering the program, along with other well-constructed modes (such as videos) connects well with the general theory upon which the program intervention is based and with best practice emerging with prevention programs. The training and support resources provided by the program developers affords the possibility of adequate delivery of these methods amidst good, ongoing communication and support.

The program has been carefully studied and has evolved consistent with successively obtained research data. It has been tested and applied in numerous types of work settings, at differing levels, and with a range of ethnic diversity.

Implications for counselors and other helpers. Work settings are an untapped resource for preventive counselor involvement. A program with various interventions, such as the *Healthy Workplace*, provides both means and evidence that a technology exists for helping employee participants to realize specific and general prevention goals. Group-based wellness and prevention methods, such as this one, use a particular skill set of most counselors and of many other mental health practitioners.

The issue is that counselors need to expand their horizons to consider the workplace to be an actual setting for counselor participation. Mental health and school settings, although critically important, are not the only settings of importance in people's lives. Taking the skills that counselors possess, for instance in group work, and applying these skills within workplace wellness and prevention programs affords a potential for change that needs to be exercised. The Healthy

Workplace program provides a means for organizing and delivering such counseling projects.

Coping With Work and Family Stress Project (Formerly Known as the Yale Work and Family Stress Project)

What is the Coping With Work and Family Stress Project? This is a workplace wellness and prevention intervention designed to teach employees 18 years and older how to deal with stressors at work and at home. It is being implemented in 22 sites within the United States and in Trinidad and Tobago, including around 1,500 participants in total.

The project includes studies in two broad areas: (a) conducting evaluations of work-based coping interventions aimed at reducing negative behavioral and psychological consequences of work and family stressors; and (b) examining relationships between particular risk and protective factors in relation to psychological symptomatology, work adjustment factors, and substance use. In this project, work and family stressors and poor coping strategies serve as risk factors. Conversely, perceived social support and adaptive coping strategies operate as protective factors. In general, it is suggested in this model that psychological symptoms arise from multiple contexts (such as the workplace), and are influenced by the interaction of individual and situational risk and protective factors over time. As you can readily see, this rationale is consistent with the Counseling for Wellness and Prevention Model discussed in chapter 4.

How is it done? Sixteen 90-minute sessions are typically provided weekly to small groups of 15–20 employees. (Once again, note the importance of small groups). These sessions focus on teaching effective methods for reducing risk factors (stressors and avoidance coping) and enhancing protective factors (active coping and social support) through behavior modification (e.g., methods to modify or eliminate sources of stress), information sharing (e.g., didactic presentations, group discussions), and skill development (e.g., learning effective communication and problem-solving skills, expanding use of social network). The curriculum emphasizes the role of stress, coping, and social support in relation to substance use and psychological symptoms. The sessions are led by a facilitator who typically has a master's-level education; is experienced in group dynamics, system theory, and cognitive and other behavior interventions; and is able to manage group process. Facilitator training in the program curriculum is required (NREPP, 2014b).

The Coping With Work and Family Stress project has conducted several studies to examine wellness and prevention programs and their effects on women. The typical intervention to be summarized below (Snow & Kline, 1995) was intended to teach participants new strategies to decrease the negative influence of specific risk factors while increasing the beneficial aspects of protective factors. The women who participated in the wellness and prevention intervention, as compared with the control participants, were expected to report: (a) lower levels of role, work-family, and work environment stressors; (b) higher perceived social support from both work and from non-work sources; (c) higher behavioral and cognitive coping and lower avoidance coping; (d) less psychological symptomatology; and (e) lower tobacco, alcohol, and illicit drug use.

A 15-session workplace, coping-skills intervention was conducted for female employees located at one of four corporate job sites in Connecticut. Intervention participants met in small groups of about 10–12 employees led by a facilitator for 1.5 hours per week over 15 weeks. Sessions occurred during work hours, using release time, and were held at the company site. The preventive intervention includes a hierarchy of coping mechanisms: (a) responses to change a situation (i.e., proactive measures to eliminate sources of stress); (b) responses to control the meaning of the stressful experience (i.e., cognitive restructuring); and (c) responses to control the stress after it has emerged and cannot be removed at the source (i.e., stress management techniques, such as relaxation).

The wellness and prevention sessions to improve coping with work and family stress with the female participants in this study included:

Session 1: Focus on women, multiple roles and stress
Session 2: Identifying and examining stressful situations
Session 3: Problem solving
Session 4: Managing stress (Part A): Deep breathing and muscle relaxation are learned and used throughout the whole program.
Session 5: Attacking the problem (Part A): Effective communication skills are discussed and practiced.
Session 6: Attacking the problem (Part B): Empathic listening and responding are learned as skills.
Session 7: Attacking the problem (Part C): Direct expression of needs and identifying how to overcome communication barriers.
Session 8: Attacking the problem (Part D): Integration of communication skills.
Session 9: Personal networks and social support
Session 10: Group strategies
Session 11: Rethinking the problem (Part A): Self statements are explored.
Session 12: Rethinking the problem (Part B): Alternative thinking modes are reviewed.
Session 13: Managing the stress (Part B): Visualization and self-suggestion are developed.
Session 14: Personal stress management plan (Part A): Problem solving, cognitive restructuring, and stress management are integrated in relation to family and work experiences.
Session 15: Personal stress management plan (Part B): Implementation of the plan in gradual steps is discussed, participants review their accomplishments during the program, and process termination issues.

What works? The program described above sought to assess the effectiveness of workplace coping skills intervention by teaching participants strategies to reduce negative influences of risk factors and to enhance beneficial effects of protective factors. Experimental and no-treatment control conditions were established. Participants were 239 female, clerical staff who were assigned randomly to either the preventive intervention (*n* = 136) or control (*n* = 103), within a pre-, post-, and delayed post-test design. The experimental condition involved the weekly, 15-session coping skills intervention. The control condition involved completion of surveys only. Variables of interest included demographic and background factors, role stressors (employee, spouse/partner, parent), work and family stressors, active and avoidance coping strategies, work and non-work social support, and substance use and psychological symptoms. A repeated measures analysis of variance was conducted, including time periods of posttest and a 6-month follow-up.

All findings favored the coping skills intervention, supporting the risk and protective factor model that was used. Certain risk and protective factors were modified positively, with corresponding reductions in alcohol use and reliance on alcohol for reduction of tension. Overall, the project results indicate that preventive interventions in the workplace that focus on coping skills enhancement can substantially benefit women working in secretarial and clerical positions.

In longer-term follow-up (22 months), results indicated that program effects were attenuated at follow-up. The researchers note that it's reasonable to assume that a person-centered, coping skills intervention, such as this one, holds more potential for changing individual behavior than to decrease risk factors that are linked to organizational variables. A valid criticism is that such person-centered programs may inadvertently teach participants how to adapt successfully to stressful conditions in the workplace instead of implementing strategies to change system-level conditions that lead to stressors. As I have noted throughout this book, a strengths-based approach to both personal and environmental factors can increase the potency of a wellness and prevention intervention.

The Coping With Work and Family Stress Project has been evaluated by the Substance Abuse and Mental Health Administration in 2003 as a Model prevention program. NREPP lists it as an evidence-based program.

Effectiveness trials are being conducted for this program with new populations, including medial residents in training at university medical schools. In addition, the program has entered a phase of being actively disseminated nationally and internationally.

Why does it work? This program is effective because, as with many other wellness and prevention programs that make a positive difference, it includes and combines needed elements. It is grounded in identifying risk and protective factors both in the workplace and at home, uses interactive and often small group change vehicles to decrease stressors while increasing coping skills and strategies, and integrates social support all along the way.

Implications for counselors and other helpers. The Coping With Work and Family Stress project again demonstrates that well-constructed psychoeducation group coping skills interventions can produce positive wellness and prevention effects, with enhanced skills for coping with life demands and for dealing with the more specific challenges targeted in the program (e.g., reducing future substance abuse). As I have stressed, counselors are well prepared to engage in such programs, as are many other professionals. Additionally, these results point to the importance of including system-level change approaches within workplace prevention programs. A more comprehensive program, with both person-and system-change components, may yield more enduring preventive effects.

Finally, as has been observed earlier, wellness and prevention programs in work settings are relatively infrequent, compared to family, school, and community settings. Counselors can make a special contribution by adding the work setting to their repertoire.

The JOBS Project for the Unemployed

What is the JOBS Project for the Unemployed? The JOBS Project is intended to prevent and reduce negative effects on mental health associated with unemployment and job-seeking stress, while promoting high-quality reemployment. Structured as a job search seminar, the program teaches participants effective strategies for finding and obtaining suitable employment as well as for anticipating and dealing with the inevitable setbacks they will encounter. The program also incorporates elements to increase participants' self-esteem, sense of control, and job search self-efficacy. By improving their job-seeking skills and sense of personal mastery, the program helps to inoculate participants against feelings of helplessness, anxiety, depression, and other stress-related mental health problems.

The JOBS Project is a wellness and prevention program intended to assist unemployed people to re-enter the labor market. JOBS was developed by researchers at the Michigan Prevention Research Center (MPRC). The MPRC focuses on a program of prevention research on problems of employment, economic stress, and well-being over the life span. In addition, the MPRC scientifically examines relationships between employment conditions and mental and physical health, while also expanding policy and practice opportunities to the public and private sector.

The JOBS Project is funded partially by the National Institute for Mental Health. It seeks to develop job-seeking skills in the recently unemployed in order to prevent feelings of anxiety, helplessness, and depression and to promote re-employment.

The JOBS Project is based on a theoretical rationale taken from several areas. Vigilant coping holds that people under pressure frequently restrict their search for solutions and directions, tending to invest prematurely on one single course of action. To counteract this orientation, the JOBS Project works with unemployed persons to open up their orientation through learning how to explore, diagnose and understand their situation and how to generate alternatives for re-employment. JOBS adapts a stress inoculation strategy from cognitive behavioral theory, based on the concept that setbacks in the job search are inevitable and people need to learn how to inoculate themselves against these setbacks through a reserve on inoculation coping skills. *JOBS* also focuses on self-efficacy, the powerful belief that one can succeed in attempts rather than fail, as providing a strong motivational force for trying out new and/or difficult behaviors. A last component of the JOBS Project is derived from theory identifying the critical importance of social support in behavior change. Confiding in and drawing support from others can provide a needed buffer against the adversity of job loss and the challenges of moving forward to seek and find re-employment.

How is it done? The JOBS Project is concerned with questions about unemployed persons, such as: How can social support be enhanced? How can a sense of mastery be increased? How can motivation be kindled? What is the impact of a wellness and prevention intervention that is designed to be sensitive to these kinds of questions? What can be learned by studying such a program applied to unemployed persons?

Again, a central feature of the JOBS Project is using psychoeducation group learning, along with large-group discussions, modeling, and role-playing. In groups of from 15 to 20 persons, recently unemployed participants engage in a training program facilitated by a male-female team. The group-based program is delivered in five 4-hour sessions during one week. The sessions include exercises to identify and convey one's job-related skills, use social networks to obtain job leads, contact potential employers, prepare job applications and resumes, and go through a job interview. Problem-solving exercises help participants prepare for and cope with the stresses of unemployment, the job search process, and setbacks Small group activities are constructed to involve participants actively in discussions, to elicit social support among each other, and to enhance their mastery through developing effective job search skills.

The JOBS Program is delivered in employment offices, social service settings, community settings, and outplacement programs. Participants can be recruited from central organizational settings such as state employment offices or outplacement programs in corporate human resources departments. Seminars are provided to groups of 12–20 participants by a pair of trainers who receive approximately 160 hours of formal training, during which they learn about group processes and the theoretical bases of the intervention, undergo extensive rehearsal, and practice the delivery of the intervention (NREPP, 2014c).

Participants in the Project are selected carefully and in accord with its prevention goals. They typically are free from diagnosable mental health disorders and have been "recently" unemployed, that is, within the previous four months.

The JOBS Project group activities include (a) addressing reemployment obstacles; (b) identifying marketable skills; (c) identifying sources of job leads; (d) using social networks to discover job leads; (e) conducting an information interview; and (f) managing emotions related to unemployment. The project seeks to maximize opportunities for the participants to engage actively throughout the process, operating with the contention that participants are much more likely to accept what they come up with themselves. For example, they brain-storm diagnoses of problems, alternative solutions to those problems, and ways to overcome barriers. They role play employment interviews. They give and receive feedback. They are led to identify what meaning they are taking from their training experiences. As Choi, Price, & Vinokur (2003) observed in relation to a follow-on program to JOBS, called "Winning New Jobs," the purpose for trainers is to help people identify internal strengths rather than to teach them specific skills, while taking full advantage of learning from one other in a supportive environment.

What works? The JOBS Project was cited as an Excellent prevention program by the APA Task Force and described in detail in *14 Ounces of Prevention* (Price et al., 1988), and as Effective by the Substance Abuse and Mental Health Services Association. The project also is featured in the video *An Ounce of Prevention* (Annenberg, 1992), a resource I have used consistently when teaching my class on preventive counseling. Studies of the JOBS Project have demonstrated that it produces preventive impacts on mental health while maintaining favorable cost-benefit results. Effects also were differential, with more positive benefits accruing to women, to those with less formal education, and to those at highest risk psychologically.

The following summary of results is taken from an update of the Project provided by the Michigan Prevention Research Center (MPRC; 2004). Eight sets of outcomes have been identified, indicating that the JOBS Project, compared to a control group, promotes the following:

1. Lower levels of depression. Two and one-half years following a randomized trial evaluating the JOBS Project showed that participants experienced significantly fewer depressive symptoms (Price, van Ryn, & Vinokur, 1992).
2. Skills, support, and inoculation. Results support that a carefully designed preventive intervention, such as the *JOBS* Project, can assist the recently unemployed (and especially those who are at risk) to acquire new job skills and a sense of mastery, provide social support, and inoculate against the setbacks that may occur in the job search.
3. Social resources that reduce vulnerability. Attention to social support and acquiring a sense of mastery through skill building contribute to a set of social resources that can serve as protective factors against the mental health risks of involuntary job loss (Price et al., 1992).
4. Positive outcomes especially for unemployed women and workers with less education. Results indicated clearly that mental health and economic benefits were strongest for those at higher risk and who would be most disadvantaged by job loss (Vinokur et al., 1995).
5. Higher paying jobs with cost-benefit. Results showed that people in the JOBS

Project obtained higher paying jobs and higher quality work than others, yielding more income while generating increased tax revenues. Thus, the intervention appears to develop preventive mental health benefits while being cost effective. For instance, this program can be implemented in unemployment offices in the U.S. at approximately $300 per participant. In addition, estimates suggest that the JOBS intervention can pay for itself through increased tax revenues in as few as seven months following re-employment.

Another reasonable test of a wellness and prevention program is the degree to which it has spread successfully. More than 20,000 individuals have participated in the program. It has been implemented successfully in social service agencies in Michigan and Baltimore, Maryland; in community service agencies in California (including the Winning New Jobs, 2004), and increasingly in other countries, including Northern Ireland and the Republic of Ireland, Finland, Korea, and China.

Why does it work? The JOBS Project for the Unemployed is grounded in a strong theoretical base and ties its method directly to it. It carefully selects participants who have not yet begun to experience the conditions that the program seeks to prevent, such as depression, and who can benefit from the active ingredients of the program, including social support and self-efficacy. The program uses small groups as the engine to drive the intervention and these groups are facilitated in such a way as to empower participants to identify and develop their own solutions and directions. A comprehensive trainer's manual is available to help facilitators guide the process and to maintain a level of treatment integrity (Curran, Wishart, & Gingrich, 1999). The program is set within a research design that is sensitive to identifying the prevention of dysfunction (e.g., of depression), competencies developed for the job search (e.g., skills and inoculation strategies), job search outcomes (i.e., securing re-employment), and cost benefits.

Implications for counselors and other helpers. As with most of the wellness and prevention programs that have been reviewed at the family, school, community, and work setting levels the JOBS Project requires provider roles and skills that are well-within the repertoire of counselors and other helpers. Its emphasis on small group intervention, that is both guided and seeks to draw out the resources of participants for mutual problem solving, fits directly with counselor training and role. Therefore, the question is not, "Can counselors and other professionals do wellness and prevention?" The question is: "How can counselors and other professional helpers become more involved in doing it?"

Conclusion: Workplace Programs

When conducting workplace wellness and prevention programs it is important to integrate the success factors identified by the Centers for Disease Control and Prevention and in the large RAND study that were discussed at the beginning of this section. The three workplace prevention programs examined in this chapter also provide direction about what works. A successful set of employee well-being programs not discussed (IBM, 2014), points to the importance of reducing employee health risks through creating a culture of wellness and enhancing diversity. Tools used include health assessment risk assessment, web-based platforms to deliver programs, and behavioral-based programming.

These programs tend to emphasize competency enhancement, that is, the building of skills and knowledge among employees, as the primary route. Related competencies include collaborating with other health professionals, (e.g., nutritionists and fitness experts), fluency leading groups, motivational interviewing, mindfulness, capitalizing on the connection between physical and mental health, and psychoeducation (Firth, 2014). These competencies are similar to those featured in other wellness and prevention applications and they reside prominently in the "wheelhouse" of counselors, psychologists, and other mental health professionals.

At the same time, these professionals need to confront barriers to their involvement in workplace wellness and prevention programs. They often experience discomfort in what they feel as "selling" themselves and their expertise to work organizations, they are more accustomed to providing individual and remedial work than consultation, training, and program development and evaluation, and work organizations themselves frequently are uncertain or apprehensive about how to build counselor expertise into their wellness and prevention programming. Once again, the call is for graduate training programs to increasingly emphasize wellness and prevention approaches and competencies, for counselor advocacy to be targeted at workplace initiatives, and for counselors themselves to become more flexible, versatile, creative, and adaptive in how they define and use their robust skill sets (Firth, 2014).

It also is important to consider how prevention can occur at the level of the work setting itself. Becker and Steele (1995) have developed a workplace focus they term "organizational ecology." This is an approach to creating healthy workplaces that centers on the totality of the workplace, all the places where one works. Organizational ecology seeks to consider an integrated workplace strategy that integrates two parts: the scope of the physical settings and the social processes that are used to plan, manage, and link the physical settings over time (Conyne & Clack, 1981; Rapin, 2004).

Quick et al. (1997) addressed a workplace approach, as well as competency enhancement, from the perspective of preventing stress within organizations. In what these authors refer to more particularly as "organizational prevention," two major approaches can be taken: (a) job and physical demands can become the target for improvement; and/or (b) work relationships can be enhanced. In either case, the aim is to modify and shape the organization/work setting, altering demands placed on employees, so that sources of stress are removed or minimized.

In terms of altering job and physical demands, Quick, et al. describe five strategies for improving job and physical demands: (a) job redesign, to improve person-job fit; (b) participative management, to increase employee involvement and control in decision making; (c) flexible work schedules, to provide greater flexibility for employees in managing their work and personal demands; (d) career development, where career paths and opportunities are opened; and (e) design of physical settings, where noxious elements are reduced and nourishing ones are increased, thus better supporting task functioning.

With regard to enhancing work relationships, Quick, et al. identify addressing role and relationship demands. Once again, five strategies are described: (a) role analysis, where an employee's work role is assessed and clarified to better connect the expected role with what is enacted; (b) goal setting, where the employee-supervisor relationship is addressed in terms of performance goals; (c) social support, which can buffer work stress, through emotional, informational, appraisal, and instrumental support; (d) team building, where an intact work group's functioning is assessed and enhanced; and (e) diversity programs, various talents and perspectives are valued and used.

Programs with the organization/work setting that are aimed at stress prevention seek to contribute to a healthy organization. They can focus on the organization itself (for which fewer documented programs of excellence exist), or by focusing on individuals in the organization (these programs tend to dominate).

Rapin (2004) (a counseling psychologist and counselor educator), referred to above, reported on a fascinating 17-month organization development intervention she delivered within an in-house laboratory of a large medical center. The nature of this preventive and ecological work centered on assessing the laboratory's social climate, using the Work Environment Scale (Moos & Insel, 1974), and integrating these data with other sources of information about the work setting. Organization change interventions were implemented, including team building within the management staff and between the management staff and line staff, and a number of communication enhancement measures, including both skill development and reconfiguring communication patterns. An example of the latter was the creation of a monthly laboratory newsletter to better distribute information and to increase awareness of ongoing events.

Work setting wellness and prevention is an area under represented by the efforts of counselors, counseling psychologists, and other professional helpers. Work is an important, abiding life context, as Freud underscored. Counselors are well prepared to enter and to contribute wellness and prevention efforts to it.

Issues for Reflection and Discussion

1. Communities are rather "messy." There is a lot to them: They are characterized by complexity, competition and cooperation, political dynamics, ethnic and racial issues, resource questions, and many other factors. Communities also can be supportive and nourishing or unfriendly and toxic. For some mental health practitioners, this messiness is perceived as an attractor; for others, it is a detractor. Where do you stand on this dimension? How appealing—or unappealing—is community-based wellness and prevention for you?

2. Pair up with a partner. Together discuss the six programs outlined in this chapter. Select one for further study. Identify what each of you might look for, for example, program goals, program methods, program results, participant involvement. Learn more about it through your research and come back in 2 weeks ready to share what you have learned.
3. Get back with your partner. Continue with that same program. Now ask yourselves this question: How could such a program be introduced/adapted into the local community or work setting (define this so you both agree)? That is, identify what factors should be considered in any plan to try bringing this program here.
4. How might a counselor with a wellness and prevention orientation function in relation to community and work settings? What kinds of roles come to mind? List three roles. Pick one and expand it. How could you make such a role come to life? What would that look like?

References

American Psychological Association. (2014a). Prevention guidelines for psychology. *American Psychologist, 69*, 285–296. doi:10.1037/a0034569

American Psychological Association. (2014b). *Coping with stress at work*. Retrieved from http://www.apa.org/helpcenter/work-stress.aspx

Annenberg/CPB Collection. (1992). *An ounce of prevention* (Video No. 13 in "The World of Abnormal Psychology" series).

Baicker, K., Cutler, D., & Song, Z. (2010). Workplace wellness programs can generate savings. *Health Affairs, 29*, 304–311.

Bandura, A. (1997). *Self-efficacy: The exercise of control*. New York, NY: Freeman.

Becker, F., & Steele, F. (1995). *Workplace by design: Mapping the high-performance work scape. San Francisco*, CA: Jossey-Bass.

Berry, L., Mirabito, A., & Baun, W. (2010, December). What's the hard return on employee wellness programs? *Harvard Business Review*. Retrieved from http://hbr.org/2010/12/whats-the-hard-return-on-employee-wellness-programs/ar/1

Choi, J., Price, R.H., & Vinokur, A.D. (2003). Self-efficacy change in groups: Effects of diversity, leadership, and group climate. *Journal of Organizational Behavior, 24*, 357–372.

Civic Enterprises & Peter D. Hart Research Associates. (2010). *Untapped potential: Fulfilling the promise of Big Brothers Big Sisters and the bigs and littles they represent*. Washington, DC: Civic Enterprises. Retrieved from http://www.civicenterprises.net/MediaLibrary/Docs/untapped_potential.pdf

Coalition for Evidence-Based Policy. (2012). *Big Brothers Big Sisters*. Retrieved from http://evidencebasedprograms.org/1366–2/117–2

Coalition for Evidence-Based Policy. (2013). *Communities Mobilizing for Change on Alcohol*. Retrieved from http://www.promisingpractices.net/program.asp?programid=174

Conyne, R. (1975). Environmental assessment: Mapping for counselor action. *Personnel and Guidance Journal, 54*, 150–155.

Conyne, R., & Clack, R. (1981). *Environmental assessment and design: A new tool for the applied behavioral scientist*. New York, NY: Praeger.

Cook, R. (1985). The alternatives approach revisited: A biopsychological model and guidelines for application. *International Journal of the Addictions, 20*, 1399–1419. doi:10.3109/10826088509047773

Cook, R., Back, A., Trudeau, J., & McPherson, T. (2002). Integrating substance abuse prevention into health promotion programs in the workplace: A social-cognitive intervention targeting the mainstream user. In J. Bennett & W. Lehman (Eds.), *Preventing workplace substance abuse: Beyond drug testing to wellness* (pp. 97–133). Washington, DC: American Psychological Association. doi:10.1037/10476–003

Cook, R. F., Hersch, R. K., Back, A. S., & McPherson, T. L. (2004). The prevention of substance abuse among construction workers: A field test of a social cognitive program. *Journal of Primary Prevention, 25*(3), 337–358. doi:10.1023/b:jopp.0000048025.11036.32

Crozier, M., Rokutani, L., Russett, J., Godwin, E., & Banks, G. (2010). A multisite program evaluation of Families and Schools Together (FAST): Continued evidence of a successful multifamily community-based prevention program. *The School Community Journal, 20*, 187–208. Retrieved from http://files.eric.ed.gov/fulltext/EJ891838.pdf

Cook, R., & Schlenger, W. (2002). Prevention of substance abuse in the workplace: Review of research on the delivery of services. *Journal of Primary Prevention, 23*, 115–142. doi:10.1023/a:1016543300433

Curran, J., Wishart, P., & Gingrich, J. (1999). *JOBS: A manual for teaching people successful job search strategies*. Retrieved from http://webservices.itcs.umich.edu/drupal/mprc/publications/jobs

Deitz, D., Cook, R. F., & Hersch, R. (2005). Workplace health promotion and utilization of health services: Follow-up data findings. *Journal of Behavioral Health Services and Research, 32*, 306–319. doi:10.1097/00075484–200507000–00006

Families and Schools Together. (2014). Retrieved from https://www.familiesandschools.org/; http://www.familiesandschools.org/about/why-how.php

Firth, P. (2014, July 16). *Healthcare reform and increased opportunities for mental health counselors in the workplace.* Poster presented at the annual meeting of the American Mental Health Counselors Association, Seattle, WA.

Gullotta, T., & Bloom, M. (Eds.). (2003). *Encyclopedia of primary prevention and health promotion*. New York, NY: Kluwer.

Harris Interactive (2009, June 18). *Adult Little survey: Exploring the value of Big Brothers Big Sisters*. Retrieved from www.harrisinteractive.com

Herrera, C., Grossman, A., Kauh, T., Feldman, A., McMaken, J., & Jucovy, L. (2007). *Making a difference in schools: The Big Brothers Big Sisters school-based mentoring impact study*. Retrieved from http://www.bbbs.org/site/c.9iILI3NGKhK6F/b.5961035/ k.A153/Big_impact8212proven_results.htm

IBM. (2014). IBM's *global wellness initiatives*. Retrieved from https://www.ibm.com/ibm/responsibility/employees_global_wellness.shtml

Kline, M., & Snow, D. (1994). Effects of a worksite coping skills intervention on the stress, social support, and health outcomes of working mothers. *Journal of Primary Prevention, 15*, 105–121. doi:10.1007/bf02197142

Mancini, J., Martin, J., & Bowen, G. (2003). Community capacity. In T. Gullotta & M. Bloom (Eds.), *Encyclopedia of primary prevention and health promotion* (pp. 319–330). New York, NY: Kluwer. doi:10.1007/978–1–4615–0195–4_45

Mattke, S., Liu, H., Caloyeras, J., Huang, C., VanBusam, K., Khodyakov, D., & Shier, V. (2013). Workplace wellness programs study: Final report. *RAND Health*. Retrieved from http://www.dol.gov/ebsa/pdf/workplacewellnessstudyfinal.pdf

McGill, D. E., Mihalic, S. F., & Grotpeter, J. K. (1998). *Big Brothers Big Sisters of America: Blueprints for Violence Prevention*, Book 2. Boulder, CO: Center for the Study and Prevention ofViolence, Institute of Behavioral Science, University of Colorado.

Michigan Prevention Research Center. (2004). *Winning new jobs: A promising job search program for unemployed workers*. Retrieved from http://www.isr.umich.edu/src/seh/mprc/wnj.html

Miller, D., Lipsedge, M., & Litchfield, P. (Eds.). (2002). *Work and mental health: An employers' guide*. London, England: Gaskell.

Moos, R., & Insel, P. (Eds.). (1974). *Issues in social ecology: Human milieus*. Palo Alto, CA: National Press.

National Registry of Evidence-Based Programs and Practices. (2014a). *Communities Mobilizing for Change on Alcohol*. Retrieved from http://nrepp.samhsa.gov/ViewIntervention.aspx?id=117

National Registry of Evidence-Based Programs and Practices. (2014b). *Coping With Work and Family Stress*. Retrieved from http://nrepp.samhsa.gov/ViewIntervention.aspx?id=103.

National Registry of Evidence-Based Programs and Practices. (2014c). *JOB's Program*. Retrieved from http://www.nrepp.samhsa.gov/ViewIntervention.aspx?id=170

Prevention Institute. (1999). *The Spectrum of Prevention: Developing a comprehensive approach to injury prevention*. Retrieved from http://preventioninstitute.org/component/jlibrary/article/id-105/127.html

Price, R., Cowen, E., Lorion, R., & Ramos-McKay, J. (Eds.). (1988). *14 ounces of prevention: A casebook for practitioners*. Washington, DC: American Psychological Association.

Price, R., van Ryn, M., & Vinokur, A. (1992). Impact of a preventive job search intervention on the likelihood of depression among the unemployed. *Journal of Health and Social Behavior, 33*, 158–167. doi:10.2307/2137253

Promising Practices Network. (2013). Big Brothers Big Sisters of America. Retrieved from http://www.promisingpractices.net/program.asp?programid=125

Public/Private Ventures (2007). *Making a difference in school: The Big Brothers Big Sisters school-based mentoring impact study: Executive summary*. Retrieved from HYPERLINK "http://www.publicprivate_ventures_53.pdf" www.publicprivate_ventures_53.pdf Conyne

Quick, J. C., Quick, J. D., Nelson, D., & Hurrell, J., Jr. (1997). *Preventive stress management in organizations*. Washington, DC: American Psychological Association. doi:10.1037/10238–000

Rapin, L. (2004). Ecological applications to organizational consultation. In R. Conyne & E. P. Cook (Eds.), *Ecological counseling: An innovative approach to conceptualizing person-environment interaction* (pp. 265–288). Alexandria, VA: American Counseling Association.

Reynolds, C., Barry, M. M., & Gabhainn, S. N. (2010). Evaluating the impact of the Winning New Jobs Programme on the re-employment and mental health of a mixed profile of unemployed people. *International Journal of Mental Health Promotion, 12*, 32–41. doi:10.1080/14623730.2010.9721812

Rosenstock, I., Strecher, V., & Becker, M. (1988, Summer). Social learning theory and the health belief mode. *Health Education Quarterly, 15*(2), 175–183. doi:10.1177/109019818801500203

Snow, D. (2009). Coping with work and family stress. Interview by J. Casey and K. Corday, Sloan Work and Family Research Network, Boston College, Chestnut Hill, MA. Retrieved from http://wfnetwork.bc.edu/The_Network_News/65/experts.htm

Snow, D., & Kline, M. (1995). Preventive interventions in the workplace to reduce the negative psychiatric consequences of work and family stress. In C. Mazure (Ed.), *Does stress cause psychiatric illness?* (pp. 221–270). Washington, DC: American Psychological Association.

Snow, D., Swan, S., Raghavan, C. Connell, C., & Klein, I. (2003). The relationship of work stressors, coping, and social support to psychological symptoms among female secretarial employees. *Work and Stress, 17*, 241–263. doi:10.1080/02678370310001625630

Van Ryn, M., & Vinokur, A. (1992). How did it work? An examination of the mechanisms through which an intervention for the unemployed promoted job-search behavior. *American Journal of Community Psychology, 20*, 577–597. doi:10.1007/bf00941773

Vinokur, A., Price, R., & Schul, Y. (1995). Impact of the JOBS intervention on unemployed workers varying in risk for depression. *American Journal of Community Psychology, 23*, 39–74. doi:10.1007/bf02506922

Vinokur, A., Schul, Y., Vuori, J., & Price, R. (2000). Two years after a job loss: Long term impact of the JOBS program on reemployment and mental health. *Journal of Occupational Health Psychology, 5*, 32–47. doi:10.1037/1076–8998.5.1.32

Wagenaar, A., Gehan, J., Jones-Webb, R., Wolfson, M., Toomey, T., Forster, J., & Murray, D. (1999). Communities mobilizing for change on alcohol: Lessons and results from a 15-community randomized trial. *Journal of Community Psychology, 27*, 315–326.

Wagenaar, A., Murray, D., Gehan, J., Wolfson, M., Forster, J., Toomey, T., . . . Jones-Webb, R. (1998). Communities mobilizing for change on alcohol: Outcomes from a randomized community trial. *Journal of Studies on Alcohol, 61*, 85–94.

Wagenaar, A., Murray, D., & Toomey, T. (2000). Communities mobilizing for change on alcohol (CMCA): Effects of a randomized trial on arrests and traffic crashes. *Addiction, 95*, 209–217. doi:10.1046/j.1360–0443.2000.9522097.x

Wandersman, A., & Florin, P. (2003). Community interventions and effective prevention. *American Psychologist, 58*, 441–448. doi:10.1037/0003–066x.58.6–7.441

Werner, E. (1996). Vulnerable but invincible—High-risk children from birth to adulthood. *European Child & Adolescent Psychiatry, 5*, 47–51.

Wootan, A. (2010). *Program evaluations in youth development nonprofits: What works?* Bloomington, IN: Indiana University School of Public and Environmental Affairs. Retrieved from http://www.indiana.edu/~spea/pubs/undergrad-honors/volume-4/wootan_allison.pdf

8

WELLNESS AND PREVENTION INITIATIVES WITH COLLECTIVES

Systems

> The *National Prevention Strategy* will move us from a system of sick care to one based on wellness and prevention.
>
> —Benjamin (2011, p. 3)

Systems Strongly Influence Our Lives

How do policies and other external systems influence wellness and prevention counseling? In this chapter we will consider the outer ring of the ecological context to examine wellness and prevention initiatives at the *systems* level.

By "systems" I mean large, complex institutions and the policies, legislation, laws, and regulations that can strongly influence our lives and the social order of life. Examples include a large institution such as the Internal Revenue Service or the Department of Health and Human Services, as well as legislation and policies associated with the areas of health care, finance, government, and religion to name a few. These systems may seem remote to our daily lives existing, in a sense, somewhere out there in the ether. Yet their impacts are experienced daily and often cogently. When social security benefits are threatened, new legislation is passed to provide greater access to higher education, or a significant economic downturn occurs—people on the ground, you and me or someone we know—are affected.

It's important for counselors to be aware of systemic resources and to actually infuse and apply principles and practices drawn from them in their work. In fact, the second major goal for this chapter is to examine how counselors and other mental health professionals can involve themselves directly at the systems level. A prime example is how these helping professionals can assist systems they are involved with (e.g., schools and communities) to become safe and healthy. The counseling for wellness and prevention model, discussed in chapter 4, can be a helpful resource in this overall goal.

Regrettably, system-level involvement often is unaddressed in graduate training other than to say something like, "being aware and involved at the systems level is important." But, *how* is the question. That is the purpose of this final chapter.

Systems are powerful influencers of people—positive, negative, and in between. In fact, systems represent the largest source of impact possible. Think, for instance, of how empowering it is for a previously uninsurable person due to a preexisting health condition to now be enrolled and covered as a consequence of the Patient Protection and Affordable Care Act, or of how access to mental health care is equivalent to that for physical health care.

Social problems within systems are all too prevalent. In one view, they emerge from three sources (Jimenez, Pasztor, & Chambers, 2014): (a) the interaction of unique ideologies and historical social values, (b) the economic structure, and (c) the legacy of discrimination and oppression against women, certain ethnic groups, and people with different sexual orientations. These sources also contribute to and in some cases restrict social policies and legislation that are developed to address social problems occurring in systems. As Jiminez et al. (2014) suggest, "each policy demonstrates the power or our ideologies and values. . . the continuing inequities of the market economy. . . and fails to meet the needs of groups who have experienced discrimination and oppression" (p. 4).

Moreover, some of the unintentional effects of systems on people may be experienced as pernicious or just plain burdensome. Governmental policy and legislation, for instance, are intended to benefit the broad populace, but they may sometimes impinge on selected groups or, in fact, may be incompatible with human dignity. Historic examples included Apartheid in South Africa and Jim Crow laws in the American South.

Indeed, caustic conditions sometimes virtually cry out for needed systems-level action. Bullying in schools is a national damaging phenomenon. Oppression against those who are different from the mainstream is not isolated to a few locales but is broadly experienced by many throughout the country. The income gap between the very rich and the very poor is expanding. Homelessness on our sidewalks and under our bridges is an inescapable daily presence. Obesity is a national epidemic. Killings occur in our communities throughout the country and are the subject of nearly every evening television news broadcast. And shooting rampages in schools and workplaces take place with alarming frequency. Every month or even week, it seems, we learn of another shooting rampage occurring in an American school or workplace. These conditions and events are the warp and woof of mental disturbance.

One Example: Incarceration Tied to Policy

Let's take a quick look at simply one pernicious problem in America, that of incarceration (Collier, 2014). It is shocking to realize that the United States imprisons more of its citizens than does any other country in the world—and by far. Research of the National Research Council (NRC; 2014) indicates that 707 of

100,000 citizens are behind bars in the United States (amounting to an annual jail population of around 13 million people, equivalent to the combined populations of New York City, Chicago, and Los Angeles), with the next closest two slots occupied by the Russian Federation (474) and Ukraine (286). Our gentler neighbor to the north clocks in at 118 per 100,000, and Finland brings up the rear, with a "mere" 58. One of the many reasons for the steep numbers in the United States is due to the mental health crisis in our country: "We have an enormous number of people who are suffering from very treatable illnesses who are not getting treatment and who end up getting caught in the criminal justice system as opposed to the mental health system" (Tangney, as cited in Collier, 2014, p. 59).

Policy changes and other solutions are needed. For instance, the NRC urges that the rate of incarceration be reduced through revised criminal justice policies, that resources be committed to support prisoners' reentry to society, and that policy makers target the deeper socioeconomic conditions that give rise to crime initially, such as the lack of education, poverty, and drug addiction.

What often roadblocks the development and implementation of broad systems-level action in response to these kinds of crushingly interminable problems is due to many factors. The problems are both incredibly complex to get a good grasp on and how to proceed in approaching them is fraught with controversy evolving from a host of factors—contentious beliefs, practices, politics, and cultural and regional divides in American society—as well as the resources it might take to concertedly make a positive difference.

Some Public Policy and Legislative Gains

Yet successes in legislation and public policy certainly have occurred, so all is not doom and gloom. The Civil Rights Act of 1964, state laws allowing for same sex marriage, the Surgeons General reports over the decades to support healthy living (e.g., 2014 marks the 50th year of the first such report, the *U.S. Surgeon General Report on Smoking*, which introduced America to the deleterious health effects of nicotine and smoking cigarettes), the Patient Protection and Affordable Care Act, Healthy People 2020, and international initiatives sponsored by the World Health Organization (WHO) come to mind.

Healthy People 2020 serves as the foundation for prevention effort for the U.S. Department of Health and Human Services (HHS). It supports HHS efforts to create a healthier Nation. In the next box, find 15 prevention initiatives listed that are associated with Healthy People and the Department Health and Human Services. These are hyperlinks, allowing you to click and go directly to the indicated initiative, such as the First Lady's Let's Move Campaign, discussed in chapter 2, and the National Prevention Strategy (Healthypeople.gov, 2014), which has been referred to at various points in this book and is considered in more detail later in this chapter.

Healthy People Initiatives Supporting Wellness and Prevention

Systems-Level Directions for Counselors

- Tobacco Control Strategic Action Plan
- HHS Initiative on Multiple Chronic Conditions
- Action Plan for the Prevention, Care, and Treatment of Viral Hepatitis
- Healthcare-Associated Infection (HAI)
- Public Health System, Finance, and Quality Program
- HHS Action Plan to Reduce Racial and Ethnic Health Disparities
- National Prevention Strategy
- National HIV/AIDS Strategy
- National Drug Control Strategy
- Let's Move Campaign
- President's Food Safety Working Group
- Global Health Initiative
- U.S. National Vaccine Plan
- National Action Plan to Improve Health Literacy
- HHS Environmental Justice

Policies at the local, state, and national levels affect health. Let's consider, once again, the Patient Protection and Affordable Care Act (PPCA), colloquially referred to as "Obamacare." A concise summary of the many prevention and health promotion features of the act are contained in Engel (2010), "Prevention in Health Care Reform: The Time Has Come." The PPACA includes provisions that "ensure that all Americans have access to free preventive services under their health insurance plans and invests in prevention and public health to encourage innovations in health care that prevent illness and disease before they require more costly treatment" (p. 259). One aspect of the act is to assure that most health plans cover a range of preventive services, such as immunizations and screenings at no cost to the individual. For those of us particularly interested in mental health, preexisting conditions no longer matter in acquiring health insurance, including mental illness conditions. The creation of health care marketplaces to make available affordable health insurance for those 40 million Americans presently without it will provide a safety net for them that has not been available before, as well as reduce health care costs. Moreover, in November 2013, final steps of the 2008 Mental Health Parity and Addiction Equity Act were completed. Now insurers must cover care for mental health and addiction on a par with physical illnesses.

This requirement results in full parity and it also extends to all those who are now included within the Affordable Care Act. This combined legislation is expected to improve access to mental health care and contribute to the de-stigmatization of counseling and therapy. Still excluded, however, is parity coverage for the millions on Medicaid and on Medicare, so there is more room for growth.

These macro-level legislative advancements in support of mental health access and coverage are expressions of prevention in health care reform (Engel, 2010). Positive steps such as these can be expected to contribute to wellness and prevention in our society. The stakes seem to be getting higher. A case in point refers to the 12 mass shootings and 88 deaths that have rocked the country from about October 2012 to November 2013. Mental illness has been implicated in many of these events, although the situations are complex and involve many factors. But being able to more easily access covered mental health services in a fairer and more accepting environment should make for a healthier population and social system.

Public policy and systems are intertwined. The country's financial solvency depends to an appreciable degree on policies adopted by the U.S. Federal Reserve Board. Policies of the Roman Catholic Church on issues such as abortion, homosexuality, or the role of women in the church set guidance for world-wide behavior of its members.

As we have seen, existing and changing health care policy in the United States shapes the system that evolves. Two noteworthy examples on the near horizon relate to obesity, a point discussed in chapter 2. In the first case, pending requirements of the Affordable Care Act that large restaurant chains must post calories immediately alongside food prices are leading several of them to respond early by reducing calories contained in their offerings. A large study by the Johns Hopkins Bloomberg School of Public Health shows that these calorie reductions, mostly in salads and sandwiches, are in the average of 12% (Bleich, Wolfson, & Jarlenski, 2014; Horovitz, 2014). Relatedly, top U.S. soda makers have voluntarily agreed to reduce calories in their soft drinks over the next decade by slimming down drink portions and marketing a range of healthier options. This groundbreaking initiative results from cooperation between the soda companies (Coca Cola Company and PepsiCo Americas Beverages) and the Alliance for a Healthier Generation, an anti-obesity organization created by the American Heart Association and the Clinton Foundation (HealthDay News, 2014).

In this section, we will examine three examples of significant policy statements that affect mental health practitioners and clients and the entire system of mental health in this country and around the world. Of significance is the relationship of these policies to wellness and prevention, which is our focus in this book, and which tapes a deep vein running throughout the healthcare system.

We will begin at the largest span of system, the whole world, by considering a recent initiative of the World Health Organization (2013), its comprehensive Mental Health Action Plan. Subsequent attention is given to the National

Prevention Council's (2011) National Prevention Strategy, which is geared to change mental health practice from an emphasis on illness to one of wellness and prevention. Last, we take up the issue of gun violence and its prevention by considering a report of the American Psychological Association (APA; 2013), Gun Violence Prediction, Prevention, and Policy, which emphasizes the role of primary and secondary prevention. These examples are important for wellness and prevention are highlighted in the next box.

Three Significant Policy Statements for Wellness and Prevention

WHO: *Comprehensive Mental Health Action Plan*
National Prevention Council: *National Prevention Strategy*
American Psychological Association: *Gun Violence, Prediction, Prevention, & Policy*

The World Health Organization's Comprehensive Mental Health Action Plan: An Initiative for the World

Most of the attention throughout this book has been placed on conditions occurring within the United States. However, it's important to realize that wellness and prevention needs are a world-wide concern. Initiatives of relevance for counselors and other mental health professionals also extend beyond our national borders. We are a global and interdependent world, after all, where conditions on the other side of the world are impactful and meaningful locally.

The WHO contributes significant systems-level schemes, such as those contained in its documents addressing violence and health (World Health Organization [WHO], 2002), social determinants of health (WHO, 2008) and on the healthy workplace framework and model (WHO, 2010). The work of the WHO is centered on world and global conditions, as its name indicates. The United States is a member country and supporter.

The WHO's most recent offering is its *Comprehensive Mental Health Action Plan 2013–20* (WHO, 2013), which the 66th World Health Assembly adopted in May 2013 and launched in October, 2013 (Clay, 2014). This plan is aimed at improving mental health services across the world. It is premised on the harsh reality that up to 85% of people experiencing mental disorders are from low- and middle-income countries where cruel living conditions persist as well as health care facilities that are debasing and injurious. In the United States, of course, we are not immune in terms of low income and income disparities, or in related issues such as equitable access to good health and mental health care. For instance, the U.S. Census Bureau reported that 15% of the population in the United States lived at or below the poverty level in 2012, totaling some 46.5 million persons (U.S. Census Bureau, 2013).

Objectives. Called a landmark achievement by the WHO Director-General Margaret Chan, MD, the comprehensive mental health plan contains four main objectives:

1. *Strengthen mental health leadership in member countries* through developing a mental health plan and supporting mental health legislation to protect human rights
2. *Locate comprehensive health and mental health services in local communities*, leading to increasing service coverage for severe mental disorders by 20% and reducing suicide rate by 10%
3. *Implement prevention and mental health promotion strategies*, with at least two multifaceted programs put into place by 80% of member countries, and
4. *Enhance research, information systems, and evidence for mental health* through a core set of mental health indicators being routinely collected and reported by 80% of member countries.

Clay (2014), writing about this plan for psychologists in the APA *Monitor*, identifies roles for American psychologists. First, because psychologists and other mental health professionals contributed to the plan's development, its content is relevant. According to Michelle Funk (as cited in Clay, 2014), a psychologist at WHO, some of the plan's attractions to psychologists are as follows:

- Its incorporation of not only treatment and the medical model but, more important, its emphasis on a holistic model
- Use of a coordinated social services approach addressing mental health issues in the context of a several related domains, including education, social care, employment, and others
- An emphasis on human rights as a primary route to improved mental health status in impoverished countries and environments often means addressing the causal conditions giving rise to emotional problems, such as oppressive systems, poverty, and broad human rights abuses. This focus fits well with underpinnings for wellness and prevention efforts in prevention and social justice.
- Specification of concrete actionable goals for mental health achievement through 2020, for the first time. Reducing the suicide rate by 10% in member countries over that time period is one example.

Psychologists specifically are set to contribute to the plan's enactment in two major ways (Ritchie, as cited in Clay, 2014). The first is they will aid in identifying what psychological interventions may fit circumstances prevailing in member countries. Second, they will help assess progress and goal accomplishment in relation to the indices.

National Prevention Strategy: Moving From a System of Sick Care to One of Wellness and Prevention

This major strategy was introduced by the National Prevention, Health Promotion, and Public Health Council, chaired by Regina M. Benjamin, MD, Surgeon General of the United States and Council Chair, on June 16, 2011. Membership on the National Prevention Council is broad. It is comprised of 17 heads of agencies, departments, and offices from the Federal government that are vested with promoting wellness and prevention. Its sweep is just as wide, seeking to influence wellness and prevention practices not only in the federal government but extending to state and local policy makers, business leaders, communities, families, and individuals. The Council seeks to support and advocate for those policies and programs required to promote and ensure the health of all Americans.

As the Surgeon General and Council Chair stated in her introduction to the Strategy (Benjamin, 2011), "*the National Prevention Strategy will move us from a system of sick care to one based on wellness and prevention*" (p. 3; italics added). This aspirational quotation, you may recall, introduced this chapter because of its aspirational significance. It is to be pursued to a large degree by establishing and working through partnerships among Federal, state, tribal, local, and territorial governments; industry, business and other private sector groups; community and faith-based organizations, philanthropic groups; and everyday citizens to advance health and wellness through prevention. This means working not only through the health care system directly but, also, through systems lying outside it, in housing, education, transportation, workplaces, and the physical environment. As Benjamin (2011) puts it, "This is why the National Prevention Strategy helps us understand how to weave prevention into the fabric of our everyday lives" (p. 3).

Consequently, the vision of the National Prevention Strategy (National Prevention Council, 2011) is as follows:

> Working together to improve the health and quality of life for individuals, families, and communities by moving the nation from a focus on sickness and disease to one based on prevention and wellness.

Strategic directions. The Strategy includes four strategic directions and seven specifically targeted priorities pointing toward a "prevention society" that increases the health of Americans at all stages of life (U.S. Department of Health and Human Services, 2014). The directions emphasize: (a) the importance of healthy and safe community environments that promote health and wellness through prevention; (b) prevention services through available and integrated clinical and community prevention; (c) empowering people by helping them to make positive and healthy life choices; and (d) eliminating health disparities existing among people, such as unequal access to good health care, as a way of improving the quality of life. All of these directions are essential to the wellness and prevention approach that is the thesis of this book.

Priorities. Increasing the health and wellness of the U.S. population includes giving specific attention to those who are unduly affected by poorer health, more injuries, and challenging living conditions. Seven evidence-based priorities are part of the National Prevention Strategy, including (a) tobacco-free living, (b) preventing drug abuse and excessive alcohol use, (c) healthy eating, (d) active living, (e) injury and violence-free living, (f) reproductive and sexual health, and (g) mental and emotional well-being. While, of course, all of these independent priorities are essential to wellness and prevention, addressing their mutual interdependence can yield broader and deeper results. For counselors and other mental health professionals the mental and emotional well-being priority stands out.

Mental and emotional well-being. The National Prevention Strategy seeks to support positive mental and emotional wellness through prevention. Its province includes quality relationships with family and friends, workplaces that maintain a positive environment, safe and healthy schools, communities that encourage their members to contribute and participate, and the availability of and access to appropriate mental health services. Four broad recommendations are contained to advance mental and emotional well-being, each containing examples of actions that can be taken by providers:

- *Promote positive early childhood development.* Successful approaches can include conducting evidence supported positive parenting practices and programs, violence reduction programs, family intervention such as home visitations and parenting training, and comprehensive early childhood development programs. Educating parents on normal child development and behavior is important for counselors to do, as well as delivering interventions to enhance the emotional well-being of children and providing support to parents through home visits and other means.
- *Facilitate social connections and community engagement throughout the lifespan.* Connect clients with safe and healthy spaces (Cornell & Sheras, 2006), such as neighborhood parks, community organizations, schools, workplaces, and families where people can interact freely and positively all characterize this recommendation. This includes supporting those older adults who wish and are able to maintain their independence to remain in their home and communities (termed "aging in place"), and assisting people with disabilities with access to transportation, health, and suitable employment opportunities.
- *Support individuals and families to maintain positive mental well-being.* Teach problem-solving and coping skills strategies, which can enhance positive decisions and relationships, and social development strategies that can empower people to better manage social situations and seek help when necessary. Encourage regular exercise, which can promote thinking skills, lower depression, improve physical health, and quality sleep. Engage or support community-wide public awareness programs and public policy, which can increase awareness of and actions regarding positive mental health.

- *Advance early identification of mental health needs and improve access to quality services.* At the individual counseling level, screen and identify mental health needs as early as possible for prevention, treatment, and referral. Work to reduce the stigma attached to counseling and mental health services to improve access and use of these services. With client consent, increase appropriate communication and data sharing across social service networks so that those in need might be identified and helped.

See Figure 8.1, which displays the directions and priorities of the strategy.

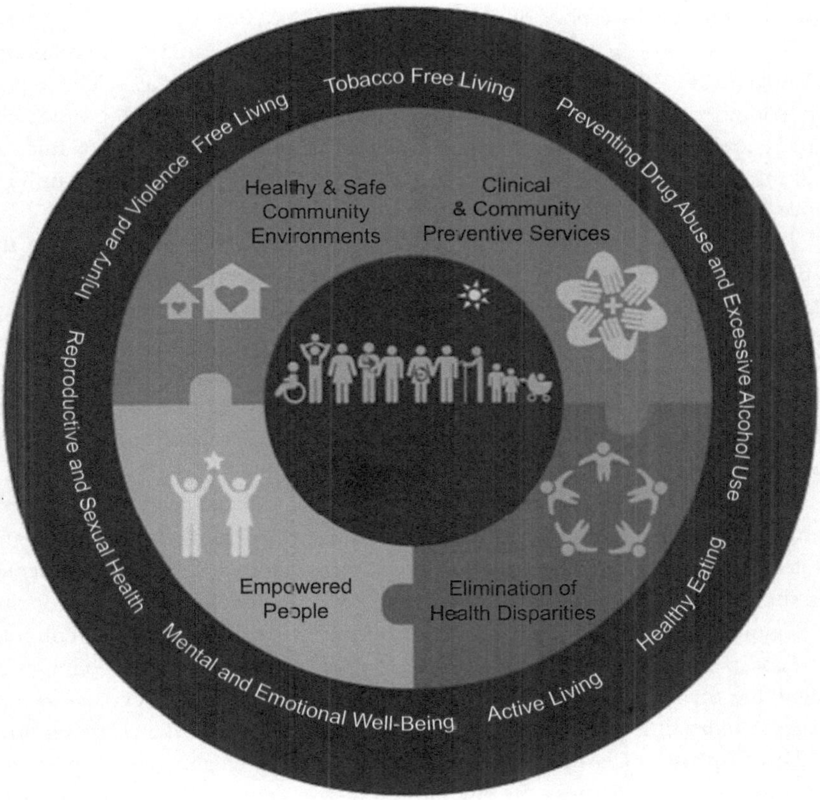

FIGURE 8.1 National Prevention Strategy: America's plan for better health and wellness. The vision is to move from sickness and disease to wellness and prevention.

Gun Violence Prediction, Prevention, and Policy: Addressing an Urgent Societal Problem

Let's turn now to examine an urgent, complex and controversial public issue in the United States, gun violence. As President Obama stated after the Sandy Hook Elementary School tragedy, "We won't be able to stop every violent act, but if there is even one thing we can do to prevent any of these events, we have a deep obligation, all of us, to try" (White House, 2013). The plan from the White House contains four main elements: (a) close background loopholes to prevent guns from getting to dangerous people; (b) ban military-style assault weapons and high-capacity gun magazines; (c) make schools safer; and (d) increase access to mental health services. Notably, this plan and others we will consider, do not include what is an extreme approach and un-recommended approach to school safety that is gaining some momentum, that of school officials becoming licensed to carry concealed weapons on school grounds (Clark, 2014).

We will consider a panel of experts report issued by the American Psychological Association (2013), *Gun Violence Prediction, Prevention, and Policy*. This report was commissioned by APA following the mass shootings at Sandy Hook Elementary School and at the Aurora, Colorado movie theater, both in 2012. Its findings will inform the ongoing work of APA's Policy Review Task Force on Gun Violence Prediction and Prevention.

The report under discussion draws from an extensive research base on the topic of gun violence to provide conclusions and recommendations aimed at reducing the incidence of gun violence by homicide, suicide, or by mass shootings and killings. Of course, it is the latter category of mass shootings that has intensified concerns related to gun-deaths. That this is so is certainly understandable. Since the mass shootings at Sandy Hook Elementary School in New Jersey in 2012 that killed 23, another 23 similar mass shooting events have occurred, killing more than 100 (Pace, Gunter, Oliver, Palmer, & Lawler, 2013).

The research paper contributes important evidence-based analysis and accompanying recommendations to the scientific and public conversation about gun violence. It examines antecedents to gun violence, focusing on developmental, gender and culture issues. It then summarizes what has been effective in reducing gun violence, examining prediction and prevention at the individual, community and policy levels. The paper concludes with recommendations. Highlighted below are themes addressing developmental issues and what has been shown to work in addressing gun violence, but I encourage you to read the entire report.

Developmental issues. No single profile exists to reliably predict who will use a gun violently because the risk and protective factors involved are so many and so interactive over time. So, there is no one developmental path leading concretely to gun violence. As with other conditions, the best predictor of future violent behavior is past violent behavior. Yet, the report concludes that prevention efforts supported by research on developmental risks can reduce the likelihood of firearms being used during conflicts or criminal acts.

For example, research suggests that the following conditions are associated with increased risk for gun violence: (a) early childhood rule-breaking and aggression; (b) socialization into criminal behaviors by parents and others who are themselves involved; (c) exposure in childhood to many adverse family and community experiences; (d) social dislocation due to school underachievement or failure; (e) continuing affiliation with peers or gangs involved in deviant activities and with attitudes supporting use of guns; (f) wide exposure to sociocultural influences, such as mass media, where gun violence is shown as an effective way to achieve; (g) males and females seem to generally hold different attitudes about gun control policies, with females tending to be much more positive; and (h) preliminary evidence suggests efforts to modify social norms and culture associated with stereotypic masculinity may assist in reducing gun violence.

What works. Following are summarizes of what approaches have shown some success, with implications for applications by counselors, psychologists, social workers, and other professional helpers. A recent analysis by Conyne and Firth (in press) specifies extant research and available strategies for the prevention of school shootings. It emphasizes the importance of threat assessment and other promising gun control strategies falling within an umbrella of a comprehensive school wellness and prevention framework, such as the model highlighted in this book.

Prevention is important. It can diminish the use of guns by those who are depressed or, more rarely, who suffer severe mental illness. Prevention programs also can be geared to assist in uncoupling cultural scripts that closely tie masculinity with guns and shooting. More broadly, the point of this book is that wellness and prevention counseling programs hold high promise for promoting healthy conditions in an environment while reducing or, in some cases, eliminating undesirable or dangerous behaviors.

Policies and procedures supporting behavioral threat assessment are needed, as it is a necessary and important strategy for addressing at risk individuals. School shootings can benefit from a behavioral threat assessment approach. These mass shootings in schools, such as in Columbine or in Sandy Hook, are highly traumatic events but the report points out that it's important to remember that school environments are highly safe compared with other community settings (e.g., less than 2% of all school-aged homicides occur in schools). Their relative infrequency does not allow for development of reliable student profiles or checklists of potential shooters.

Rather, a behavioral threat assessment approach (Miller, 2014) is indicated, where students who threaten actual violence or are involved in noticeable threatening behavior are identified, with individualized interventions administered to prevent threats from being turned into action. The behavioral health assessment approach is especially useful, I suggest, when it is an integral aspect of an overall wellness and prevention model being implemented at the system level in a school, workplace, or community.

Mental health treatment at the individual level with those who are at risk for violence due to mental illness, suicidal thoughts, and feelings of desperation often can prevent gun violence. Behavioral threat assessment is becoming a standard of care for preventing violence in schools, colleges and the workplace and against government and other public officials. The report stresses that urgent attention is needed to address this area, which involves identifying and intervening with individuals or with a smaller group of people who have communicated threats or have been planning or preparing to commit violence. Threat assessment teams gather and analyze information to assess if a person poses a threat of violence or self-harm, and if so, take steps to intervene.

Threat assessment ("TA") emerged within the FBI's Critical Incident Group, which has spawned Behavioral Analysis units, one of which specializes in analyzing threats as part of a "pathway to violence." For an instructive discussion of threat assessment and mass shooters, see Junod (2014) in *Esquire* magazine, as well as the scholarly sources cited. An important point made is that prospective mass shooters "want to be known, not through the infamy of a massacre, but before they have to go through with it" (p. 83). Threat assessment rests on the assumption that mass killings can be prevented if the pathway to violence can be intersected, which first takes a bystander to notice and then for an at risk person to be connected with an organization with a treat assessment protocol in place.

The prevention of violence needs to be understood within a continuum. Beginning with early childhood, programs need to be developed to help parents and caregivers nurture emotionally healthy children and proceeding to bring wellness and prevention programs to bear throughout the life span. The report emphasizes that the mental health community must take the lead in advocating for community-based collaborative problem-solving models to address gun violence.

A new community-based model needs to be created. Such a model would break down silos by organizing community stakeholders together in a collaborative, problem-solving model, with a goal of preventing individuals from engaging in gun violence, whether directed at others or self-inflicted.

Basic safety precautions are required. Actions such as how to store guns safely, need to be communicated by parents to children and to physicians, and mental health professionals to patients and clients in the regular course of their work. Public health messages about gun safety also are recommended.

Public policies and laws need to be addressed. Current U.S. policies that are in place focus on gun users, with relatively few of them addressing the "lifespan of guns." This lifespan includes their design and manufacture, distribution, advertising, sales and purchases—as well as use. Research is needed in all these areas to determine which existing policies work and what other ones might be needed.

The report calls for a multifaceted approach to reducing gun violence that incorporates the areas addressed above. Wellness and prevention approaches are an essential part of this multifaceted approach, with their emphasis on developing competencies throughout the life span and on removing or reducing harmful risk factors.

The Importance of Public Policy and Legislative Awareness for Counselors

Public policy and legislation are one vital aspect of a system, and a wealth of public policy resources is available that supports wellness, prevention, and social justice. Alas, it goes largely untapped by too many counselors and other professional mental health practitioners. This is so because these resources and, in fact, the whole question of system-level change, typically is not included in counselor preparation. To advance wellness and prevention it is important that practitioners need to become aware of public policy resources and of how they can inform the work of counselors.

Embedded in the discussion of the three systems-level initiatives considered earlier in this chapter are suggestions for how counselors and other mental health professionals can be involved at the systems level. Return to those sections for a refresher. In general, mental health professionals need to keep aware of the recommendations contained in documents such as those summarized and then find how they can use their skills of education, collaboration, consultation, and advocacy to enact whatever recommendations fit the issues and contexts of their local communities. Perhaps the key point is *to become aware of the systems-level and public policy and legislative resource documents that are available*. The evidence-supported position papers and policies of organizations, such as the World Health Organization and the U.S. Department of Health and Human Services, provide a wealth of information that needs to be followed up on by professionals in the field to guide local research and action.

Take a look at the wellness and prevention-oriented public policy and legislation initiatives in selected areas (e.g., nicotine, suicide prevention) that are contained in Table 8.1. They represent steps of accomplishment in the public policy arena to advance wellness, prevention, and social justice and they provide opportunities for counselor action with clients and client systems. This content is adapted from material previously summarized in narrative form by Pirog and Good (2013). Please also refer to the extensive analysis and summaries of social welfare policies and programs in the United States provided by Jimenez et al. (2014).

A Successful Initiative: Preventing Cigarette Smoking

As we have discussed periodically in this book, cigarette smoking and other uses of tobacco (e.g., chewing it) are known threats to wellness and health. Worse, long-term use of tobacco products can cause death.

Fifty years ago the U.S. Surgeon General launched a public health prevention campaign aimed at reducing deaths attributed to smoking. In fact, the goal was to eliminate smoking from the landscape of America. Of course, the power of tobacco companies, the severe challenges associated with nicotine's powerful addictive

TABLE 8.1 Illustrative Public Policy and Prevention Initiatives: Programs and Outcomes

Area addressed	*Public policy and legislation*	*Example programs*
Nicotine	Family Smoking Prevention and Control Act (Tobacco Control Act) *Implemented in 2009.* Enables the FDA to control the retail, marketing and manufacture of tobacco products. Among other stipulations, mandates that large warning labels be placed on all cigarette packs.	Center for Tobacco Products The Center for Tobacco Products has multiple functions, one of which is the running of a national media campaign designed to target youth who have started smoking or are exploring it as an option. Other campaigns will target other at risk youth populations (Federal Drug Administration, 2014).
Substance abuse	The Safe and Drug Free Schools and Community Act *Implemented in 1994* Provides grants to fund evidence based, effective community programming designed to reduce school violence and substance use.	Safe Schools Healthy Students Initiative Received funding in 2011. This grant program dispersed funds to various partners working to create safe communities (U.S. Department of Education, Office of Safe and Drug-Free Schools, 2011).
Suicide prevention	The Joshua Omvig Veterans Suicide Prevention Act *Implemented in 2007* Emphasized increased training for VA staff, increase suicide assessment use, veteran mental health research, the creation of suicide prevention counselors, among other stipulations.	Veteran's Suicide Prevention Hotline This hotline was the result of the act's requirement that there is 24 hour mental health care available to veterans.
Health care	Patient Protection and Affordable Care Act (PPACA) *Implemented in 2010* Requires that individuals have health care insurance, that states provide health care coverage, and that businesses provide health care options. Incorporates an emphasis on prevention and preventive services, such that certain preventive services, including mental health, must be covered by all insurance plans.	Wellness Programs Wellness and preventive services and programs are now a required part of insurance policies. Specifically, employees who reach specific health standards through participation in wellness programs may pay less for insurance. Small employers are also pushed to incorporate wellness and prevention programs though the legislation's provision of wellness program grant money. Medicare Preventive Benefits This part of the PPACA legislation ensures that Medicare enrollee's also have access to preventive services, including personalized prevention plans and comprehensive health risk assessment.

Eating disorders	The Federal Response to Eliminate Eating Disorders Act (FREED) *Implemented in 2011* Designates funding for research, education, and training on eating disorders.	Task Force on Eating Disorders Prevention in Educational Institutions A program designed to train educational professionals working in schools on eating disorder identification and prevention.
Mental Illness and the law	America's Law Enforcement and Mental Health Project and Mentally Ill Offender Treatment and Crime Reduction Act *Implemented in 2004* Provides funding for psychological training for police officers, prisoner access to mental health counseling both while in prison and after release, and alternatives to incarceration.	Mental Health Courts Mental Health Courts provide psychological intervention to individuals with mental illness through collaboration with community mental health centers as an alternative to incarceration.
Gun control and mental health	Brady Handgun Violence Protection Act *Implemented in 1993* Individuals who want to purchase a handgun must go through a background check.	National Instant Criminal Background Check System (NICS) This system started running in 1998. Requires cashiers to call in background checks to the FBI before completing a sale for firearms or explosives. Since 1998 there have been more than 100 million checks, and 700,000 denials. Has kept guns out of the hands of 1.9 million high-risk individuals (Federal Bureau of Investigation, 2014).

qualities, and the prevailing attitude among many that smoking is "cool," made this goal seem improbable, at best. However, it seems that such progress has been made that experts now increasingly envision the end of smoking in this country, anticipating that the smoking rate in the U.S. will drop to 10% over the next 10 years and to 5% by 2050 from the current 18%. According to Acting U.S. Surgeon General Boris Lushniak, these results can be accelerated to reach 0% by that date, because of the public health policies and procedures now available (Stobbe, 2014).

It is instructive to review the steps that have accumulated to lead to this possibility, as a TA protocol discussion (Curry School of Education, 2013), and the treatment by them illustrate the power that public policy and programs can have on behavior change:

–Cigarette tax increases, from about \$1.75/pack in the early 1990s to over \$5.00/pack

–Laws banning smoking in restaurants, bars, and workplaces
–Public attitude change, that smoking generally is no longer perceived as being acceptable
–Antismoking advertising by federal agencies, such as the CDC and FDA
–2009 federal law giving FDA authority to regulate tobacco products (still awaiting actions)
–Significant legal setbacks experienced by tobacco companies
–Changes in retailing cigarettes (notably, CVS Caremark, the country's second largest pharmacy chain, which stopped selling tobacco products in October 2014)
–Development of cigarette cessation programs

In addition, wellness and prevention approaches throughout all areas of health have contributed to a building awareness that lifestyle matters in the quality and length of life.

An Initiative Yet Unfulfilled: Suicide Prevention

Suicide is a major mental health problem that is completely preventable. Yet it remains a crisis in this country, the 10th leading cause for death overall, coming in at number three for people between the ages of 15 and 24 in 2009. Shockingly, nearly 4 deaths occur by suicide every hour of every day, amounting to 40,000 per year (American Foundation for Suicide Prevention, 2014; National Institute of Mental Health, 2014). These alarming figures are exacerbated when considering that the national budget assigned to suicide prevention lags far behind other diseases. For example, National Institutes of Health research dollars in millions spent from 2009–2013 were for: (a) suicide: $165; (b) heart disease: $5,045; (c) prostate cancer: $1,182; (d) breast cancer: $3,000; (e) colorectal cancer: $1,187; and (f) HIV/AIDS: $12,237 (Zoroya, 2014). The release by the U.S. Office of the Surgeon General (2012) of a National Strategy for Suicide Prevention points to a coordinated plan of attack. Investing more funds in suicide prevention and mobilizing professional and public motivation to help enact the Strategy are desperately needed.

Public Policy and Legislation Systems-Level Resources of Professional Associations

A treasure trove of resources also is generated, collated, and maintained by professional associations. Psychologists can turn to the American Psychological Association (APA) and to relevant Divisions and Societies to which they may belong. Journals, newsletters, conferences, and web-based resources are within reach. The same situation exists for counselors (the American Counseling Association, ACA), and its divisions and for social workers (the National Association of Social Workers, NASW, and its divisions), and so on.

I want to point attention to the category of the web-based system level resources maintained by a professional association for its members, because I believe they are consistently overlooked while holding significant opportunity for wellness and prevention. Let's take a look at four examples drawn from American Psychological Association and American Counseling Association Web sites.

APA Web Site Resources: Public Education and Outreach

- Public Education and Outreach (American Psychological Association [APA], 2014d). A major initiative that arches *public education campaigns* to educate the public about mental health issues, *the Psychologically Healthy Workplace Program* to educate about the link between work organizations and employee health and well-being, and the *Disaster Resource Network* that connects volunteer psychologists with providing disaster relief. These resources arm psychologists with powerful tools they can use in their practice and for wider public education and advocacy efforts.
- Public Interest Government Relations Office (APA, 2014a). This initiative seeks to influence and shape federal policy to advance psychology in serving the public interest. Particular emphasis is placed on children, youth, and families; disability issues; ethnic minority affairs; and on lesbian, gay, bisexual and transgender issues, although a number of other matters are of concern, too, such as socioeconomic status and women's issues. Take the area of children, youth, and families, where advocacy efforts are launched in child abuse, child care, mental health, family medical leave, early intervention, and violence prevention, all areas of high concern for psychologists and other mental health practitioners.
- Advancing Psychology: Guide to Federal Advocacy (APA, 2014b). Obviously, all citizens—including mental health professionals and their practices—are directly affected by policies and legislation established at local, state, and national levels. Yet, too few people exercise their right and privilege to participate in the political process (APA, 2014b). Three guides are available to psychologists to assist them in establishing and maintaining contact with their U.S. representatives and senators to advocate for psychology and psychological issues that are important to them. These guides outline valuable concrete actions psychologists can take to help move these issues along. By taking advantage of this opportunity, psychologists can channel their training and expertise proactively to contribute to federal policies and programs.

The three advocacy guides are (a) *Advancing Psychology Education and Training: A Psychologist's Guide to Federal Advocacy*; (b) *Advancing Psychology in the Public Interest: A Psychologist's Guide to Participation in Federal Policymaking*; and (c) *Advancing the Science: A Psychologist's Guide to Participation in Federal Policymaking*.

American Counseling Association Web Site Resource

- Governmental Affairs (American Counseling Association, 2014). ACA continually works on federal policy issues to advance the counseling profession and the capacity of counselors to more effectively deliver wellness, prevention, and remedial services. Among the advocacy projects underway address how counselors can support: (a) the initiative for gaining counselor access to the Veteran's Administration; (b) the passage of Bill S. 562, the "Seniors Mental Health Access Improvement Act of 2013," which would permit Medicare coverage for licensed professional counselors; (c) the work of school counselors through three pieces of legislation that need to be funded: the Elementary and Secondary School Counseling Program, the Safe School Healthy Students Initiative, and the Integration of School and Mental Health Systems; and (d) the Student Support Act to reduce the student to counselor ratio, and the Mental Health in Schools Act (introduced January 31, 2013 and awaiting passage) to increase collaboration of local education agencies with community-based health and social service organizations. In all these (and other) cases, the ACA Government Affairs office makes briefing papers or advocacy kits available for counselors to use in their advocacy efforts to advance important wellness, prevention, and social justice causes with elected officials.

You've already noted a number of ways that counselors, psychologists and other mental health professionals can become involved with systems-level work, including becoming aware of advancements in public policy legislation affecting wellness, prevention, and social justice. Education, Behavioral Threat Assessment, consultation, and advocacy with and on behalf of clients are other chief action strategies they can use. A summation, so far, of systems-level change approaches is presented in the next box.

Important Systems-Level Change Approaches Considered So Far

- Educate clients and the public regarding wellness and prevention approaches
- Screen
- Develop behavioral threat assessment policies and procedures
- Work to reduce mental health stigma
- Collaborate with other mental health and social service providers
- Develop, implement, and evaluate wellness and prevention programs (the counseling for wellness and prevention model can be helpful here)
- Consult with agencies and policy-level groups related to systems change
- Advocate using collaborative, community-based approach
- Become aware of public policy and legislative initiatives

Additional Systems-Level Involvement and Change Approaches

Counselors and other mental health professionals also can be involved at the systems-level in more individual ways, not necessarily as a part of a more broadly organized effort. Pirog and Good (2013) enumerated several examples that are summarized next.

Take advantage of "windows of opportunity." Scan your environment. Note significant events that occur that connect directly with wellness and prevention; these may provide opportunities for action. In a well-known example from 1966, Ira Iscoe, the director of the Counseling Center at the University of Texas at Austin, was able to obtain increased funding for providing campus counseling and psychological services following his immediate follow-up to the mass shootings by an engineering student, Charles Whitman, in which he killed 16 and wounded 32.

Use the media to help advocate change or establish a blog, Web site, or tweet. Social media provide vehicles for education and advocacy. In chapter 2 I mentioned several of these kinds of resources.

Be persistent and patient. Change at the systems level usually results from two steps forward and one step back, and sometimes, the reverse. The *Guidelines for Prevention in Psychology* that I discussed in chapter 1 took some 10 years to see the light of day.

Build or join an advocacy group, or volunteer with efforts to promote systems change. If there is a particular wellness and prevention issue that you think needs to be pushed forward (e.g., reducing mental health stigma), you might consider joining an existing organization in this area, such as Bringchange-2mind (2014), or an advocacy group within your professional association, such as the Public Interest Directorate of APA. If none exists, then consider joining with others of like mind and passion to start one. This is how Mothers Against Drunk Driving (MADD), and many other advocacy groups, took flight.

Whistle blowing. This approach is high-stakes, reserved perhaps when all else fails or when the situation is thought to be of dire consequences. Some famous cases of whistle blowing have been featured in the popular media, such as Erin Brockovich's action and subsequent movie (*Erin Brockovich*, 2000) addressing deadly environmental conditions. The Society for the Psychological Study of Social Issues (Costanzo, Gerrity, & Lykes, n.d.) strongly called into question the role of psychologists in torture at the U.S. Guantanamo prison in Cuba and the American Psychological Association, after considerable debate of the controversial matter, issued a policy statement (APA, 2014c) which remains a source of discussion (e.g., the Institute on Medicine as a Profession [IMAP], 2014, has criticized it and offered its own recommendations).

Know and contact your legislator. State and national professional associations provide briefings and offer specific training to members about how to reach out to legislators through mediated contact (e.g., by letter) or in person. Issues can be pressed forward in this way that address matters of importance for professional practice (e.g., aspects of licensure or insurance coverage) and for service to clients (e.g., increasing funding for suicide prevention).

Run for political office. Sometimes the best way for a professional to make a big difference is to be elected to public office. Members of the U.S. Congress come from many occupations, but the largest numbers, by far, are from business and the law. Mental health occupations are hardly noticeable: in 2011–1012, the 112th Congress, there were two psychologists in the House, seven social workers in the House and two in the Senate, and one psychiatrist in the Senate. No counselors were listed (Congressional Research Service, 2013). It perhaps is safe to say that we need more mental health professionals in political office, or maybe we could say, not entirely tongue in cheek, that such positions clearly represent a "growth industry" for mental health professionals. In terms of an appointed position, one of the more prominent roles occupied by a mental health professional was that of Patrick DeLeon (a former President of APA) who for 38 years served as chief of staff to Senator Daniel Inouye of Hawaii.

Get assigned to a board or commission. Look to your local community. What are the significant issues and needs? What is missing? Are there governmental committees, boards, or commissions that address these matters? Are they looking for members? Could you apply for membership? Or consult with the group? One example I was involved with for years was as an appointed commissioner with the Human Relations Commission of the city in which I was a resident. It was a spot from which I was able to educate and advocate for equity.

Teach and train students. If you are teacher or faculty member, opportunities present themselves to develop courses that speak directly to wellness, prevention, social justice and system change, or you can infuse this material within existing courses (Conyne, Newmeyer, Kenny, Romano, & Matthews, 2008). Education and training are primary methods for social change, as well as individual learning.

Provide continuing education related to public policy issues. Practitioners in the field are in positions of high importance in relation to service delivery. Given their work context, they can introduce wellness and prevention approaches and seek to influence system change to empower people. Most likely, though, having completed their degree programs some time ago, they may not have been exposed to these concepts and supporting competencies. Therefore, continuing education is a vital means to bring this important material to practitioners. Tying offerings to provisions of licensure or certification can help to increase attendance at events that are offered. For instance, a course to satisfy part of an ethics requirement might be titled, "Ethical Considerations in System Change Approaches."

Publish research and action findings, not only in scholarly journals but through electronic media, op-ed pieces, etc. Academics hold an obligation to produce scholarly work in peer-reviewed professional journals, conference presentations, and in books and monographs. Doing so is critically important, because significant knowledge and practice advancements are limited in their impact unless they are disseminated to others. In addition to the typical scholarly sources wellness, prevention, and system change advancements can and should be disseminated through non-traditional channels in an effort to reach more people. Articles in local newspapers, TV and radio interviews, op-ed pieces, and use of social media (such as blogs) need to be used, as well.

See the following box, which summarizes these additional ways of approaching system-level change and wellness and prevention.

Additional Public Policy and Legislation Systems-Level Strategies

–Take advantage of "windows of opportunity" (Pirog & Good, 2013, p. 62)
–Use the media to help advocate change or establish a blog, Web site, or tweet (p. 63)
–Be persistent and patient
–Build or join an advocacy group
–Become aware of and participate in public health advocacy work of professional associations of which you are a member
–Whistle blowing sometimes might be necessary
–Know and contact your legislators
–Run for political office
–Volunteer with efforts to promote systems change
–Get assigned to a board or commission
–Teach and train students
–Provide continuing education related to public policy issues
–Publish research and action findings, not only in scholarly journals but through electronic media, op-ed pieces, etc.

Final Thoughts on Counseling for Wellness and Prevention

Whether applied at the individual or system level, or someplace in between, wellness and prevention counseling is an important accompaniment to therapeutic services. The counseling for wellness and prevention model discussed in chapter 4 is one of several approaches that can be helpful in promoting health and preventing dysfunction.

There is much remaining to be accomplished in order to strengthen people and their communities against the significant mental health stressors that abound. Substantial health challenges continue to plague far too many people, and settings and systems remain too slow to broadly adopt best practices. But there also is significant progress being made. Wellness and prevention initiatives enjoy a strong evidence base and they also are able to generate significant cost savings.

You may recall that the opening of this book started with the following statement:

> It's more than time that counselors and other mental health professionals take the steps necessary to elevate wellness and prevention to occupy a prominent place in mental health delivery that effectively complements the important role of treatment.

May we all find ways to participate in this positive movement.

Issues for Reflection and Discussion

1. Early in this chapter, you read, "It's important for counselors to be aware of systemic resources and to actually infuse and apply principles and practices drawn from them in their work." What is your opinion of this assertion? What is meant by the term *systemic resources*?
2. Identify three ways that counselors can become involved at the systems level. Choose one of these ways and provide an example. Discuss with a partner.
3. What do you still need to learn to become involved effectively at this level? What competencies do you presently possess that can be applied?

References

American Counseling Association. (2014). *Governmental affairs*. Retrieved from www.counseling.org/government-affairs/current-issues

American Foundation for Suicide Prevention. (2014). *Understanding suicide*. Retrieved from http://www.afsp.org/understanding-suicide

American Psychological Association. (2013). *Gun violence: Prediction, prevention, and policy*. Retrieved from http://www.apa.org/pubs/info/reports/gun-violence-prevention.aspx

American Psychological Association. (2014a). *Public interest government relations office*. Retrieved from http://www.apa.org/about/gr/pi/index.aspx

American Psychological Association. (2014b). *Advancing psychology: A psychologist's guide to federal advocacy*. Retrieved from www.apa.org/about/gr/advocacy/guide.aspx

American Psychological Association. (2014c). *Position on ethics and interrogation*. Retrieved from http://www.apa.org/ethics/programs/position/

American Psychological Association. (2014d). *Practice Central: Public education and outreach*. Retrieved from http://www.apapracticecentral.org/outreach/index.aspx

Benjamin, R. (2011). *Message from the chair of the National Prevention, Health Promotion, and Public Health Council*. Retrieved from http://www.healthcare.gov/center/councils/nphpphc

Bleich, S., Wolfson, S., & Jarlenski, M. (2014, October 7). Calorie changes in chain restaurant menu items: Implications for obesity and evaluation of menu labeling. *American Journal of Preventive Medicine.* doi:10.1016/j.amepre.2014.08.026

Bringchange2mind. (2014, June 4). *Start the conversation. Stop the stigma.* Retrieved from http://www.bringchange2mind.org

Clark, M. (2014, October 20). Coming to these halls: Principal packing a gun. *The Cincinnati Enquirer,* pp. A1, A4.

Clay, R. A. (2014, January). Introducing the Mental Health Action Plan: The World Health Organization launches a comprehensive plan to improve services worldwide. *Monitor on Psychology, 45*(1). Retrieved from http://www.apa.org/monitor/

Collier, L. (2014). Incarceration nation. *Monitor on Psychology, 45*(9), 56–60, 62.

Congressional Research Service. (2013). *Annual Report of the Congressional Research Services of the Library of Congress for Fiscal Year 2012 to Joint Committee on the Library United States Congress.* Washington, DC: Author.

Conyne, R., & Firth, P. (in press). Preventing school shootings from a United States and European perspective. In M. Israelashvili & J. Romano (Eds.), *Cambridge handbook of international prevention science.* Cambridge: Cambridge University Press.

Conyne, R., Newmeyer, M., Kenny, M., Romano, J., & Matthews, C. (2008). Two key strategies for teaching prevention: Specialized course and infusion. *Journal of Primary Prevention, 29,* 375–401. doi:10.1007/s10935–008–0146–8

Cornell, D., & Sheras, P. (2006). *Guidelines for responding to student threats of violence.* Longmont, CO: Sopris West.

Costanzo, M., Gerrity, E., & Lykes, M. B. (n.d.). SSPI policy statement: The use of torture and other cruel, inhumane, or degrading treatment as interrogation devices. Retrieved from http://www.spssi.org/index.cfm?fuseaction=page.viewpage&pageid=1460

Curry School of Education. (2013). *Report: Threat assessment most effective way to prevent gun violence* [Press release]. Retrieved from http://curry.virginia.edu/press-releases/report-threat-assessment-most-effective-way-to-prevent-gun-violence

Engel J. (2010). Prevention in healthcare reform: The time has come. *North Carolina Medical Journal, 71,* 259–262.

Federal Bureau of Investigation. (2014, October 14). *National Instant Criminal Background Check System.* Retrieved from http://www.fbi.gov/about-us/cjis/nics

Federal Drug Administration. (2014, February 2). *Protecting and promoting your health: Public education campaigns.* Retrieved from http://www.fda.gov/AboutFDA/CentersOffices/OfficeofMedicalProductsandTobacco/AbouttheCenterforTobaccoProducts/PublicEducationCampaigns/default.htm

HealthDay News. (2014, October 9). *Soda giants pledge to make calorie cuts in their drinks.* Retrieved from http://www.healthfinder.gov/News/Article.aspx?id=692063&source=govdelivery&utm_medium=email&utm_source=govdelivery

Healthy people.gov. (2014). *Federal prevention initiatives.* Retrieved from http://www.healthypeople.gov/2020/tools-and-resources/Federal-Prevention-Initiatives

Horovitz, B. (2014, October 9). Restaurant chains trim the fat, study shows. *USA Today,* p. 8B.

Institute on Medicine as a Profession. (2014). *Medical, military, and ethics experts say health professionals designed and participated in cruel, inhumane, and degrading treatment and torture of detainees; seek policies to assure conformance with ethical principles.* Retrieved from http://www.imapny.org/medicine_as_a_profession/interrogation torture-and-dual- loyalty

Jimenez, J., Pasztor, E. M., & Chambers, R. M., with Fujii, C. P. (2014). Social policy and social change: Toward the creation of social and economic justice (2nd ed.). Thousand Oaks, CA: Sage.

Junod, T. (2014, October). Everything we think we know about mass shooters is wrong. *Esquire*, pp. 82–97, 160.

Miller, A. (2014, May). Stop gun violence. *Monitor on Psychology, 45*(5). Retrieved from http://www.apa.org/monitor/2014/05/gun-violence.aspx

National Institute of Mental Health. (2014). *Suicide: A major preventable mental health problem*. Retrieved from http://www.nimh.nih.gov/health/publications/suicide-a-major-preventable-mental-health-problem-fact-sheet/index.shtml

National Prevention Council. (2011). *National Prevention Strategy*. Washington, DC: U.S. Department of Health and Human Services, Office of the Surgeon General.

National Research Council. (2014). *The growth of incarceration in the United States: Exploring causes and consequences*. Retrieved from http://www.nap.edu/catalog.php?record_id=18613

Pace, A., Gunter, J., Oliver, M., Palmer, D., & Lawler, D. (2013, December 14). Mass shootings in America: The year since Sandy Hook. *News Today Online*. Retrieved from http://newsatw.com/

Pirog, M.A., & Good, E.M. (2013). *Public policy and mental health: Avenues for prevention*. Thousand Oaks, CA: Sage.

Stobbe, M. (2014, February 10). The end of cigarette smoking in America. Real Clear Science. Retrieved from http://www.realclearscience.com/

U.S. Census Bureau. (2013). Poverty. Retrieved from http://www.census.gov/hhes/www/poverty/about/overview/

U.S. Department of Education Office of Safe and Drug-Free Schools. (2011). *Safe and Drug-Free Schools and Communities National Activities (CFDA84.184)*. Retrieved from http://www2.ed.gov/about/offices/list/osdfs/programs.html

U.S. Department of Health and Human Services. (2014, September 23). HHS prevention strategies. *Healthy People 2020*. Retrieved from http://healthypeople.gov/2020/about/prevStrategies.aspx

U.S. Office of the Surgeon General. (2012). *National strategy for suicide prevention: Goals and objectives for action*. Washington, DC: Department of Health and Human Services. Retrieved from http://www.ncbi.nlm.nih.gov/books/NBK109917/

White House. (2013, January 16). *Now-Is-the-Time: The president's plan to protect our children and our communities by reducing gun violence*. Retrieved from http://www.whitehouse.gov/sites/default/files/docs/wh_now_is_the_time_full.pdf

World Health Organization. (2002). *World report on violence and health*. Geneva, Switzerland: Author. Retrieved from http://whqlibdoc.who.int/publications/2002/9241545615_eng.pdf

World Health Organization. (2008). *Closing the gap in a generation: Health equity through action on the social determinants of health*. Geneva, Switzerland: Author.

World Health Organization. (2010). *WHO healthy workplace framework and model: Background and supporting literature and practice* (Joan Burton, author). Geneva, Switzerland: Author.

World Health Organization. (2013). *Comprehensive mental health action plan 2013–2020*. Retrieved from http://www.who.int/mentalhealth/publications/action_plan/en/

Zoroya, G. (2014, October 10). 40,000 suicides annually, yet USA shrugs. *USA Today*, p. 2B. Retrieved from http://www.usatoday.com/longform/news/nation/2014/10/09/suicide-mental-health-prevention-research/15276353/

INDEX

Accreditation of Counseling 53
advocacy: competencies 68, 111, 144; efforts 11, 229–30
Ajzen, I. 81, 84, 109
Albee, G. 10, 15–16, 41–2, 91
Aldarondo, E. 17, 39, 78–9, 112–13
Alexander, J., Waldron, H., Robbins, M., & Neeb, A. 147–8, 150, 174, 178
American Counseling Association (ACA) 68–9, 109–13, 143–5, 228–9
American Psychological Association (APA) 109–13, 208–10, 228–9, 234; *see Guidelines for Prevention in Psychology*; gun violence
APA Gun Violence, Prediction, Prevention, and Policy 222–5
assets 121, 123–4, 130, 190
assist developmental transitions strategy 72–3; *see* wellness and prevention strategies
Association for Specialists in Group Work (ASGW) 40, 75, 91, 134

Bandura, A. 81, 84, 109
Behavioral Threat Assessment: approach 223; process 103–4
behavior change wheel 81, 85–6
Bell, L. 68, 75, 91, 109
best practices, group 136–8
Bierman, K, Coie, J., Dodge, K., Greenberg, B., Lochman, J., & McMahon, R. 147, 151, 174
Big Brothers/Big Sisters of America 181–4
Blueprints for Healthy Youth Development 118, 170, 174
Borden, L., Schultz, T., Herman, K., & Brooks, C. 135, 141–3
Botvin, G. 35, 159–61, 174–5
Bronfenbrenner, U. 39, 40, 42, 81, 87, 126
bullying 53–4, 60, 103–4, 130, 169–71, 174

caregivers, natural 124–5, 131
Catalano, R., Berglund, L., Ryan, J., Lonczak, H., & Hawkins, J. 147, 159, 167, 175–7
Centers for Disease Control and Prevention 26, 31, 43, 49
change: person-centered 98; system-centered 98
change models 97, 98
Chestnut, J. 48–9, 132, 210
chronic diseases 4, 14, 16, 73
Clanton Harpine, E. 59, 108–9, 135, 143
client systems 7, 20, 69, 90
clinical and educational wellness model 96
clinical mental health counseling 52–4
collaboration 54, 76, 106–8, 135–6
collective levels of wellness 7
Communities Mobilizing for Change on Alcohol (CMCA) 181, 185–8, 208, 210–11
Communities that Care (CTC) 159, 165–6, 168, 183

community and workplace programs 179
community counseling model 56, 69, 93, 97
community development 65–6, 75, 159, 189
Community Development Society 67
community organizing and systems intervention; *see* COSI
competencies 105–6, 108, 110, 205–6
Complementary and Alternative Medicine (CAM) 36–7, 73
comprehensive mental health counseling model 94–5
Conduct Problems Prevention Research Group 151, 153, 175
consultation 41, 68–9, 75–8, 105–8
Conyne, R. 75–8, 109–10, 133–5, 143–5
Conyne, R., & Cook, E.P. 38, 40, 56, 58
Conyne, R., Horne, A., & Raczynski, K. 105
Cook, E.P., 43, 143–5, 194–5, 208–10
Coping with Work and Family Stress Project 194, 199–202
COSI (community organizing and systems intervention) 56, 65–70, 100–101, 180–1; *see* wellness and prevention strategies
counseling, remedial 125, 130
counseling for wellness and justice model 93, 98–9
counseling for wellness and prevention 81, 83, 85, 101–5
counseling for wellness and prevention model 99–104, 199
counseling for wellness model 93, 96
counseling model for positive behavioral change 97
counseling psychology 11, 16–17, 54–5, 112–13
counselor education 52–5
counselors, preventive 98, 173
Crozier, M., Rokutani, L., Russett, J., Godwin, E., & Banks, G. 181, 209

Dahlgren, G., & Whitehead, M. 89, 110
Department of Health and Human Services 212, 214, 219, 236
DiClemente, R. 81–2, 113
dimensions of counselor functioning 77, 94, 112, 144
disease prevention 10, 14, 26, 30, 36
diseases and disorders 4, 7–8, 10–11, 19, 26, 49, 219

eating, healthy 91, 93–5, 97–8, 143, 145, 220; model 6, 56, 87–9, 177; perspective 38, 86–7, 110–11, 143–5
ecological 6–7, 13, 38, 76, 83, 86–90
ecological counseling 87, 93, 95–6
ecological techniques 126–9
ecosystem 91–2, 95, 148
educational strategy 56–7, 59, 60–1, 82, 208; competency 123; context 12, 72–9; redesign 70, 100–101, 124; *see* wellness and prevention strategies
encourage everyday wellness and prevention strategy 73–4; *see* wellness and prevention strategies
environmental redesign strategy 70–2; *see* wellness and prevention strategies
environments, natural 39, 70–1
European Code Against Cancer 27, 44
Evans, S., & Prilleltensky, I. 98–9
everyday wellness and prevention 19, 20, 21, 41, 56, 73, 125, 138–9
evidence-based programs 155–6, 160, 170, 210

families and schools 115–16, 181, 189, 209
family and school programs 146
FAST (Families and Schools Together) 116, 181, 189–91, 209
Fast Track prevention project 151, 153, 175
Fishbein, M. 81, 84, 111
functional family therapy (FFT) 147–51, 174, 178

general behavioral change frameworks supporting wellness and prevention 80–1
general process for wellness and prevention approaches 100, 122
general strategies of wellness and prevention 55–6
Gerig, M. 56, 76, 95
Granello, P. 93, 96–8, 111, 144
groups 57–9, 63–4, 134–44, 163–6; dynamics 135, 143–4, 199; small 171, 173, 189, 195–7, 199–200
group work 113–14, 119–20, 133–4, 143–5; counseling 77–8, 131, 134, 143–5; psychoeducation groups 34, 131, 134, 161–3
Guidelines for Prevention in Psychology 11, 12, 41, 66, 68, 208; *see* American Psychological Association
Gullotta, T. 76, 112, 163, 209

Gullotta, T., & Bloom, M. 55–7, 63, 65, 70
gun violence 217, 234–6; *see* APA Gun Violence, Prediction, Prevention, and Policy

Hage, S., & Kenny, M. 10
Hage, S., & Romano, J. 111
Hage, S., Schwartz, J., & Murray, M. 11–12, 16–17, 111, 113
Haggerty, K. 111, 164–6, 176
happiness 23–4, 27, 34, 71
Hawkins, D. 105, 111, 159, 175–7
health, optimal 121
Health and Human Services (HHS) 15–16, 214
health belief model (HBM) 81, 83, 114, 195
health care 20–1, 36–7, 67, 69; mental 20, 213, 216–17, 226; reform 77, 215–16; system 14, 32, 37, 219
health insurance 64, 193, 215
health promotion 13, 106–7, 195–6, 198
healthy: communities 8, 25, 179; lifestyle 6, 15, 36, 42
Healthy People 117, 214–15, 236
Healthy Workplace program 195–9
heart disease 4–5, 31, 74, 83
helpers, natural 65, 75
helping professionals 9–20, 62, 64, 94
Hettler, B. 28, 44
HHS prevention strategies 236
history of counseling and counselor education 52
Horne, A, Bartolomucci, C., & Newmay-Carlson, D. 76

incarceration 213
Incredible Years Parent Training Program 135
individual- and intrapersonal-level focus 81
individual clients 41, 51, 121, 126
individual counseling 119–22, 124–5, 127, 130–1, 221
interconnection 107–8, 133, 137
Interpersonal Cognitive Problem Solving (ICPS) 4, 14–15, 26, 168, 214–15
interpersonal skills 23, 53, 150, 160
interventions, system 7, 48, 80, 107
Ivey, A. 34, 44, 58, 77

JOBS Project for the Unemployed 194, 202–5, 211

justice 13, 25, 93, 98–101; *see* social justice

Katz, D. 4–5, 16
Kenny, M. 16–17, 39, 44, 110–11
Kenny, M., Horne, A., Orpinas, P., & Reese, L. 81
Keyes, C., & Lopez, S. 9, 40, 44

levels: collective 7–9, 11, 91, 101; ecological 69, 94, 115–16, 170–1
Lewin, K. 87, 111
Lewis, J., Lewis, M., Daniels, J., & D'Andrea, M. 68–9, 91, 93–4, 111
life: challenges 58, 63, 132; contexts 41, 63, 73, 121; healthy 19, 192, 195, 197–8
Life Skills Training (LST) 159–60, 162, 174–5
lifestyle-induced disorders 4–5
Lopez, S., & Snyder, C. 29, 34, 38, 81, 90, 112, 114

mass shootings 102, 216, 222–3, 231; *see* school shootings
Maton, K. 39, 45, 78
McGill, D., Mihalic, S., & Grotpeter, J. 181, 184
McWhirter, B., & McWhirter, E.M. 24, 40, 45
medical model 48–51, 74, 90, 107; in relation to wellness and prevention 48
mental and emotional behaviors (MEB) 11
mental health counseling model 94
mental health counselors 70, 97, 209
mental health practitioners 39, 198, 207, 216
mental health services 70, 73, 218, 220–2
Michie, S., Van Stralen, M., & West, R. 81, 85–6, 112
Michigan Prevention Research Center (MPRC) 202, 204, 209
Morrill, W., Oetting, E., & Hurst, J. 56, 93
Myers, J., & Sweeney, T. 7–8, 16–17, 28, 45, 93, 96, 112

National Association of School Psychologists (NASP) 68
National Association of Social Workers (NASW) 68, 228
National Center for Complementary and Alternative Medicine (NCCAM) 36–7
National Prevention Council 219, 236

National Prevention Strategy 212, 214–5, 217, 219–22
National Registry of Effective Programs and Practices 116, 119, 187
National Registry of Evidence-Based Programs and Practices 155, 177, 210
natural care-giving strategy 62–5; *see* wellness and prevention strategies

Office of Disease Prevention and Health Promotion 30, 36
Olweus, D. 159, 177
Olweus Bullying Prevention Program 159, 169, 171, 177
oppression 10, 92, 100–101, 213
optimism 15, 22–3, 106, 108
optimum health 7, 10, 13
outreach 41, 68–9, 97–8, 229

parent training 147, 152–3
personal wellness 19, 25–6, 120–1, 123
person-environment psychology 43–4, 46–7
perspectives supporting wellness and prevention 86
Pirog, M., & Good, E. 41, 67, 68, 117, 233, 236
Positive Parenting Program 148, 154, 178
positive psychology 12, 22–4, 44–6, 90, 114
practices: clinical 17, 78–9, 109, 112–13; person-centered 21–2
practice wellness 25
preventing: bullying 87, 112, 169, 177; cigarette smoking 225; school shootings 235
prevention: benefits 14, 180; classic 10–11; competencies 1, 105–6; concepts 4, 37, 55; efforts 207, 214, 218, 222; ounces of 175, 178, 210; teaching 110, 112, 235
prevention research and science 12, 79, 84, 174, 177, 202
Prevention Section 11–12, 17
preventive counseling 16, 91, 94, 98
Price, R., Cowen, E., Lorion, R., & Ramos-McKay, J., 175
Price, R., Van Ryn, M., & Vinokur, A. 210
Prilleltensky, I. 45, 113
Prilleltensky, I., Dokecki, P., Frieden, G., & Wang, O. 6–8, 87, 91–3
primary prevention 16, 76, 110, 209
Principles of Good Practice in Community Development 66; *see* Community Development Society
processes, protective 100–101, 146–50, 156–7, 164–7, 199
Prochaska, J. 81–2, 113
program development 12, 84, 109, 119
psychoeducation 58–9, 125, 136, 144, 159
psychotherapy 5, 27, 113–14, 143–4
public health 10, 48–9, 111, 176–7, 215–16
public policy 67–8, 117, 119, 224–5
public policy and legislation systems 228–9

Raczynski, K., Waldo, M., Schwartz, J., & Horne, A. 82
Ratts, M. 39, 91, 111, 113
relational wellness 146–7, 149, 151, 153
relational wellness and prevention 181, 183, 185, 187
resilience 23, 40, 44–5, 96
risk: factors 101, 167, 199, 201; levels 151–2
Rogers, E.M. 81, 114
ROI (return on investment) 14, 156, 176, 193–4
Romano, J. 12, 81, 113, 116, 119, 235
Romano, J., & Hage, S. 11–12, 105, 113
Rosenstock, I. 81, 83

Sanders, M. 148, 154–5, 177
Sandy Hook Elementary School 222
school: bullying 169–70; counseling 52–4, 172; culture 103–4; professionals 102–4; school settings 79, 147, 154, 157–8, 223; strengths 102, 104
school counselors 172
school shootings 70, 101–4, 109, 144, 170; *see* mass shootings
Seligman, M. 24–5, 45–6, 90, 114
sickness 54–5, 219, 221
signature strengths 24–5
SLT *see* social learning theory
smoking 5, 60, 225, 227–8
Snow, D. 199, 210
Snyder, C. 44–6, 90, 112, 114
Snyder & Lopez 34, 38, 81, 90
social competency facilitation strategy 61–2; *see* wellness and prevention strategies
Social Development Research Group (SDRG) 58, 159, 163–7, 169
social justice 77–9, 91–3, 106–9, 111–14; counseling 17, 45, 94, 113; interventions 41, 68; principles 91

social learning theory (SLT) 81, 84, 109, 114
social media 29–30, 60–1, 94, 164–5
social support 194, 199–201, 203–5, 209–10
spectrum of prevention 151, 179, 210
strategies in wellness and prevention for individual counseling 125
Strengthening Families Program 135, 144
strengths 24–5, 123–4, 130, 148–51
strengths in wellness and prevention 130
stress 32, 192, 197–200, 208–10
Substance Abuse and Mental Health Services Administration 66, 170, 197
suicide prevention 225–6, 228, 232, 234
Sweeney, T. 16–17, 95–6, 112, 114
systems: change approaches 15, 121, 230–3; ecological 7, 87; healthcare 55, 80, 216; intervention 65–6, 68; level 212–13, 225, 231, 234

theory 80–2, 84–6, 111–13, 143–4
therapeutic life changes (TLC) 5–6, 26–7, 55–6, 136–9
threat assessment 223–4, 235
Toporek, R. 91, 98, 111, 115
transtheoretical model (TTM) 81–2
treatment 50–1, 54–5, 147–8, 150–1
Triple P-Positive Parenting Program 148, 154–6

unemployment 69, 89, 92, 202–4
UNICEF (United Nations International Children's Emergency Fund) 35, 46

Vera, E. 16–17, 42–3, 112, 114

Wagenaar, A. 181, 186–7, 211
Waldo, M., Schwartz, J., Horne, A., & Cote, L. 112–13
Walsh, R. 26–7, 43–4, 46, 73
Walsh, W., Craik, K., & Price, R. 46
Ward, D. 144–5, 158, 175, 177
well-being 8–9, 21–2, 111–12, 196
wellness: collective 85, 92, 99, 103–4; effective 14, 116–18, 146, 156; individual 99, 131; integrated 100–101; social justice 99
wellness and prevention: counseling 93, 105, 172; initiatives 213, 215, 217, 219; paradigm 48; strategies 49, 51, 53, 55; *see* wellness and prevention strategies
wellness and prevention strategies: assist developmental transitions 72–3; COSI 65–70; education 56–61; encourage everyday wellness and prevention 73–4; environmental redesign 70–2; natural care-giving 62–5; social competency facilitation 61–2
wellness dimensions and domains 6, 28, 33–5, 98
Wellness Evaluation of Lifestyle 124; five factor 96
White House 31, 46, 222, 236
Wilson, F.R. 123, 126, 138, 145
Witmer, J., & Sweeney, T. 95
workplace health promotion programs 197
World Health Organization (WHO) 43, 214, 216–17, 235–6; WHO Comprehensive Mental Health Action Plan 217–18

Zimbardo, P. 22, 38, 39, 41, 47